History of Egypt, Chaldea, Syria, Babylonia and Assyria

by A. S. Rappoport

Volume 5

Translated by M. L. McCLURE, Member of the Committee of the Egypt Exploration Fund

ISBN: 978-1-63923-895-8

All Rights reserved. No part of this book maybe reproduced without written permission from the publishers, except by a reviewer who may quote brief passages in a review to be printed in a newspaper or magazine.

Printed: March 2023

Published and Distributed By:
Lushena Books
607 Country Club Drive, Unit E
Bensenville, IL 60106
www.lushenabks.com

ISBN: 978-1-63923-895-8

CONTENTS

CHAPTER I.

THE EIGHTEENTH THEBAN DYNASTY (*Continued*)

Thûtmosis III.: The Organization of the Syrian Provinces — Amenôthes III.: The Worshippers of Atonû 3

CHAPTER II.

THE REACTION AGAINST EGYPT

The XIXth Dynasty: Harmhabî — The Hittite Empire in Syria and in Asia Minor — Seti I. and Ramses II. — The People of the Sea: Mînephtah and the Israelite Exodus 117

CHAPTER III.

THE CLOSE OF THE THEBAN EMPIRE

Ramses III. — The Theban City under the Ramessides — Manners and customs 287

LIST OF ILLUSTRATIONS

	PAGE
Temple of Hypetre — Philæ	*Frontispiece*
A procession of negroes bringing the tribute of Kûsh	7
A Syrian town and its outskirts after an Egyptian army has passed through it	15
The Lotanû and the Goldsmiths' work constituting their tribute	31
Painted tablet in the Hall of the Harps in the fifth Tomb of the Kings to the East. Thebes (Bŷhan el Molouk)	33
The bear and elephant brought as tribute in the tomb of Rakhmiri	34
The Mummy of Thûtmosis III.	40
Head of the Mummy of Thûtmosis III.	41
Amenôthes II., from the statue at Turin	44
The great Sphinx and the chapel of Thûtmosis IV.	47
The Simoom. Sphinx and Pyramids at Gizeh	49
The Stele of the Sphinx of Gizeh	50
Queen Mûtemûaû	52
Amenôthes III., from the Tomb of Khâmâit	53
A gang of Syrian prisoners making brick for the temple of Amon	58
One of the Rams of Amenôthes III.	59
One of the lions of Gebel-Barkal	62
Island of Elephantinê and Roman Baths	64
The Temple of Elephantinê, as it was in 1799	65
The great court of the temple of Luxor during the inundation	66
Part of the Avenue of Rams, between the temples of Amon and Maût	67
The Pylons of Thûtmosis III. and Harmhabî at Karnak	69
The sacred lake and the southern part of the Temple of Karnak	70
The two colossi of Memnon in the Plain of Thebes	73
A party of tourists at the foot of the vocal statue of Memnon	76

LIST OF ILLUSTRATIONS

	PAGE
Marriage Scarabæus	79
The decorated pavement of the Palace of Khûniatonû at El-Amarna	87
The mask of Khûniatonû	95
Amenôthes IV., from the statuette in the Louvre	96
Khûniatonû with his wife upon his knees	97
Khûniatonû and his wife rewarding one of the great officers of the court	98
The door of a tomb at Tel El-Amarna	100
Interior of a tomb at Tel El-Amarna	103
Profile of head of a mummy (female) (Thebes Tomb)	104
Two of the daughters of Khuniatonû	106
Sarcophagus of the Pharaoh Aî	110
The great Hypostyle Hall at Karnak, seen from the southern side of the Sacred Lake	117
The First Pylon of Harmhabî at Karnak	123
Amenôthes IV., from a fragment used again by Harmhabî	126
Harmhabî	128
The vaulted passage of the Rock-Tomb at Gebel Silsileh	129
The triumph of Harmhabî in the Sanctuary of Gebel Silsileh	131
Three heads of Hittite soldiers	135
A Hittite King	138
A Hittite Chariot with its three occupants	140
Ramses I.	160
The return of the north wall of the Hypostyle Hall at Karnak, where Seti I. represents some episodes in his first campaign	163
Representation of Seti I. vanquishing the Libyans and Asiatics on the walls, Karnak	166
A fortified station on the route between the Nile and the Red Sea	168
The temple of Seti I. at Redesieh	169
Fragment of the map of the gold-mines	170
The three standing columns of the Temple of Sesebi	171
An avenue of one of the aisles of the Hypostyle Hall at Karnak	173
The gratings of the central colonnade in the Hypostyle Hall at Karnak	174
One of the Colonnades of the Hypostyle Hall in the Temple of Seti I. at Abydos	176
The Façade of the temple of Seti I. at Abydos	177
The Temple of Qurnah	181
One of the pillars of the tomb of Seti I.	184
Ramses II. puts the negroes to flight	187
The Shardana guard of Ramses II.	193
Two Hittite spies beaten by the Egyptian soldiers	195
The Egyptian camp and the council of war on the morning of the Battle of Qodshû	196

LIST OF ILLUSTRATIONS ix

	PAGE
The fugitives welcomed by the garrison of Qodshû	197
The garrison of Qodshû issuing forth to help the Prince of Khâti	198
The taking of Dapur in Galilee	205
Khâtusaru, Prince of Khâti, and his daughter	215
Phœnician boats landing at Thebes	218
The projecting columns of the Speos of Gerf-Hosseîn	221
The Caryatides of Gerf-Hossein	222
The two colossi of Abu Simbel to the south of the doorway	224
The interior of the Speos of Abu Simbel	225
The face of the rock at Abu Simbel	227
Ramses II. pierces a Libyan chief with his lance	229
Ramses II. strikes a group of prisoners	230
The façade of the little Speos of Hathor at Abu Simbel	231
The Chapel of Thûtmosis III. and one of the Pylons of Ramses II. at Luxor	233
The colonnade of Seti I. and the three colossal statues of Ramses II. at Luxor	235
Paintings of chairs in the fifth Tomb of the Kings to the East. Thebes (Bŷban el Molouk)	236
The remains of the colossal statue of Ramses II. at the Ramesseum	237
The Ramesseum	238
The ruins of the Memnonium of Ramses II. at Abydos	240
The colossal statue of Ramses II. at Mitrahineh	242
The Chapel of the Apis of Amenôthes III.	244
Statue of Khâmoîsît	246
Stele of the Nahr El-Kelb	247
The Bas-relief of Ninfi	248
Coffin of Ramses II.	249
Ramses II.	249
A Libyan	253
Statue of Mînephtah	260
The Chapels of Ramses II. and Mînephtah at Silsileh	263
Statue of Seti II.	264
Seti II.	265
Amenmesis	268
The Battle of the Rats and Cats, a parody of the Egyptian Wars	287
Nakhtûsît	289
One of the Libyan chiefs vanquished by Ramses III.	299
The wagons of the Pulasati	300
Pulasati	301
A Shagalasha Chief	304

LIST OF ILLUSTRATIONS

	PAGE
The army of Ramses III. on the march, and the Lion-hunt	307
The defeat of the peoples of the sea at Magadîl	309
The captive chiefs of Ramses III. at Medinet-Habu	313
Ramses III. binds the chiefs of the Libyans	315
The Prince of Khâti	318
The colossal Osirian figures in the first court at Medinet-Habu	321
The first Pylon of the temple of Medinet-Habu, the façade looking into the first court	323
The Mummy of Ramses III.	327
A Ramses of the XXth Dynasty	331
Pectoral of Ramses II.	345
The ram-headed Sparrow-Hawk in the Louvre	347
Ordinary furniture of the Theban period	350
The Cat and the Jackal go off to the fields with their flocks	357
The Cat before its judge	358
A concert of animals devoted to Music	359

THE EIGHTEENTH THEBAN DYNASTY—(continued)

THÛTMOSIS III.: THE ORGANISATION OF THE SYRIAN PROVINCES—AMENÔTHES III.: THE WORSHIPPERS OF ATONÛ.

Thûtmosis III.: the taking of Qodshû in the 42nd year of his reign—The tribute of the south—The triumph-song of Amon.

The constitution of the Egyptian empire—The Crown vassals and their relations with the Pharaoh—The king's messengers—The allied states—Royal presents and marriages; the status of foreigners in the royal harem—Commerce with Asia, its resources and its risks; protection granted to the national industries, and treaties of extradition.

Amenôthes II., his campaigns in Syria and Nubia—Thûtmosis IV.; his dream under the shadow of the Sphinx and his marriage—Amenôthes III. and his peaceful reign—The great building works—The temples of Nubia: Soleb and his sanctuary built by Amenôthes III., Gebel Barkal, Elephantinê—The beautifying of Thebes: the temple of Mût, the temples of Amon at Luxor and at Karnak, the tomb of Amenôthes III., the chapel and the colossi of Memnon

The increasing importance of Amon and his priests: preference shown by Amenôthes III. for the Heliopolitan gods, his marriage with Tii—The influence of Tii over Amenôthes IV.: the decadence of Amon and of Thebes, Atonû and Khûîtniatonû—Change of physiognomy in Khûniaton, his character, his government, his relations with Asia: the tombs of Tel el-Amarna and the art of the period—Tûtankhamon, Aî: the return of the Pharaohs to Thebes and the close of the XVIII^h dynasty.

CHAPTER I

THE EIGHTEENTH THEBAN DYNASTY—(*continued*)

Thûtmosis III.: the organisation of the Syrian provinces—Amenôthes III.: the royal worshippers of Atonû.

IN the year XXXIV. the Egyptians reappeared in Zahi. The people of Anaugasa having revolted, two of their towns were taken, a third surrendered, while the chiefs of the Lotauû hastened to meet their lord with their usual tribute. Advantage was taken of the encampment being at the foot of the Lebanon to procure wood for building purposes, such as beams and planks, masts and yards for vessels, which were all shipped by the Kefâtiu at Byblos for exportation to the Delta. This expedition was, indeed, little more than a military march through the country. It would appear that the Syrians soon accustomed themselves to the presence of the Egyptians in their midst, and their obedience henceforward could be fairly relied on. We are unable to ascertain what were the circumstances or the intrigues which, in the year XXXV., led to a sudden outbreak among the tribes settled on the Euphrates and the Orontes. The King of Mitanni rallied round him the princes of Naharaim, and awaited the attack of the

Egyptians near Aruna. Thûtmosis displayed great personal courage, and the victory was at once decisive. We find mention of only ten prisoners, one hundred and eighty mares, and sixty chariots in the lists of the spoil. Anaugasa again revolted, and was subdued afresh in the year XXXVIII.; the Shaûsû rebelled in the year XXXIX., and the Lotanû or some of the tribes connected with them two years later. The campaign of the year XLII. proved more serious. Troubles had arisen in the neighbourhood of Arvad. Thûtmosis, instead of following the usual caravan route, marched along the coast-road by way of Phœnicia. He destroyed Arka in the Lebanon and the surrounding strongholds, which were the haunts of robbers who lurked in the mountains; then turning to the northeast, he took Tunipa and extorted the usual tribute from the inhabitants of Naharaim. On the other hand, the Prince of Qodshû, trusting to the strength of his walled city, refused to do homage to the Pharaoh, and a deadly struggle took place under the ramparts, in which each side availed themselves of all the artifices which the strategic warfare of the times allowed. On a day when the assailants and besieged were about to come to close quarters, the Amorites let loose a mare among the chariotry of Thûtmosis. The Egyptian horses threatened to become unmanageable, and had begun to break through the ranks, when Amenemhabî, an officer of the guard, leaped to the ground, and, running up to the creature, disembowelled it with a thrust of his sword; this done, he cut off its tail and presented it to the king. The besieged were eventually obliged to shut themselves within their newly built walls, hoping by this means to tire out the patience of their assailants; but a picked body of men, led by the same brave Amenemhabî who had killed the mare, succeeded in making a breach and forcing an entrance into the town. Even the numerous successful campaigns we have mentioned, form but a part, though indeed an important part, of the wars undertaken by Thûtmosis to "fix his frontiers in the ends of the earth." Scarcely a year elapsed without the viceroy of Ethiopia having a conflict with one or other of the tribes of the Upper Nile; little merit as he might gain in triumphing over such foes, the spoil taken from them formed a considerable adjunct to the treasure collected in Syria, while the tributes from the people of Kûsh and the Ûaûaiû were paid with as great regularity as the taxes levied on the Egyptians themselves. It comprised gold both from the mines and from the rivers, feathers, oxen with curiously trained horns, giraffes, lions, leopards, and slaves of all ages. The distant regions explored by Hâtshopsîtû continued to pay a tribute at intervals. A fleet went to Pûanît to fetch large cargoes of incense, and from time to time some Ilim chief would feel himself honoured by having one of his daughters accepted as an inmate of the harem of the great king. After the year XLII. we have no further records of the reign, but there is no reason to suppose that its closing years were less eventful or less prosperous than the earlier. Thûtmosis III., when conscious of failing powers, may have delegated the direction of his armies to his sons or to his generals, but it is also quite possible that he kept the supreme command in his own hands to the end of his days. Even when old age approached and threatened to abate his vigour, he was upheld by the belief that his father Amon was ever at hand to guide him with his counsel and assist him in battle. "I give to thee, declared the god, the rebels that they may fall beneath thy sandals, that thou mayest crush the rebellious, for I grant to thee by decree the earth in its length and breadth. The tribes of the West and those of the East are under the place of thy countenance, and when thou goest up into all the strange lands with a joyous heart, there is none who will withstand Thy Majesty, for I am thy guide when thou treadest them underfoot. Thou hast crossed the water of the great curve of Naharaim[1] in thy strength and in thy power, and I have commanded thee to let them hear thy roaring which shall enter their dens, I have deprived their nostrils of the breath of life, I have granted to thee that thy deeds shall sink into their hearts, that my uræus which is upon thy head may burn them, that it may bring prisoners in long files from the peoples of Qodi, that it may consume with its flame those who are in the marshes,[2] that it may cut off the heads of the Asiatics without one of them being able to escape from its clutch. I grant to thee that thy conquests may embrace all lands, that the uræus

[1] The Euphrates, in the great curve described by it across Naharaim, after issuing from the mountains of Cilicia.

[2] The meaning is doubtful. The word signifies pools, marshes, the provinces situated beyond Egyptian territory, and consequently the distant parts of the world—those which are nearest the ocean which encircles the earth, and which was considered as fed by the stagnant waters of the celestial Nile, just as the extremities of Egypt were watered by those of the terrestrial Nile.

A PROCESSION OF NEGROES BRINGING THE TRIBUTE OF KÛSH.

Drawn by Faucher-Gudin, from photographs taken at Beît-Wally by Insinger.

which shines upon my forehead may be thy vassal, so that in all the compass of the heaven there may not be one to rise against thee, but that the people may come bearing their tribute on their backs and bending before Thy Majesty according to my behest; I ordain that all aggressors arising in thy time shall fail before thee, their heart burning within them, their limbs trembling!

"I.—I am come that I may grant unto thee to crush the great ones of Zahi, I throw them under thy feet across their mountains,—I grant to thee that they shall see Thy Majesty as a lord of shining splendour when thou shinest before them in my likeness!

"II.—I am come, to grant thee that thou mayest crush those of the country of Asia, to break the heads of the people of Lotanû,—I grant thee that they may see Thy Majesty, clothed in thy panoply, when thou seizest thy arms, in thy war-chariot.

"III.—I am come, to grant thee that thou mayest crush the land of the East, and invade those who dwell in the provinces of Tonûtir,—I grant that they may see Thy Majesty as the comet which rains down the heat of its flame and sheds its dew.

"IV.—I am come, to grant thee that thou mayest crush the land of the West, so that Kafîti and Cyprus shall be in fear of thee,—I grant that they may see Thy Majesty like the young bull, stout of heart, armed with horns which none may resist.

"V.—I am come, to grant thee that thou mayest crush those who are in their marshes, so that the countries of Mitanni may tremble for fear of thee,—I grant that they may see Thy Majesty like the crocodile, lord of terrors, in the midst of the water, which none can approach.

"VI.—I am come, to grant thee that thou mayest crush those who are in the isles, so that the people who live in the midst of the Very-Green may be reached by thy roaring,—I grant that they may see Thy Majesty like an avenger who stands on the back of his victim.

"VII.—I am come, to grant that thou mayest crush the Tihonu, so that the isles of the Ûtanâtiû may be in the power of thy souls,—I grant that they may see Thy Majesty like a spell-weaving lion, and that thou mayest make corpses of them in the midst of their own valleys.[1]

"VIII.—I am come, to grant thee that thou mayest crush the ends of the earth, so that the circle which surrounds the ocean may be grasped in thy fist,—I grant that they may see Thy Majesty as the sparrow-hawk, lord of the wing, who sees at a glance all that he desires.

"IX.—I am come, to grant thee that thou mayest crush the peoples who are in their "duars," so that thou mayest bring the Hirû-shâitû into captivity,—I grant that they may see Thy Majesty like the jackal of the south, lord of swiftness, the runner who prowls through the two lands.

"X.—I am come, to grant thee that thou mayest crush

[1] The name of the people associated with the Tihonu was read at first Tanau, and identified with the Danai of the Greeks. Chabas was inclined to read Ûtena, and Brugsch, Ûthent, more correctly Utanâtiû, Utanâti, the people of Uatanît. The juxtaposition of this name with that of the Libyans compels us to look towards the west for the site of this people: may we assign to them the Ionian Islands, or even those in the western Mediterranean?

the nomads, so that the Nubians as far as the land of Pidît are in thy grasp,—I grant that they may see Thy Majesty like unto thy two brothers Horus and Sît, whose arms I have joined in order to establish thy power."

The poem became celebrated. When Seti I., two centuries later, commanded the Poet Laureates of his court to celebrate his victories in verse, the latter, despairing of producing anything better, borrowed the finest strophes from this hymn to Thûtmosis III., merely changing the name of the hero. The composition, unlike so many other triumphal inscriptions, is not a mere piece of official rhetoric, in which the poverty of the subject is concealed by a multitude of common-places whether historical or mythological. Egypt indeed ruled the world, either directly or through her vassals, and from the mountains of Abyssinia to those of Cilicia her armies held the nations in awe with the threat of the Pharaoh.

The conqueror, as a rule, did not retain any part of their territory. He confined himself to the appropriation of the revenue of certain domains for the benefit of his gods.[1] Amon of Karnak thus became possessor of seven Syrian towns which he owed to the generosity of the victorious Pharaohs.[2] Certain cities, like Tunipa, even begged for statues of Thûtmosis for which they built a temple and instituted a cultus. Amon and his fellow-gods

[1] The seven towns which Amon possessed in Syria are mentioned, in the time of Ramses III., in the list of the domains and revenues of the god.

[2] In the year XXIII., on his return from his first campaign, Thûtmosis III. provided offerings, guaranteed from the three towns Anaûgasa, Inûâmû, and Hûrnikarû, for his father Amonrâ.

too were adored there, side by side with the sovereign the inhabitants had chosen to represent them here below.[1] These rites were at once a sign of servitude, and a proof of gratitude for services rendered, or privileges which had been confirmed. The princes of neighbouring regions repaired annually to these temples to renew their oaths of allegiance, and to bring their tributes "before the face of the king." Taking everything into account, the condition of the Pharaoh's subjects might have been a pleasant one, had they been able to accept their lot without any mental reservation. They retained their own laws, their dynasties, and their frontiers, and paid a tax only in proportion to their resources, while the hostages given were answerable for their obedience. These hostages were as a rule taken by Thûtmosis from among the sons or the brothers of the enemy's chief. They were carried to Thebes, where a suitable establishment was assigned to them,[2] the younger members receiving an education which practically made them Egyptians. As soon as a vacancy occurred in the

[1] The statues of Thûtmosis III. and of the gods of Egypt erected at Tunipa are mentioned in a letter from the inhabitants of that town to Amenôthes III. Later, Ramses II., speaking of the two towns in the country of the Khâti in which were two statues of His Majesty, mentions Tunipa as one of them.

[2] The various titles of the lists of Thûtmosis III. at Thebes show us "the children of the Syrian chiefs conducted as prisoners" into the town of Sûhanû, which is elsewhere mentioned as the depôt, the prison of the temple of Amon. W. Max Muller was the first to remark the historical value of this indication, but without sufficiently insisting on it; the name indicates, perhaps, as he says, a great prison, but a prison like those where the princes of the family of the Ottoman sultans were confined by the reigning monarch — a palace usually provided with all the comforts of Oriental life.

succession either in Syria or in Ethiopia, the Pharaoh would choose from among the members of the family whom he held in reserve, that prince on whose loyalty he could best count, and placed him upon the throne.[1] The method of procedure was not always successful, since these princes, whom one would have supposed from their training to have been the least likely to have asserted themselves against the man to whom they owed their elevation, often gave more trouble than others. The sense of the supreme power of Egypt, which had been inculcated in them during their exile, seemed to be weakened after their return to their native country, and to give place to a sense of their own importance. Their hearts misgave them as the time approached for them to send their own children as pledges to their suzerain, and also when called upon to transfer a considerable part of their revenue to his treasury. They found, moreover, among their own cities and kinsfolk, those who were adverse to the foreign yoke, and secretly urged their countrymen to revolt, or else competitors for the throne who took advantage of the popular discontent to pose as champions of national independence, and it was difficult for the vassal prince to counteract the intrigues of these adversaries without openly declaring himself hostile to his foreign master.[2] A

---

[1] Among the Tel el-Amarna tablets there is a letter of a petty Syrian king, Adadnirari, whose father was enthroned after a fashion in Nûkhassi by Thûtmosis III.

[2] Thus, in the Tel el-Amarna correspondence, Zimrida, governor of Sidon, gives information to Amenôthes III. on the intrigues which the notables of the town were concocting against Egyptian authority. Ribaddû relates in one of these despatches that the notables of Byblos and the

time quickly came when a vestige of fear alone constrained them to conceal their wish for liberty; the most trivial incident then sufficed to give them the necessary encouragement, and decided them to throw off the mask,— a repulse or the report of a repulse suffered by the Egyptians, the news of a popular rising in some neighbouring state, the passing visit of a Chaldæan emissary who left behind him the hope of support and perhaps of subsidies from Babylon, and the unexpected arrival of a troop of mercenaries whose services might be hired for the occasion.[1] A rising of this sort usually brought about the most disastrous results. The native prince or the town itself could keep back the tribute and own allegiance to no one during the few months required to convince Pharaoh of their defection and to allow him to prepare the necessary means of vengeance; the advent of the Egyptians followed, and the work of repression was systematically set in hand. They destroyed the harvests, whether green or ready for the sickle, they cut down the palms and olive trees, they tore up the vines, seized on the flocks, dismantled the strongholds, and took the inhabitants prisoners.[2] The rebellious prince had to

women of his harem were urging him to revolt; later, a letter of Amûnirâ to the King of Egypt informs us that Ribaddû had been driven from Byblos by his own brother.

[1] Bûrnabûriash, King of Babylon, speaks of Syrian agents who had come to ask for support from his father, Kûrigalzû, and adds that the latter had counselled submission. In one of the letters preserved in the British Museum, Azîrû defends himself for having received an emissary of the King of the Khâti.

[2] Cf. the raiding, for instance, of the regions of Arvad and of the Zahi by Thûtmosis III., described in the *Annals*, ll. 4, 5. We are still

THE CONDITION OF THE VASSAL STATES 15

deliver up his silver and gold, the contents of his palace, even his children,[1] and when he had finally obtained peace by means of endless sacrifices, he found himself a vassal as before, but with an empty treasury, a wasted country, and a decimated people. In spite of all this, some head-

A SYRIAN TOWN AND ITS OUTSKIRTS AFTER AN EGYPTIAN ARMY HAD PASSED THROUGH IT.[2]

strong native princes never relinquished the hope of freedom, and no sooner had they made good the breaches in their walls as far as they were able, than they entered

in possession of the threats which the messenger Khâni made against the rebellious chief of a province of the Zahi—possibly Azîru.

[1] See, in the accounts of the campaigns of Thûtmosis, the record of the spoils, as well as the mention of the children of the chiefs brought as prisoners into Egypt.

[2] Drawn by Boudier, from a photograph by Gayet.

once more on this unequal contest, though at the risk of bringing irreparable disaster on their country. The majority of them, after one such struggle, resigned themselves to the inevitable, and fulfilled their feudal obligations regularly. They paid their fixed contribution, furnished rations and stores to the army when passing through their territory, and informed the ministers at Thebes of any intrigues among their neighbours.[1] Years elapsed before they could so far forget the failure of their first attempt to regain independence, as to venture to make a second, and expose themselves to fresh reverses.

The administration of so vast an empire entailed but a small expenditure on the Egyptians, and required the offices of merely a few functionaries.[2] The garrisons which they kept up in foreign provinces lived on the country, and were composed mainly of light troops, archers, a certain proportion of heavy infantry, and a few minor detachments of chariotry dispersed among the principal fortresses.[3] The

---

[1] We find in the *Annals*, in addition to the enumeration of the tributes, the mention of the foraging arrangements which the chiefs were compelled to make for the army on its passage. We find among the tablets letters from Azîru denouncing the intrigues of the Khâti; letters also of Ribaddu pointing out the misdeeds of Abdashirti, and other communications of the same nature, which demonstrate the supervision exercised by the petty Syrian princes over each other.

[2] Under Thûtmosis III. we have among others "Mir," or "Nasi sitû mihâtîtû," "governors of the northern countries," the Thûtîi who became afterwards a hero of romance. The individuals who bore this title held a middle rank in the Egyptian hierarchy.

[3] The archers—*pidâtiû, pidâti, pidâte*—and the chariotry quartered in Syria are often mentioned in the Tel el-Amarna correspondence. Steindorff has recognised the term *ûâû aûîtû*, meaning infantry, in the word *ûeû, ûiû*, of the Tel el-Amarna tablets.

officers in command had orders to interfere as little as possible in local affairs, and to leave the natives to dispute or even to fight among themselves unhindered, so long as their quarrels did not threaten the security of the Pharaoh.[1] It was never part of the policy of Egypt to insist on her foreign subjects keeping an unbroken peace among themselves. If, theoretically, she did not recognise the right of private warfare, she at all events tolerated its practice. It mattered little to her whether some particular province passed out of the possession of a certain Ribaddû into that of a certain Azîru, or *vice versâ*, so long as both Ribaddû and Azîru remained her faithful slaves. She never sought to repress their incessant quarrelling until such time as it threatened to take the form of an insurrection against her own power. Then alone did she throw off her neutrality; taking the side of one or other of the dissentients, she would grant him, as a pledge of help, ten, twenty, thirty, or even more archers.[2] No doubt the discipline and personal courage of these veterans exercised a certain influence on the turn of events, but they were after all a mere handful of men, and their individual action in the

[1] A half at least of the Tel el-Amarna correspondence treats of provincial wars between the kings of towns and countries subject to Egypt—wars of Abdashirti and his son Azîru against the cities of the Phœnician coast, wars of Abdikhîba, or Abdi-Tabba, King of Jerusalem, against the chiefs of the neighbouring cities.

[2] Abimilki (Abisharri) demands on one occasion from the King of Egypt ten men to defend Tyre, on another occasion twenty; the town of Gûla requisitioned thirty or forty to guard it. Delattre thinks that these are rhetorical expressions answering to a general word, just as if we should say "a handful of men"; the difference of value in the figures is to me a proof of their reality.

combat would scarcely ever have been sufficient to decide the result; the actual importance of their support, in spite of their numerical inferiority, lay in the moral weight they brought to the side on which they fought, since they represented the whole army of the Pharaoh which lay behind them, and their presence in a camp always ensured final success. The vanquished party had the right of appeal to the sovereign, through whom he might obtain a mitigation of the lot which his successful adversary had prepared for him; it was to the interest of Egypt to keep the balance of power as evenly as possible between the various states which looked to her, and when she prevented one or other of the princes from completely crushing his rivals, she was minimising the danger which might soon arise from the vassal whom she had allowed to extend his territory at the expense of others.

These relations gave rise to a perpetual exchange of letters and petitions between the court of Thebes and the northern and southern provinces, in which all the petty kings of Africa and Asia, of whatever colour or race, set forth, either openly or covertly, their ambitions and their fears, imploring a favour or begging for a subsidy, revealing the real or suspected intrigues of their fellow-chiefs, and while loudly proclaiming their own loyalty, denouncing the perfidy and the secret projects of their neighbours. As the Ethiopian peoples did not, apparently, possess an alphabet of their own, half of the correspondence which concerned them was carried on in Egyptian, and written on papyrus. In Syria, however, where Babylonian civilization maintained itself in spite of its conquest by Thûtmosis, cuneiform

THE PHARAOH'S DIVINITY ACKNOWLEDGED   19

writing was still employed, and tablets of dried clay.[1] It had, therefore, been found necessary to establish in the Pharaoh's palace a department for this service, in which the scribes should be competent to decipher the Chaldæan character. Dictionaries and easy mythological texts had been procured for their instruction, by means of which they had learned the meaning of words and the construction of sentences. Having once mastered the mechanism of the syllabary, they set to work to translate the despatches, marking on the back of each the date and the place from whence it came, and if necessary making a draft of the reply.[2] In these the Pharaoh does not appear, as a rule, to have insisted on the endless titles which we find so lavishly used in his inscriptions, but the shortened protocol employed shows that the theory of his divinity was as fully acknowledged by strangers as it was by his own subjects. They greet him as their sun, the god before whom they prostrate themselves seven times seven, while they are his slaves, his dogs, and the dust beneath his feet.[3] The runners to whom these documents were entrusted, and who delivered them with their own hand, were not, as a rule,

---

[1] A discovery made by the fellahin, in 1887, at Tel el-Amarna, in the ruins of the palace of Khûniaton, brought to light a portion of the correspondence between Asiatic monarchs, whether vassals or independent of Egypt, with the officers of Amenôthes III. and IV., and with these Pharaohs themselves.

[2] Several of these registrations are still to be read on the backs of the tablets at Berlin, London, and Gizeh.

[3] The protocols of the letters of Abdashirti may be taken as an example, or those of Abimilki to Pharaoh, sometimes there is a development of the protocol which assumes panegyrical features similar to those met with in Egypt.

persons of any consideration; but for missions of grave importance "the king's messengers" were employed, whose functions in time became extended to a remarkable degree. Those who were restricted to a limited sphere of activity were called "the king's messengers for the regions of the south," or "the king's messengers for the regions of the north," according to their proficiency in the idiom and customs of Africa or of Asia. Others were deemed capable of undertaking missions wherever they might be required, and were, therefore, designated by the bold title of "the king's messengers for all lands." In this case extended powers were conferred upon them, and they were permitted to cut short the disputes between two cities in some province they had to inspect, to excuse from tribute, to receive presents and hostages, and even princesses destined for the harem of the Pharaoh, and also to grant the support of troops to such as could give adequate reason for seeking it.[1] Their tasks were always of a delicate and not infrequently of a perilous nature, and constantly exposed them to the danger of being robbed by highwaymen or maltreated by some insubordinate vassal, at times even running the risk of mutilation or assassination by the way.[2] They were obliged to brave the dangers of the forests of

[1] The Tel el-Amarna correspondence shows the messengers in the time of Amenôthes III. and IV. as receiving tribute, as bringing an army to the succour of a chief in difficulties, as threatening with the anger of the Pharaoh the princes of doubtful loyalty, as giving to a faithful vassal compliments and honours from his suzerain, as charged with the conveyance of a gift of slaves, or of escorting a princess to the harem of the Pharaoh.

[2] A letter of Ribaddu, in the time of Amenôthes III., represents a royal messenger as blockaded in Byblos by the rebels.

Lebanon and of the Taurus, the solitudes of Mesopotamia, the marshes of Chaldæa, the voyages to Pûanît and Asia Minor. Some took their way towards Assyria and Babylon, while others embarked at Tyre or Sidon for the islands of the Ægean Archipelago.[1] The endurance of all these officers, whether governors or messengers, their courage, their tact, the ready wit they were obliged to summon to help them out of the difficulties into which their calling frequently brought them, all tended to enlist the public sympathy in their favour.[2] Many of them achieved a reputation, and were made the heroes of popular romance. More than three centuries after it was still related how one of them, by name Thûtîi, had reduced and humbled Jaffa, whose chief had refused to come to terms. Thûtîi set about his task by feigning to throw off his allegiance to Thûtmosis III., and withdrew from the Egyptian service, having first stolen the great magic wand of his lord; he then invited the rebellious chief into his camp, under pretence of showing him this formidable talisman, and killed him after they had drunk together. The cunning

[1] We hear from the tablets of several messengers to Babylon, and the Mitanni, Rasi, Mani, Khamassi. The royal messenger Thûtîi, who governed the countries of the north, speaks of having satisfied the heart of the king in "the isles which are in the midst of the sea." This was not, as some think, a case of hyperbole, for the messengers could embark on Phœnician vessels; they had a less distance to cover in order to reach the Ægean than the royal messenger of Queen Hâtshopsîtû had before arriving at the country of the Somalis and the "Ladders of Incense."
[2] The hero of the *Anastasi Papyrus*, No. 1, with whom Chabas made us acquainted in his *Voyage d'un Égyptien*, is probably a type of the "messenger" of the time of Ramses II.; in any case, his itinerary and adventures are natural to a "royal messenger" compelled to traverse Syria alone.

envoy then packed five hundred of his soldiers into jars, and caused them to be carried on the backs of asses before the gates of the town, where he made the herald of the murdered prince proclaim that the Egyptians had been defeated, and that the pack train which accompanied him contained the spoil, among which was Thûtîi himself. The officer in charge of the city gate was deceived by this harangue, the asses were admitted within the walls, where the soldiers quitted their jars, massacred the garrison, and made themselves masters of the town. The tale is, in the main, the story of Ali Baba and the forty thieves.

The frontier was continually shifting, and Thûtmosis III., like Thûtmosis I., vainly endeavoured to give it a fixed character by erecting stelæ along the banks of the Euphrates, at those points where he contended it had run formerly. While Kharu and Phœnicia were completely in the hands of the conqueror, his suzerainty became more uncertain as it extended northwards in the direction of the Taurus. Beyond Qodshû, it could only be maintained by means of constant supervision, and in Naharaim its duration was coextensive with the sojourn of the conqueror in the locality during his campaign, for it vanished of itself as soon as he had set out on his return to Africa. It will be thus seen that, on the continent of Asia, Egypt possessed a nucleus of territories, so far securely under her rule that they might be actually reckoned as provinces; beyond this immediate domain there was a zone of waning influence, whose area varied with each reign, and even under one king depended largely on the activity which he personally displayed.

SUBMISSION TO THE EGYPTIAN YOKE

This was always the case when the rulers of Egypt attempted to carry their supremacy beyond the isthmus; whether under the Ptolemies or the native kings, the distance to which her influence extended was always practically the same, and the teaching of history enables us to note its limits on the map with relative accuracy.[1] The coast towns, which were in maritime communication with the ports of the Delta, submitted to the Egyptian yoke more readily than those of the interior. But this submission could not be reckoned on beyond Berytus, on the banks of the Lykos, though occasionally it stretched a little further north as far as Byblos and Arvad; even then it did not extend inland, and the curve marking its limits traverses Cœle-Syria from north-west to south-east, terminating at Mount Hermon. Damascus, securely entrenched behind Anti-Lebanon, almost always lay outside this limit. The rulers of Egypt generally succeeded without much difficulty in keeping possession of the countries lying to the south of this line; it demanded merely a slight effort, and this could be furnished for several centuries without encroaching seriously on the resources of the country, or endangering its prosperity. When, however, some province ventured to break away from the control of Egypt, the whole mechanism of the government was put into operation to provide soldiers

[1] The development of the Egyptian navy enabled the Ptolemies to exercise authority over the coasts of Asia Minor and of Thrace, but this extension of their power beyond the indicated limits only hastened the exhaustion of their empire. This instance, like that of Mehemet Ali, thus confirms the position taken up in the text.

and the necessary means for an expedition. Each stage of the advance beyond the frontier demanded a greater expenditure of energy, which, with prolonged distances, would naturally become exhausted. The expedition would scarcely have reached the Taurus or the Euphrates, before the force of circumstances would bring about its recall homewards, leaving but a slight bond of vassalage between the recently subdued countries and the conqueror, which would speedily be cast off or give place to relations dictated by interest or courtesy. Thûtmosis III. had to submit to this sort of necessary law; a further extension of territory had hardly been gained when his dominion began to shrink within the frontiers that appeared to have been prescribed by nature for an empire like that of Egypt. Kharû and Phœnicia proper paid him their tithes with due regularity; the cities of the Amurru and of Zahi, of Damascus, Qodshû, Hamath, and even of Tunipa, lying on the outskirts of these two subject nations, formed an ill-defined borderland, kept in a state of perpetual disturbance by the secret intrigues or open rebellions of the native princes. The kings of Alasia, Naharaim, and Mitanni preserved their independence in spite of repeated reverses, and they treated with the conqueror on equal terms.[1] The tone of their letters to the Pharaoh, the polite formulas with which they addressed him, the special protocol which the Egyptian ministry had drawn up for their reply, all differ widely from those

[1] The difference of tone between the letters of these kings and those of the other princes, as well as the consequences arising from it, has been clearly defined by Delattre.

THE SUBJECTS AND ALLIES OF EGYPT 25

which we see in the despatches coming from commanders of garrisons or actual vassals. In the former it is no longer a slave or a feudatory addressing his master and awaiting his orders, but equals holding courteous communication with each other, the brother of Alasia or of Mitanni with his brother of Egypt. They inform him of their good health, and then, before entering on business, they express their good wishes for himself, his wives, his sons, the lords of his court, his brave soldiers, and for his horses. They were careful never to forget that with a single word their correspondent could let loose upon them a whirlwind of chariots and archers without number, but the respect they felt for his formidable power never degenerated into a fear which would humiliate them before him with their faces in the dust.

This interchange of diplomatic compliments was called for by a variety of exigencies, such as incidents arising on the frontier, secret intrigues, personal alliances, and questions of general politics. The kings of Mesopotamia and of Northern Syria, even those of Assyria and Chaldæa, who were preserved by distance from the dangers of a direct invasion, were in constant fear of an unexpected war, and heartily desired the downfall of Egypt; they endeavoured meanwhile to occupy the Pharaoh so fully at home that he had no leisure to attack them. Even if they did not venture to give open encouragement to the disposition in his subjects to revolt, they at least experienced no scruple in hiring emissaries who secretly fanned the flame of discontent. The Pharaoh, aroused to indignation by such plotting, reminded them of their former oaths and treaties. The king in question would thereupon deny everything, would speak of his tried friendship, and recall the fact that he had refused to help a rebel against his beloved brother.[1] These protestations of innocence were usually accompanied by presents, and produced a twofold effect. They soothed the anger of the offended party, and suggested not only a courteous answer, but the sending of still more valuable gifts. Oriental etiquette, even in those early times, demanded that the present of a less rich or powerful friend should place the recipient under the obligation of sending back a gift of still greater worth. Every one, therefore, whether great or little, was obliged to regulate his liberality according to the estimation in which he held himself, or to the opinion which others formed of him, and a personage of such opulence as the King of Egypt was constrained by the laws of common civility to display an almost boundless generosity: was he not free to work the mines of the Divine Land or the diggings of the Upper Nile; and as for gold, "was it not as the dust of his country"?[2] He would have desired nothing better than to exhibit such liberality, had not the repeated

---

[1] See the letter of Amenôthes III. to Kallimmasin of Babylon, where the King of Egypt complains of the inimical designs which the Babylonian messengers had planned against him, and of the intrigues they had concocted on their return to their own country; see also the letter from Burnaburiash to Amenôthes IV., in which he defends himself from the accusation of having plotted against the King of Egypt at any time, and recalls the circumstance that his father Kurigalzu had refused to encourage the rebellion of one of the Syrian tribes, subjects of Amenôthes III.

[2] See the letter of Dushratta, King of Mitanni, to the Pharaoh Amenôthes IV.

ROYAL PRESENTS AND MARRIAGES 27

calls on his purse at last constrained him to parsimony; he would have been ruined, and Egypt with him, had he given all that was expected of him. Except in a few extraordinary cases, the gifts sent never realised the expectations of the recipients; for instance, when twenty or thirty pounds of precious metal were looked for, the amount despatched would be merely two or three. The indignation of these disappointed beggars and their recriminations were then most amusing: "From the time when my father and thine entered into friendly relations, they loaded each other with presents, and never waited to be asked to exchange amenities;[1] and now my brother sends me two minas of gold as a gift! Send me abundance of gold, as much as thy father sent, and even, for so it must be, more than thy father."[2] Pretexts were never wanting to give reasonable weight to such demands: one correspondent had begun to build a temple or a palace in one of his capitals,[3] another was reserving his fairest daughter for the Pharaoh, and he gave him to understand that anything he might receive would help to complete the bride's trousseau.[4] The princesses

[1] Burnaburiash complains that the king's messengers had only brought him on one occasion two minas of gold, on another occasion twenty minas; moreover, that the quality of the metal was so bad that hardly five minas of pure gold could be extracted from it.

[2] Literally, "and they would never make each other a fair request." The meaning I propose is doubtful, but it appears to be required by the context. The letter from which this passage was taken is from Burnaburiash, King of Babylon, to Amenôthes IV.

[3] This is the pretext advanced by Burnaburiash in the letter just cited.

[4] This seems to have been the motive in a somewhat embarrassing letter

thus sent from Babylon or Mitanni to the court of Thebes enjoyed on their arrival a more honourable welcome, and were assigned a more exalted rank than those who came from Kharû and Phœnicia. As a matter of fact, they were not hostages given over to the conqueror to be disposed of at will, but queens who were united in legal marriage to an ally.[1] Once admitted to the Pharaoh's court, they retained their full rights as his wife, as well as their own fortune and mode of life. Some would bring to their betrothed chests of jewels, utensils, and stuffs, the enumeration of which would cover both sides of a large tablet; others would arrive escorted by several hundred slaves or matrons as personal attendants.[2] A few of them preserved their original name,[3] many assumed an Egyptian designation,[4] and so far adapted themselves to the costumes, manners, and language of their adopted country, that they dropped all intercourse with their

which Dushratta, King of Mitanni, wrote to the Pharaoh Amenôthes III. on the occasion of his fixing the dowry of his daughter.

[1] The daughter of the King of the Khâti, wife of Ramses II., was treated, as we see from the monuments, with as much honour as would have been accorded to Egyptian princesses of pure blood.

[2] Gilukhîpa, who was sent to Egypt to become the wife of Amenôthes III., took with her a company of three hundred and seventy women for her service. She was a daughter of Sutarna, King of Mitanni, and is mentioned several times in the Tel el-Amarna correspondence.

[3] For example, Gilukhîpa, whose name is transcribed Kilagîpa in Egyptian, and another princess of Mitanni, niece of Gilukhîpa, called Tadukhîpa, daughter of Dushratta and wife of Amenôthes IV.

[4] The prince of the Khâti's daughter who married Ramses II. is an example; we know her only by her Egyptian name Mâîtnofirûrî. The wife of Ramses III. added to the Egyptian name of Isis her original name, Humazarati.

ADAPTATION TO ALTERED CIRCUMSTANCES 29

native land, and became regular Egyptians. When, after several years, an ambassador arrived with greetings from their father or brother, he would be puzzled by the changed appearance of these ladies, and would almost doubt their identity: indeed, those only who had been about them in childhood were in such cases able to recognise them.[1] These princesses all adopted the gods of their husbands,[2] though without necessarily renouncing their own. From time to time their parents would send them, with much pomp, a statue of one of their national divinities—Ishtar, for example—which, accompanied by native priests, would remain for some months at the court.[3] The children of these queens ranked next in order to those whose mothers belonged to the solar race, but nothing prevented them marrying their brothers or sisters of pure descent, and being eventually raised to the throne. The members of their families who remained in Asia were naturally proud of these bonds of close affinity with the Pharaoh, and they rarely missed an opportunity of reminding him in their letters that they stood to him in the relationship of brother-in-law, or one of his fathers-in-law; their vanity stood them in good stead, since it

[1] This was the case with the daughter of Kallimmasin, King of Babylon, married to Amenôthes III.; her father's ambassador did not recognise her.
[2] The daughter of the King of the Khâti, wife of Ramses II., is represented in an attitude of worship before her deified husband and two Egyptian gods.
[3] Dushratta of Mitanni, sending a statue of Ishtar to his daughter, wife of Amenôthes III., reminds her that the same statue had already made the voyage to Egypt in the time of his father Sutarna.

afforded them another claim on the favours which they were perpetually asking of him.[1]

These foreign wives had often to interfere in some of the contentions which were bound to arise between two States whose subjects were in constant intercourse with one another. Invasions or provincial wars may have affected or even temporarily suspended the passage to and fro of caravans between the countries of the Tigris and those of the Nile; but as soon as peace was re-established, even though it were the insecure peace of those distant ages, the desert traffic was again resumed and carried on with renewed vigour. The Egyptian traders who penetrated into regions beyond the Euphrates, carried with them, and almost unconsciously disseminated along the whole extent of their route, the numberless products of Egyptian industry, hitherto but little known outside their own country, and rendered expensive owing to the difficulty of transmission or the greed of the merchants. The Syrians now saw for the first time in great quantities, objects which had been known to them hitherto merely through the few rare specimens which made their way across the frontier: arms, stuffs, metal implements, household utensils—in fine, all the objects which ministered to daily needs or to luxury. These were now offered to them at reasonable prices, either by the hawkers who accompanied the army or by the soldiers themselves, always ready, as soldiers are, to part with their possessions in order to procure a few extra

[1] Dushratta of Mitanni never loses an opportunity of calling Amenôthes III., husband of his sister Gilukhipa, and of one of his daughters, " akhiya," my brother, and " khatani-ya," my son-in-law.

pleasures in the intervals of fighting. On the other hand, whole convoys of spoil were despatched to Egypt after every successful campaign, and their contents were distri-

THE LOTANÛ AND THE GOLDSMITHS' WORK CONSTITUTING THEIR TRIBUTE.[1]

buted in varying proportions among all classes of society, from the militiaman belonging to some feudal contingent,

[1] Drawn by Boudier, from a photograph by Insinger. The scene here reproduced occurs in most of the Theban tombs of the XVIIIth dynasty.

who received, as a reward of his valour, some half-dozen necklaces or bracelets, to the great lord of ancient family or the Crown Prince, who carried off waggon-loads of booty in their train. These distributions must have stimulated a passion for all Syrian goods, and as the spoil was insufficient to satisfy the increasing demands of the consumer, the waning commerce which had been carried on from early times was once more revived and extended, till every route, whether by land or water, between Thebes, Memphis, and the Asiatic cities, was thronged by those engaged in its pursuit. It would take too long to enumerate the various objects of merchandise brought in almost daily to the marts on the Nile by Phœnician vessels or the owners of caravans. They comprised slaves destined for the workshop or the harem,[1] Hittite bulls and stallions, horses from Singar, oxen from Alasia, rare and curious animals such as elephants from Nii, and brown bears from the Lebanon,[2] smoked and salted fish, live birds of many-coloured plumage, goldsmiths' work[3] and precious stones, of which lapis-lazuli was the chief, wood for building or for ornamental work—pine,

[1] Syrian slaves are mentioned along with Ethiopian in the *Anastasi Papyrus*, No. 1, and there is mention in the Tel el-Amarna correspondence of Hittite slaves whom Dushratta of Mitanni brought to Amenôthes III., and of other presents of the same kind made by the King of Alasia as a testimony of his grateful homage.

[2] The elephant and the bear are represented on the tomb of Rakhmirî among the articles of tribute brought into Egypt.

[3] The *Annals of Thûtmosis III.* make a record in each campaign of the importation of gold and silver vases, objects in lapis-lazuli and crystal, or of blocks of the same materials; the Theban tombs of this period afford examples of the vases and blocks brought by the Syrians. The Tel el-Amarna letters also mention vessels of gold or blocks of precious stone

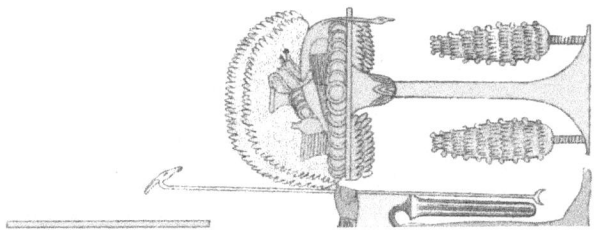
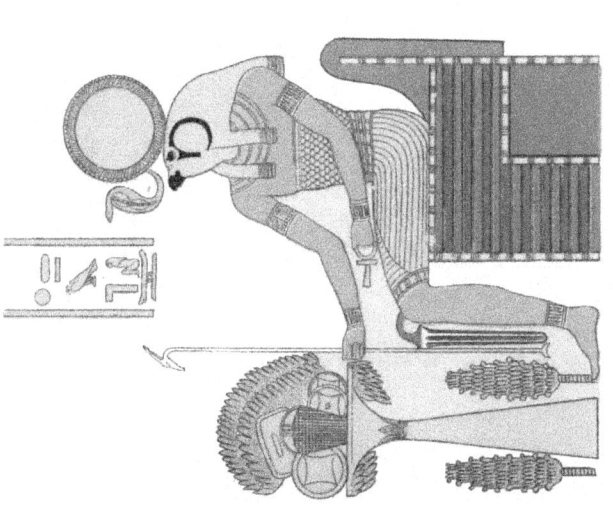

PAINTED TABLET IN THE HALL OF HARPS IN THE FIFTH TOMB OF THE KINGS TO THE EAST. THEBES (BŶBAN EL MOLOUK).

cypress, yew, cedar, and oak,[1] musical instruments,[2] helmets, leathern jerkins covered with metal scales, weapons of bronze and iron,[3] chariots,[4] dyed and embroidered stuffs,[5] sent as presents or as objects of exchange to the Pharaoh by the King of Babylon, by the King of Mitanni, by the King of the Hittites, and by other princes. The lapis-lazuli of Babylon, which probably came from Persia, was that which was most prized by the Egyptians on account of the golden sparks in it, which enhanced the blue colour; this is, perhaps, the Uknu of the cuneiform inscriptions, which has been read for a long time as "crystal."

[1] Building and ornamental woods are often mentioned in the inscriptions of Thûtmosis III. A scene at Karnak represents Seti I. causing building-wood to be cut in the region of the Lebanon. A letter of the King of Alasia speaks of contributions of wood which several of his subjects had to make to the King of Egypt.

[2] Some stringed instruments of music, and two or three kinds of flutes and flageolets, are designated in Egyptian by names borrowed from some Semitic tongue—a fact which proves that they were imported; the wooden framework of the harp, decorated with sculptured heads of Astartê, figures among the objects coming from Syria in the temple of the Theban Amon.

[3] Several names of arms borrowed from some Semitic dialect have been noticed in the texts of this period. The objects as well as the words must have been imported into Egypt, e.g. the quiver, the sword and javelins used by the charioteers. Cuirasses and leathern jerkins are mentioned in the inscriptions of Thûtmosis III.

[4] Chariots plated with gold and silver figure frequently among the spoils of Thûtmosis III.: the *Anastasi Papyrus*, No. 1, contains a detailed description of Syrian chariots — Markabûti — with a reference to the localities where certain parts of them were made;—the country of the Amurru, that of Aûpa, the town of Pahira. The Tel el-Amarna correspondence mentions very frequently chariots sent to the Pharaoh by the King of Babylon, either as presents or to be sold in Egypt; others sent by the King of Alasia and by the King of Mitanni.

[5] Some linen, cotton, or woollen stuffs are mentioned in the *Anastasi Papyrus*, No. 4, and elsewhere as coming from Syria. The Egyptian love of white linen always prevented their estimating highly the coloured and brocaded stuffs of Asia; and one sees nowhere, in the representations, any examples of stuffs of such origin, except on furniture or in ships equipped with something of the kind in the form of sails.

perfumes,[1] dried cakes, oil, wines of Kharû, liqueurs from Alasia, Khâti, Singar, Naharaim, Amurru, and beer from

THE BEAR AND ELEPHANT BROUGHT AS TRIBUTE IN THE TOMB OF RAKHMIRI.[2]

Qodi.[3] On arriving at the frontier, whether by sea or by land, the majority of these objects had to pay the custom

[1] The perfumed oils of Syria are mentioned in a general way in the *Anastasi Papyrus*, No. 1; the King of Alasia speaks of essences which he is sending to Amenôthes III.; the King of Mitanni refers to bottles of oil which he is forwarding to Gilukhîpa and to Tii.

[2] Drawn by Faucher-Gudin, from a photograph of Prisse d'Avennes' sketch.

[3] A list of cakes of Syrian origin is found in the *Anastasi Papyrus*, No. 1; also a reference to balsamic oils from Naharaim, and to various oils which had arrived in the ports of the Delta, to the wines of Syria, to palm wine and various liqueurs manufactured in Alasia, in Singar, among the Khâti, Amorites, and the people of Tikhisa; finally, to the beer of Qodi.

dues which were rigorously collected by the officers of the Pharaoh. This, no doubt, was a reprisal tariff, since independent sovereigns, such as those of Mitanni, Assyria, and Babylon, were accustomed to impose a similar duty on all the products of Egypt. The latter, indeed, supplied more than she received, for many articles which reached her in their raw condition were, by means of native industry, worked up and exported as ornaments, vases, and highly decorated weapons, which, in the course of international traffic, were dispersed to all four corners of the earth. The merchants of Babylon and Assyria had little to fear as long as they kept within the domains of their own sovereign or in those of the Pharaoh; but no sooner did they venture within the borders of those turbulent states which separated the two great powers, than they were exposed to dangers at every turn. Safe-conducts were of little use if they had not taken the additional precaution of providing a strong escort and carefully guarding their caravan, for the Shaûsû concealed in the depths of the Lebanon or the needy sheikhs of Kharû could never resist the temptation to rob the passing traveller.[1] The victims

---

[1] The scribe who in the reign of Ramses II. composed the *Travels of an Egyptian*, speaks in several places of marauding tribes and robbers, who infested the roads followed by the hero. The Tel el-Amarna correspondence contains a letter from the King of Alasia, who exculpates himself from being implicated in the harsh treatment certain Egyptians had received in passing through his territory; and another letter in which the King of Babylon complains that Chaldæan merchants had been robbed at Khinnatun, in Galilee, by the Prince of Akku (Acre) and his accomplices: one of them had his feet cut off, and the other was still a prisoner in Akku, and Burnaburiash demands from Amenôthes IV. the death of the guilty persons.

complained to their king, who felt no hesitation in passing on their woes to the sovereign under whose rule the pillagers were supposed to live. He demanded their punishment, but his request was not always granted, owing to the difficulties of finding out and seizing the offenders. An indemnity, however, could be obtained which would nearly compensate the merchants for the loss sustained. In many cases justice had but little to do with the negotiations, in which self-interest was the chief motive; but repeated refusals would have discouraged traders, and by lessening the facilities of transit, have diminished the revenue which the state drew from its foreign commerce.

The question became a more delicate one when it concerned the rights of subjects residing out of their native country. Foreigners, as a rule, were well received in Egypt; the whole country was open to them; they could marry, they could acquire houses and lands, they enjoyed permission to follow their own religion unhindered, they were eligible for public honours, and more than one of the officers of the crown whose tombs we see at Thebes were themselves Syrians, or born of Syrian parents on the banks of the Nile.[1] Hence, those who settled in Egypt without any intention of returning to their own country enjoyed all the advantages possessed by the natives, whereas those who took up a merely temporary abode there were more limited in their privileges. They were granted the permission to hold property in the country, and also the right to

[1] In a letter from the King of Alasia, there is question of a merchant who had died in Egypt. Among other monuments proving the presence of Syrians about the Pharaoh, is the stele of Ben-Azana, of the town

buy and sell there, but they were not allowed to transmit their possessions at will, and if by chance they died on Egyptian soil, their goods lapsed as a forfeit to the crown. The heirs remaining in the native country of the dead man, who were ruined by this confiscation, sometimes petitioned the king to interfere in their favour with a view of obtaining restitution. If the Pharaoh consented to waive his right of forfeiture, and made over the confiscated objects or their equivalent to the relatives of the deceased, it was solely by an act of mercy, and as an example to foreign governments to treat Egyptians with a like clemency should they chance to proffer a similar request.[1] It is also not improbable that the sovereigns themselves had a personal interest in more than one commercial undertaking, and that they were the partners, or, at any rate, interested in the enterprises, of many of their subjects, so that any loss sustained by one of the latter would eventually fall upon themselves. They had, in fact, reserved to themselves the privilege of carrying on several lucrative industries, and of disposing of the products to foreign buyers, either to those who purchased them out and out, or else through the medium of agents, to whom they intrusted certain quantities of the goods for warehousing. The King of Babylon, taking advantage of the

of Zairabizana, surnamed Ramses-Empirî: he was surrounded with Semites like himself.

[1] All this seems to result from a letter in which the King of Alasia demands from Amenôthes III. the restitution of the goods of one of his subjects who had died in Egypt; the tone of the letter is that of one asking a favour, and on the supposition that the King of Egypt had a right to keep the property of a foreigner dying on his territory.

fashion which prompted the Egyptians to acquire objects of Chaldæan goldsmiths' and cabinet-makers' art, caused ingots of gold to be sent to him by the Pharaoh, which he returned worked up into vases, ornaments, household utensils, and plated chariots. He further fixed the value of all such objects, and took a considerable commission for having acted as intermediary in the transaction.[1] In Alasia, which was the land of metals, the king appears to have held a monopoly of the bronze. Whether he smelted it in the country, or received it from more distant regions ready prepared, we cannot say, but he claimed and retained for himself the payment for all that the Pharaoh deigned to order of him.[2] From such instances we can well understand the jealous watch which these sovereigns exercised, lest any individual connected with corporations of workmen should leave the kingdom and establish himself in another country without special permission. Any emigrant who opened a workshop and initiated his new compatriots in the technique or professional secrets of his craft, was regarded by the authorities as the most dangerous of all evil-doers. By thus introducing his trade into a rival state, he deprived his own people of a good customer, and thus rendered himself liable to the penalties inflicted on those who were guilty of treason. His savings were confiscated, his house razed to the ground, and his whole family—parents, wives, and children—treated as partakers in his crime. As for

---

[1] Letter of Burnaburiash to Amenôthes IV.
[2] Letter from the King of Alasia to Amenôthes III., where, whilst pretending to have nothing else in view than making a present to his royal

himself, if justice succeeded in overtaking him, he was punished with death, or at least with mutilation, such as the loss of eyes and ears, or amputation of the feet. This severity did not prevent the frequent occurrence of such cases, and it was found necessary to deal with them by the insertion of a special extradition clause in treaties of peace and other alliances. The two contracting parties decided against conceding the right of habitation to skilled workmen who should take refuge with either party on the territory of the other, and they agreed to seize such workmen forthwith, and mutually restore them, but under the express condition that neither they nor any of their belongings should incur any penalty for the desertion of their country. It would be curious to know if all the arrangements agreed to by the kings of those times were sanctioned, as in the above instance, by properly drawn up agreements. Certain expressions occur in their correspondence which seem to prove that this was the case, and that the relations between them, of which we can catch traces, resulted not merely from a state of things which, according to their ideas, did not necessitate any diplomatic sanction, but from conventions agreed to after some war, or entered on without any previous struggle, when there was no question at issue between the two states.[1] When once the

brother, he proposes to make an exchange of some bronze for the products of Egypt, especially for gold.

[1] The treaty of Ramses II. with the King of the Khâti, the only one which has come down to us, was a renewal of other treaties effected one after the other between the fathers and grandfathers of the two contracting sovereigns. Some of the Tel el-Amarna letters probably refer to treaties of this kind; *e.g.* that of Burnaburiash of Babylon, who says that since

THE EIGHTEENTH THEBAN DYNASTY

Syrian conquest had been effected, Egypt gave permanency to its results by means of a series of international decrees, which officially established the constitution of her empire, and brought about her concerted action with the Asiatic powers.

She already occupied an important position among them, when Thûtmosis III. died, on the last day of Phamenoth, in the LVth year of his reign.[1] He was buried, probably, at Deîr el-Baharî, in the family tomb wherein the most illustrious members of his house had been laid to rest since the time of Thûtmosis I. His mummy was not

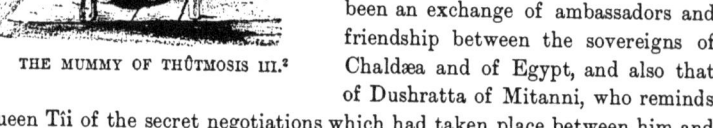

THE MUMMY OF THÛTMOSIS III.[2]

the time of Karaîndash there had been an exchange of ambassadors and friendship between the sovereigns of Chaldæa and of Egypt, and also that of Dushratta of Mitanni, who reminds Queen Tîi of the secret negotiations which had taken place between him and Amenôthes III.

[1] Dr. Mahler has, with great precision, fixed the date of the accession of Thûtmosis III. as the 20th of March, 1503, and that of his death as the 14th of February, 1449 B.C. I do not think that the data furnished to Dr. Mahler by Brugsch will admit of such exact conclusions being drawn from them, and I should fix the fifty-four years of the reign of Thûtmosis III. in a less decided manner, between 1550 and 1490 B.C., allowing, as I have said before, for an error of half a century more or less in the dates which go back to the time of the second Theban empire.

[2] Drawn by Faucher-Gudin, from a photograph taken by Émil Brugsch-Bey.

THÛTMOSIS III.

securely hidden away, for towards the close of the XXth dynasty it was torn out of the coffin by robbers, who stripped it and rifled it of the jewels with which it was covered, injuring it in their haste to carry away the spoil. It was subsequently re-interred, and has remained undisturbed until the present day; but before re-burial some renovation of the wrappings was necessary, and as portions of the body had become loose, the restorers, in order to give the mummy the necessary firmness, compressed it between four oar-shaped slips of wood, painted white, and placed, three inside the wrappings and one outside, under the bands which confined the winding-sheet. Happily the face, which had been plastered over with pitch at the time of embalming, did not suffer at all from this rough treatment, and appeared intact when the protecting mask was removed. Its appearance does not answer to our ideal of the conqueror. His statues, though not representing him as a type of manly beauty, yet give him refined, intelligent features, but a comparison with the mummy

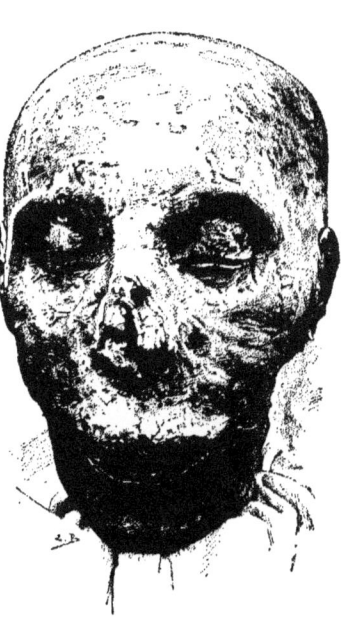

HEAD OF THE MUMMY OF THÛTMOSIS III.[1]

[1] Drawn by Boudier, from a photograph lent by M. Grébaut, taken by Émil Brugsch-Bey.

shows that the artists have idealised their model. The forehead is abnormally low, the eyes deeply sunk, the jaw heavy, the lips thick, and the cheek-bones extremely prominent; the whole recalling the physiognomy of Thûtmosis II., though with a greater show of energy. Thûtmosis III. is a fellah of the old stock, squat, thickset, vulgar in character and expression, but not lacking in firmness and vigour.[1] Amenôthes II., who succeeded him, must have closely resembled him, if we may trust his official portraits. He was the son of a princess of the blood, Hâtshopsîtû II., daughter of the great Hâtshopsîtû,[2] and consequently he came into his inheritance with stronger claims to it than any other Pharaoh since the time of Amenôthes I. Possibly his father may have associated him with himself on the throne as soon as the young prince attained his majority;[3] at any rate, his accession aroused no appreciable opposition in the country, and if any difficulties were made, they must have come from outside. It is always a dangerous moment in the existence of a newly formed empire when its founder having passed away, and the conquered people not having yet become accustomed to a subject condition, they are called upon to submit to a successor of whom they know little or nothing. It is always problematical whether the new sovereign will display as great activity and be as

[1] The restored remains allow us to estimate the height at about 5 ft. 3 in.

[2] His parentage is proved by the pictures preserved in the tomb of his foster-father, where he is represented in company with the *royal mother*, Marîtrî Hâtshopsîtû.

[3] It is thus that Wiedemann explains his presence by the side of Thûtmosis III. on certain has-reliefs in the temple of Amada.

successful as the old one; whether he will be capable of turning to good account the armies which his predecessor commanded with such skill, and led so bravely against the enemy; whether, again, he will have sufficient tact to estimate correctly the burden of taxation which each province is capable of bearing, and to lighten it when there is a risk of its becoming too heavy. If he does not show from the first that it is his purpose to maintain his patrimony intact at all costs, or if his officers, no longer controlled by a strong hand, betray any indecision in command, his subjects will become unruly, and the change of monarch will soon furnish a pretext for widespread rebellion. The beginning of the reign of Amenôthes II. was marked by a revolt of the Libyans inhabiting the Theban Oasis, but this rising was soon put down by that Amenemhabî who had so distinguished himself under Thûtmosis.[1] Soon after, fresh troubles broke out in different parts of Syria, in Galilee, in the country of the Amurru, and among the peoples of Naharaim. The king's prompt action, however, prevented their resulting in a general war.[2] He marched in person against the

[1] Brugsch and Wiedemann place this expedition at the time when Amenôthes II. was either hereditary prince or associated with his father; the inscription of Amenemhabî places it explicitly after the death of Thûtmosis III., and this evidence outweighs every other consideration until further discoveries are made.

[2] The campaigns of Amenôthes II. were related on a granite stele, which was placed against the second of the southern pylons at Karnak. The date of this monument is almost certainly the year II.; there is strong evidence in favour of this, if it is compared with the inscription of Amada, where Amenôthes II. relates that in the year III. he sacrificed the prisoners whom he had taken in the country of Tikhisa.

malcontents, reduced the town of Shamshiaduma, fell upon the Lamnaniu, and attacked their chief, slaying him

AMENÔTHES II., FROM THE STATUE AT TURIN.[1]

with his own hand, and carrying off numbers of captives. He crossed the Orontes on the 26th of Pachons, in the year II., and seeing some mounted troops in the

[1] Drawn by Faucher-Gudin.

distance, rushed upon them and overthrew them; they proved to be the advanced guard of the enemy's force, which he encountered shortly afterwards and routed, collecting in the pursuit considerable booty. He finally reached Naharaim, where he experienced in the main but a feeble resistance. Nii surrendered without resistance on the 10th of Epiphi, and its inhabitants, both men and women, with censers in their hands, assembled on the walls and prostrated themselves before the conqueror. At Akaîti, where the partisans of the Egyptian government had suffered persecution from a considerable section of the natives, order was at once re-established as soon as the king's approach was made known. No doubt the rapidity of his marches and the vigour of his attacks, while putting an end to the hostile attitude of the smaller vassal states, were effectual in inducing the sovereigns of Alasia, of Mitanni,[1] and of the Hittites to renew with Amenôthes the friendly relations which they had established with his father.[2] This one campaign, which lasted three or four months, secured a lasting peace in the north, but in the south a disturbance again broke out among the Barbarians of the Upper Nile. Amenôthes suppressed it, and, in order to prevent a

[1] Amenôthes II. mentions tribute from Mitanni on one of the columns which he decorated at Karnak, in the Hall of the Caryatides, close to the pillars finished by his predecessors.

[2] The cartouches on the pedestal of the throne of Amenôthes II., in the tomb of one of his officers at Sheikh-Abd-el-Qûrueh, represent—together with the inhabitants of the Oasis, Libya, and Kush—the Kefatiû, the people of Naharaim, and the Upper Lotanû, that is to say, the entire dominion of Thûtmosis III., besides the people of Manûs, probably Mallos, in the Cilician plain.

repetition of it, was guilty of an act of cruel severity quite in accordance with the manners of the time. He had taken prisoner seven chiefs in the country of Tikhisa, and had brought them, chained, in triumph to Thebes, on the forecastle of his ship. He sacrificed six of them himself before Amon, and exposed their heads and hands on the façade of the temple of Karnak; the seventh was subjected to a similar fate at Napata at the beginning of his third year, and thenceforth the sheîkhs of Kûsh thought twice before defying the authority of the Pharaoh.[1]

Amenôthes' reign was a short one, lasting ten years at most, and the end of it seems to have been darkened by the open or secret rivalries which the question of the succession usually stirred up among the kings' sons. The king had daughters only by his marriage with one of his full sisters, who like himself possessed all the rights of sovereignty; those of his sons who did not die young were the children of princesses of inferior rank or of concubines, and it was a subject of anxiety among these princes which of them would be chosen to inherit the crown and be united in marriage with the king's heiresses, Khûît and Mûtemûaû. One of his sons, named Thûtmosis, who resided at the "White Wall," was in the habit of betaking himself frequently to the Libyan desert to practise with the javelin, or to pursue the hunt of lions and gazelles

[1] In an inscription in the temple of Amada, it is there said that the king offered this sacrifice on his return from his first expedition into Asia, and for this reason I have connected the facts thus related with those known to us through the stele of Karnak.

THE GREAT SPHINX AND THE CHAPEL OF THÛTMOSIS IV.
Drawn by Faucher-Gudin, from the photograph taken in 1887 by Émil Brugsch-Bey

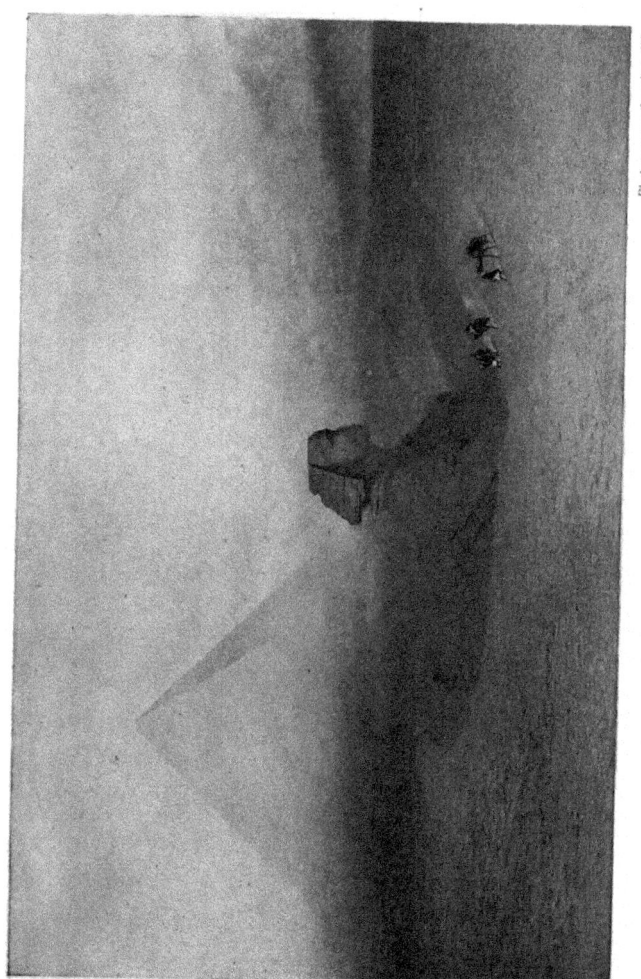

Photogravure Fougel & Cⁱᵉ

DREAM OF AMENÔTHES II.

in his chariot. On these occasions it was his pleasure to preserve the strictest incognito, and he was accompanied by two discreet servants only. One day, when chance had brought him into the neighbourhood of the Great Pyramid, he lay down for his accustomed siesta in the shade cast by the Sphinx, the miraculous image of Khopri the most powerful, the god to whom all men in Memphis and the neighbouring towns raised adoring hands filled with offerings. The gigantic statue was at that time more than half buried, and its head alone was seen above the sand. As soon as the prince was asleep it spoke gently to him, as a father to his son: "Behold me, gaze on me, O my son Thûtmosis, for I, thy father Harmakhis-Khopri-Tûmû, grant thee sovereignty over the two countries, in both the South and the North, and thou shalt wear both the white and the red crown on the throne of Sibû, the sovereign, possessing the earth in its length and breadth; the flashing eye of the lord of all shall cause to rain on thee the possessions of Egypt, vast tribute from all foreign countries, and a long life for many years as one chosen by the Sun, for my countenance is thine, my heart is thine, no other than thyself is mine! Nor am I covered by the sand of the mountain on which I rest, and have given thee this prize that thou mayest do for me what my heart desires, for I know that thou art my son, my defender; draw nigh, I am with thee, I am thy well-beloved father." The prince understood that the god promised him the kingdom on condition of his swearing to clear the sand from the statue. He was, in fact, chosen to be the husband of the queens, and immediately after his accession he fulfilled his oath ; he removed the sand, built a chapel between the paws, and erected against the breast of the statue a stele of red

THE STELE OF THE SPHINX OF GÎZEH.[1]

granite, on which he related his adventure. His reign was as short as that of Amenôthes, and his campaigns both in Asia and Ethiopia were unimportant.[2] He had suc-

[1] Drawn by Boudier, from a photograph by Émil Brugsch-Bey.
[2] The latest date of his reign at present known is that of the year VII., on the rocks of Konosso, and on a stele of Sarbût el-Khâdim. There is an allusion to his wars against the Ethiopians in an inscription of Amada, and to his campaigns against the peoples of the North and South on the stele of Nofirhaît.

ceeded to an empire so firmly established from Naharaim to Kari,¹ that, apparently, no rebellion could disturb its peace. One of the two heiress-princesses, Kûît, the daughter, sister, and wife of a king, had no living male offspring, but her companion Mûtemûaû had at least one son, named Amenôthes. In his case, again, the noble birth of the mother atoned for the defects of the paternal origin. Moreover, according to tradition, Amon-Râ himself had intervened to renew the blood of his descendants: he appeared in the person of Thûtmosis IV., and under this guise became the father of the heir of the Pharaohs.² Like Queen Ahmasis in the bas-reliefs of Deir el-Baharî, Mûtemûaû is shown on those of Luxor in the arms of her divine lover, and subsequently greeted by him with the title of mother; in another bas-relief we see the queen led to her couch by the goddesses who preside over the birth of children; her son Amenôthes, on coming into the world with his double, is placed in the hands of the two Niles, to receive the nourishment and the education meet for the children of the gods. He profited fully by them, for he remained in power forty years, and his reign

[1] The peoples of Naharaim and of Northern Syria are represented bringing him tribute, in a tomb at Sheikh-Abd-el-Qûrneh. The inscription published by Mariette, speaks of the first expedition of Thûtmosis IV. to the land of [Naharai]na, and of the gifts which he lavished on this occasion on the temple of Amon.

[2] It was at first thought that Mûtemûaû was an Ethiopian, afterwards that she was a Syrian, who had changed her name on arriving at the court of her husband. The manner in which she is represented at Luxor, and in all the texts where she figures, proves not only that she was of Egyptian race, but that she was the daughter of Amenôthes II., and born of the marriage of that prince with one of his sisters, who was herself an hereditary princess.

was one of the most prosperous ever witnessed by Egypt during the Theban dynasties.

Amenôthes III. had spent but little of his time in war. He had undertaken the usual raids in the South against the negroes and the tribes of the Upper Nile. In his fifth year, a general defection of the sheikhs obliged him to invade the province of Abhaît, near Semneh, which he devastated at the head of the troops collected by Marimosû, the Prince of Kûsh; the punishment was salutary, the booty considerable, and a lengthy peace was re-established. The object of his rare expeditions into Naharaim was not so much to add new provinces to his empire, as to prevent disturbances in the old ones. The kings of Alasia, of the Khâti, of Mitanni, of Singar,[2] of Assyria, and of Babylon did not dare to provoke so powerful a neighbour.[3] The remembrance of the

QUEEN MÛTEMÛAÛ.[1]

[1] Drawn by Faucher-Gudin, from a photograph by Daniel Héron.

[2] Amenôthes entitles himself on a scarabæus "he who takes prisoner the country of Singar;" no other document has yet been discovered to show whether this is hyperbole, or whether he really reached this distant region.

[3] The lists of the time of Amenôthes III. contain the names of Phœnicia, Naharaim, Singar, Qodshu, Tunipa, Patina, Carchemish, and Assur; that is to say, of all the subject or allied nations mentioned in the correspondence of Tel el-Amarna. Certain episodes of these expeditions had been engraved on the exterior face of the pylon constructed by the king for the temple of

victories of Thûtmosis III. was still fresh in their memories, and, even had their hands been free, would have made them cautious in dealing with his great-grandson; but they were incessantly engaged in internecine quarrels, and had

AMENÔTHES III.
FROM THE
TOMB OF KHÂMHÂÎT.[1]

recourse to Pháraoh merely to enlist his support, or at any rate make sure of his neutrality, and prevent him from joining their adversaries. Whatever might have been the nature of their private sentiments, they professed to be anxious to maintain, for their mutual interests, the

Amon at Karnak; at the present time they are concealed by the wall at the lower end of the Hypostyle Hall. The tribute of the Lotanû was represented on the tomb of Hûi, at Sheikh-Abd-el-Qûrneh.

[1] Drawn by Boudier, from a photograph by Daniel Héron.

relations with Egypt entered on half a century before, and as the surest method of attaining their object was by a good marriage, they would each seek an Egyptian wife for himself, or would offer Amenôthes a princess of one of their own royal families. The Egyptian king was, however, firm in refusing to bestow a princess of the solar blood even on the most powerful of the foreign kings; his pride rebelled at the thought that she might one day be consigned to a place among the inferior wives or concubines, but he gladly accepted, and even sought for wives for himself, from among the Syrian and Chaldæan princesses. Kallimmasin of Babylon gave Amenôthes first his sister, and when age had deprived this princess of her beauty, then his daughter Irtabi in marriage.[1] Sutarna of Mitanni had in the same way given the Pharaoh his daughter Gilukhîpa; indeed, most of the kings of that period had one or two relations in the harem at Thebes. This connexion usually proved a support to Asiatic sovereigns, such alliances being a safeguard against the rivalries of their brothers or cousins. At times, however, they were the means of exposing them to serious dangers. When Sutarna died he was succeeded by his son Dushratta, but a numerous party put forward another prince, named Artassumara, who was probably Gilukhîpa's brother, on

[1] Letter from Amenôthes III. to Kallimmasin, concerning a sister of the latter, who was married to the King of Egypt, but of whom there are no further records remaining at Babylon, and also one of his daughters whom Amenôthes had demanded in marriage; and letters from Kallimmasin, consenting to bestow his daughter Irtabi on the Pharaoh, and proposing to give to Amenôthes whichever one he might choose of the daughters of his house.

EXPLOITS OF AMENÔTHES III.

the mother's side;[1] a Hittite king of the name of Pirkhi espoused the cause of the pretender, and a civil war broke out. Dushratta was victorious, and caused his brother to be strangled, but was not without anxiety as to the consequences which might follow this execution should Gilukhîpa desire to avenge the victim, and to this end stir up the anger of the suzerain against him. Dushratta, therefore, wrote a humble epistle, showing that he had received provocation, and that he had found it necessary to strike a decisive blow to save his own life; the tablet was accompanied by various presents to the royal pair, comprising horses, slaves, jewels, and perfumes. Gilukhîpa, however, bore Dushratta no ill-will, and the latter's anxieties were allayed. The so-called expeditions of Amenôthes to the Syrian provinces must constantly have been merely visits of inspection, during which amusements, and especially the chase, occupied nearly as important a place as war and politics. Amenôthes III. took to heart that pre-eminently royal duty of ridding the country of wild beasts, and fulfilled it more conscientiously than any of his predecessors. He had killed 112 lions during the first ten years of his reign, and as it was an exploit of which he was remarkably proud, he perpetuated the memory of it in a special inscription, which he caused to be engraved on numbers of large

---

[1] Her exact relationship is not explicitly expressed, but is implied in the facts, for there seems no reason why Gilukhîpa should have taken the part of one brother rather than another, unless Artassumara had been nearer to her than Dushratta; that is to say, her brother on the mother's side as well as on the father's.

scarabs of fine green enamel. Egypt prospered under his peaceful government, and if the king made no great efforts to extend her frontiers, he spared no pains to enrich the country by developing industry and agriculture, and also endeavoured to perfect the military organisation which had rendered the conquest of the East so easy a matter. A census, undertaken by his minister Amenôthes, the son of Hâpi, ensured a more correct assessment of the taxes, and a regular scheme of recruiting for the army. Whole tribes of slaves were brought into the country by means of the border raids which were always taking place, and their opportune arrival helped to fill up the vacancies which repeated wars had caused among the rural and urban population; such a strong impetus to agriculture was also given by this importation, that when, towards the middle of the reign, the minister Khâmhâît presented the tax-gathers at court, he was able to boast that he had stored in the State granaries a larger quantity of corn than had been gathered in for thirty years. The traffic carried on between Asia and the Delta by means of both Egyptian and foreign ships was controlled by custom-houses erected at the mouths of the Nile, the coast being

SCARAB OF THE HUNT.[1]

[1] Drawn by Faucher-Gudin, from the photograph published in Mariette.

THE TEMPLES AND RELIGIONS OF NUBIA 57

protected by cruising vessels against the attacks of pirates. The fortresses of the isthmus and of the Libyan border, having been restored or rebuilt, constituted a check on the turbulence of the nomad tribes, while garrisons posted at intervals at the entrance to the Wadys leading to the desert restrained the plunderers scattered between the Nile and the Red Sea, and between the chain of Oases and the unexplored regions of the Sahara.[1] Egypt was at once the most powerful as well as the most prosperous kingdom in the world, being able to command more labour and more precious metals for the embellishment of her towns and the construction of her monuments than any other.

Public works had been carried on briskly under Thûtmosis III. and his successors. The taste for building, thwarted at first by the necessity of financial reforms, and then by that of defraying the heavy expenses incurred through the expulsion of the Hyksôs and the earlier foreign wars, had free scope as soon as spoil from the Syrian victories began to pour in year by year. While the treasure seized from the enemy provided the money, the majority of the prisoners were used as workmen, so that temples, palaces, and citadels began to rise as if by magic from one end of the valley to the other.[2] Nubia, divided into provinces, formed merely an extension of the ancient

[1] All this information is gathered from the inscription on the statue of Amenôthes, the son of Hâpi.
[2] For this use of prisoners of war, cf. the picture from the tomb of Rakhmirî on p. 58 of the present work, in which most of the earlier Egyptologists believed they recognised the Hebrews, condemned by Pharaoh to build the cities of Ramses and Pithom in the Delta.

58   THE EIGHTEENTH THEBAN DYNASTY

feudal Egypt—at any rate as far as the neighbourhood of the Tacazzeh—though the Egyptian religion had here assumed a peculiar character. The conquest of Nubia having been almost entirely the work of the Theban dynasties, the Theban triad, Amon, Maût, and Montû, and their immediate followers were paramount in this region, while in the north, in witness of the ancient Elephantinite colonisation, we find Khnûmû of the cataract being

A GANG OF SYRIAN PRISONERS MAKING BRICK FOR THE TEMPLE OF AMON.[1]

worshipped, in connexion with Didûn, father of the indigenous Nubians. The worship of Amon had been the means of introducing that of Râ and of Horus, and Osiris as lord of the dead, while Phtah, Sokhît, Atûmû, and the Memphite and Heliopolitan gods were worshipped only in isolated parts of the province. A being, however, of less exalted rank shared with the lords of heaven the favour of the people. This was the Pharaoh, who as the son of Amon was foreordained to receive divine honours, sometimes figuring, as at Bohani, as the third member of a

[1] Drawn by Faucher-Gudin, from the chromolithograph in Lepsius.

triad, at other times as head of the Ennead. Ûsirtasen III. had had his chapels at Semueh and at Kûmmeh, they were restored by Thûtmosis III., who claimed a share of the worship offered in them, and whose son, Amenôthes II., also assumed the symbols and functions of divinity. Amenôthes I. was venerated in the province of Kari, and Amenôthes III., when founding the fortress Hâit-Khâmmâît[1] in the neighbourhood of a Nubian village, on a spot now known as Soleb, built a temple there, of which he himself was the protecting genius.[2] The edifice was of considerable size, and the columns and walls

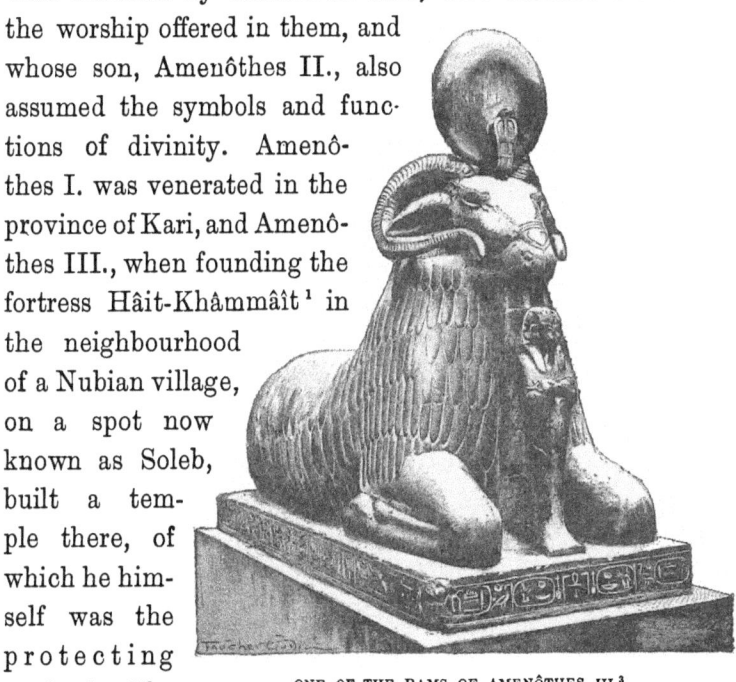

ONE OF THE RAMS OF AMENÔTHES III.[3]

[1] The name signifies literally "the Citadel of Khâmmâît," and it is formed, as Lepsius recognised from the first, from the name of the Sparrow-hawk Khâmmâît, "Maît rising as Goddess," which Amenôthes had assumed on his accession.

[2] Lepsius recognised the nature of the divinity worshipped in this temple; the deified statue of the king, "his living statue on earth," which represented the god of the temple, is there named "Nibmâûrî, lord of Nubia." Thûtmosis III. had already worked at Soleb.

[3] Drawn by Faucher-Gudin, from a photograph by Mons. de Mertens.

remaining reveal an art as perfect as that shown in the best monuments at Thebes. It was approached by an avenue of ram-headed sphinxes, while colossal statues of lions and hawks, the sacred animals of the district, adorned the building. The sovereign condescended to preside in person at its dedication on one of his journeys to the southern part of his empire, and the mutilated pictures still visible on the façade show the order and detail of the ceremony observed on this occasion. The king, with the crown upon his head, stood before the centre gate, accompanied by the queen and his minister Amenôthes, the son of Hâpi, who was better acquainted than any other man of his time with the mysteries of the ritual.[1] The king then struck the door twelve times with his mace of white stone, and when the approach to the first hall was opened, he repeated the operation at the threshold of the sanctuary previous to entering and placing his statue there. He deposited it on the painted and gilded wooden platform on which the gods were exhibited on feast-days, and enthroned beside it the other images which were thenceforth to constitute the local Ennead, after which he kindled the sacred fire before them. The queen, with the priests and nobles, all bearing torches, then passed through the halls, stopping from time to time to perform acts of purification, or to recite formulas to dispel evil spirits and pernicious influences; finally, a triumphal procession was formed, and the whole *cortége* returned to the palace, where a banquet brought the day's

---

[1] On Amenôthes, the son of Hâpi, see p. 56 of the present volume; it will be seen in the following chapter, in connection with the Egyptian accounts of the Exodus, what tradition made of him.

festivities to a close.¹ It was Amenôthes III. himself, or rather one of his statues animated by his double, who occupied the chief place in the new building. Indeed, wherever we come across a temple in Nubia dedicated to a king, we find the homage of the inhabitants always offered to the image of the founder, which spoke to them in oracles. All the southern part of the country beyond the second cataract is full of traces of Amenôthes, and the evidence of the veneration shown to him would lead us to conclude that he played an important part in the organisation of the country. Sedeinga possessed a small temple under the patronage of his wife Tîi. The ruins of a sanctuary which he dedicated to Amon, the Sun-god, have been discovered at Gebel-Barkal; Amenôthes seems to have been the first to perceive the advantages offered by the site, and to have endeavoured to transform the barbarian village of Napata into a large Egyptian city. Some of the monuments with which he adorned Soleb were transported, in later times, to Gebel-Barkal, among them some rams and lions of rare beauty. They lie at rest with their paws crossed, the head erect, and their expression suggesting both power and repose.² As we descend the Nile, traces of the work of this king are less frequent,

[1] Thus the small temple of Sarrah, to the north of Wady Halfa, is dedicated to "the living statue of Ramses II. in the land of Nubia," a statue to which his Majesty gave the name of " Ûsirmârî Zosir-Shâfi."

[2] One of the rams was removed from Gebel-Barkal by Lepsius, and is now in the Berlin Museum, as well as the pedestal of one of the hawks. Prisse has shown that these two monuments originally adorned the temple of Soleb, and that they were afterwards transported to Napata by an Ethiopian king, who engraved his name on the pedestal of one of them.

and their place is taken by those of his predecessors, as at Sai, at Semneh, at Wady Halfa, at Amada, at Ibrim, and at Dakkeh. Distant traces of Amenôthes again appear in the neighbourhood of the first cataract, and in the island of Elephantinê, which he endeavoured to restore to its ancient splendour. Two of the small buildings which he there dedicated to Khnûmû, the local god, were still in existence at the beginning of the present century. That least damaged,

ONE OF THE LIONS OF GEBEL-BARKAL.[1]

on the south side of the island, consisted of a single chamber nearly forty feet in length. The sandstone walls, terminating in a curved cornice, rested on a hollow substructure raised rather more than six feet above the ground, and surrounded by a breast-high parapet. A portico ran round the building, having seven square pillars on each of its two sides, while at each end stood two columns having lotus-shaped capitals; a flight of ten or

[1] Drawn by Faucher-Gudin, from one of the two lions of Gebel-Barkal in the British Museum.

twelve steps between two walls of the same height as the basement, projected in front, and afforded access to the cella. The two columns of the façade were further apart than those at the opposite end of the building, and showed a glimpse of a richly decorated door, while a second door opened under the peristyle at the further extremity. The walls were covered with the half-brutish profile of the good Khnûmû, and those of his two companions, Anûkit and Satît, the spirits of stormy waters. The treatment of these figures was broad and simple, the style free, light, and graceful, the colouring soft; and the harmonious beauty of the whole is unsurpassed by anything at Thebes itself. It was, in fact, a kind of oratory, built on a scale to suit the capacities of a decaying town, but the design was so delicately conceived in its miniature proportions that nothing more graceful can be imagined.[1]

Ancient Egypt and its feudal cities, Ombos, Edfû,[2] Nekhabît, Esneh,[3] Medamôt,[4] Coptos, Denderah,[5] Abydos,

[1] Amenôthes II. erected some small obelisks at Elephantinê, one of which is at present in England. The two buildings of Amenôthes III. at Elephantinê were still in existence at the beginning of the present century. They have been described and drawn by French scholars; between 1822 and 1825 they were destroyed, and the materials used for building barracks and magazines at Syene.

[2] The works undertaken by Thûtmosis III. in the temple of Edfû are mentioned in an inscription of the Ptolemaic period; some portions are still to be seen among the ruins of the town.

[3] An inscription of the Roman period attributes the rebuilding of the great temple of Esneh to Thûtmosis III. Grébaut discovered some fragments of it in the quay of the modern town.

[4] Amenôthes II. appears to have built the existing temple.

[5] The temple of Hâthor was built by Thûtmosis III. Some fragments found in the Ptolemaic masonry bear the cartouche of Thûtmosis IV.

Memphis,[1] and Heliopolis, profited largely by the generosity of the Pharaohs. Since the close of the XIIth dynasty these cities had depended entirely on their own resources, and their public buildings were either in ruins, or quite inadequate to the needs of the population, but now gold from Syria and Kûsh furnished them with the means of restoration. The Delta itself shared in this architectural revival, but it had suffered too severely under the struggle between the Theban kings and the Shepherds to recover itself as quickly as the remainder of the country. All effort was concentrated on those of its nomes which lay on the Eastern frontier, or which were crossed by the Pharaohs in their journeys into Asia, such as the Bubastite and Athribite nomes; the rest remained sunk in their ancient torpor.[2] Beyond the Red Sea the mines were actively worked, and even the oases of the Libyan desert took part in the national revival, and buildings rose in their midst of a size proportionate to their slender revenues. Thebes naturally came in for the largest share of the spoils of war. Although her kings had become the rulers of the world, they had not, like the Pharaohs of the XIIth and XIIIth dynasties, forsaken her for some more illustrious city: here they had their ordinary residence as well as

[1] Amenôthes II. certainly carried on works at Memphis, for he opened a new quarry at Tûrah, in the year IV. Amenôthes III. also worked limestone quarries, and built at Saqqârah the earliest chapels of the Serapeum which are at present known to us.

[2] Mariette and E. de Rougé, attribute this torpor, at least as far as Tanis is concerned, to the aversion felt by the Pharaohs of Egyptian blood for the Hyksôs capital, and for the provinces where the invaders had formerly established themselves in large numbers.

their seat of government, hither they returned after each campaign to celebrate their victory, and hither they sent the prisoners and the spoil which they had reserved for their own royal use. In the course of one or two generations Thebes had spread in every direction, and had enclosed within her circuit the neighbouring villages of Ashîrû, the

THE TEMPLE AT ELEPHANTINÊ, AS IT WAS IN 1799.[1]

fief of· Maût, and Apît-rîsît, the southern Thebes, which lay at the confluence of the Nile with one of the largest of the canals which watered the plain. The monuments in these two new quarters of the town were unworthy of the city of which they now formed part, and Amenôthes III.

[1] Drawn by Faucher-Gudin, from the *Description de l'Égypte, Ant.*, vol. i. p. 35. A good restoration of it, made from the statements in the *Description*, is to be found in PERROT-CHIPIEZ, *Histoire de l'Art dans l'Antiquité*, vol. i. pp. 402, 403.

consequently bestowed much pains on improving them. He entirely rebuilt the sanctuary of Maût, enlarged the sacred lake, and collected within one of the courts of the temple several hundred statues in black granite of the Memphite divinity, the lioness-headed Sokhît, whom be

THE GREAT COURT OF THE TEMPLE OF LUXOR DURING THE INUNDATION.[1]

identified with his Theban goddess. The statues were crowded together so closely that they were in actual contact with each other in places, and must have presented something of the appearance of a regiment drawn up in battle array. The succeeding Pharaohs soon came to look

[1] Drawn by Boudier, from a photograph by Beato.

upon this temple as a kind of storehouse, whence they might provide themselves with ready-made figures to decorate their buildings either at Thebes or in other royal cities. About a hundred of them, however, still remain, most of them without feet, arms, or head; some over-

PART OF THE AVENUE OF RAMS, BETWEEN THE TEMPLES OF AMON AND MAÛT.[1]

turned on the ground, others considerably out of the perpendicular, from the earth having given way beneath them, and a small number only still perfect and *in situ*. At Luxor Amenôthes demolished the small temple with which the sovereigns of the XIIth and XIIIth dynasties had

[1] Drawn by Faucher-Gudin, from a photograph by Beato.

been satisfied, and replaced it by a structure which is still one of the finest yet remaining of the times of the Pharaohs. The naos rose sheer above the waters of the Nile, indeed its cornices projected over the river, and a staircase at the south side allowed the priests and devotees to embark directly from the rear of the building. The sanctuary was a single chamber, with an opening on its side, but so completely shut out from the daylight by the long dark hall at whose extremity it was placed as to be in perpetual obscurity. It was flanked by narrow, dimly lightly chambers, and was approached through a pronaos with four rows of columns, a vast court surrounded with porticoes occupying the foreground. At the present time the thick walls which enclosed the entire building are nearly level with the ground, half the ceilings have crumbled away, air and light penetrate into every nook, and during the inundation the water flowing into the courts, transformed them until recently into lakes, whither the flocks and herds of the village resorted in the heat of the day to bathe or quench their thirst. Pictures of mysterious events never meant for the public gaze now display their secrets in the light of the sun, and reveal to the eyes of the profane the supernatural events which preceded the birth of the king. On the northern side an avenue of sphinxes and criosphinxes led to the gates of old Thebes. At present most of these creatures are buried under the ruins of the modern town, or covered by the earth which overlies the ancient road; but a few are still visible, broken and shapeless from barbarous usage, and hardly retaining any traces of the inscriptions in which Amenôthes claimed them boastingly as his work. Triumphal processions passing along this route from Luxor to Karnak would at length reach the great court before the temple of Amon, or, by turning a little to the right after passing the temple of Maût, would arrive in front of the southern façade, near the two gilded obelisks whose splendour once rejoiced the heart of the

THE PYLONS OF THÛTMOSIS III. AND HARMHABÎ AT KARNAK.[1]

famous Hâtshopsîtû. Thûtmosis III. was also determined on his part to spare no expense to make the temple of his god of proportions suitable to the patron of so vast an empire. Not only did he complete those portions which his predecessors had merely sketched out, but on the south side towards Ashîrû he also built a long row of pylons, now half ruined, on which he engraved, according to custom, the list of nations and cities which he had subdued

[1] Drawn by Boudier, from a photograph by Beato.

in Asia and Africa. To the east of the temple he rebuilt some ancient structures, the largest of which served as a halting-place for processions, and he enclosed the whole with a stone rampart. The outline of the sacred lake, on which the mystic boats were launched on the nights of festivals, was also made more symmetrical, and its margin edged with masonry. By these alterations the harmonious proportion between the main buildings and the façade had

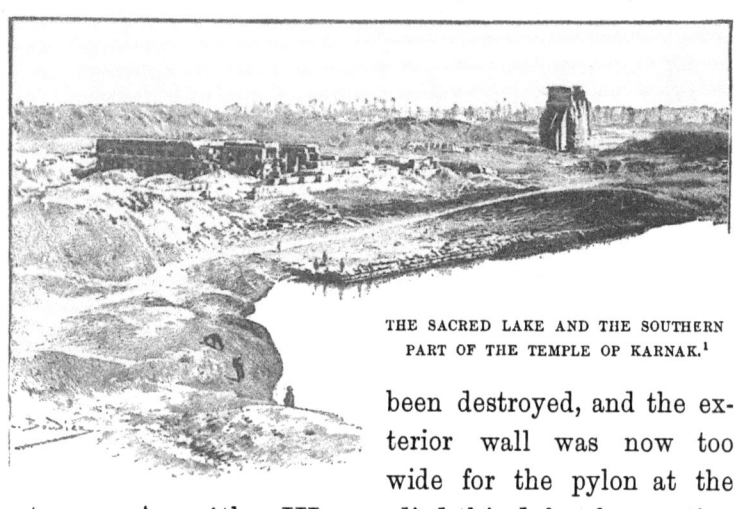

THE SACRED LAKE AND THE SOUTHERN PART OF THE TEMPLE OF KARNAK.[1]

been destroyed, and the exterior wall was now too wide for the pylon at the entrance. Amenôthes III. remedied this defect by erecting in front a fourth pylon, which was loftier, larger, and in all respects more worthy to stand before the enlarged temple. Its walls were partially covered with battle-scenes, which informed all beholders of the glory of the conqueror.[2]

[1] Drawn by Boudier, from a photograph by Beato: the building near the centre of the picture is the covered walk constructed by Thûtmosis III.

[2] Portions of the military bas-reliefs which covered the exterior face of the pylon are still to be seen through the gaps in the wall at the end of the great Hall of Pillars built by Seti I. and Ramses II.

Progress had been no less marked on the left bank of the river. As long as Thebes had been merely a small provincial town, its cemeteries had covered but a moderate area, including the sandy plain and low mounds opposite Karnak and the valley of Deir el-Baharî beyond; but now that the city had more than doubled its extent, the space required for the dead was proportionately greater. The tombs of private persons began to spread towards the south, and soon reached the slopes of the Assassîf, the hill of Sheîkh-Abd-el-Qûrnah and the district of Qûrnet-Mûrraî— in fact, all that part which the people of the country called the "Brow" of Thebes. On the borders of the cultivated land a row of chapels and mastabas with pyramidal roofs sheltered the remains of the princes and princesses of the royal family. The Pharaohs themselves were buried either separately under their respective brick pyramids or in groups in a temple, as was the case with the first three Thûtmosis and Hâtshopsîtû at Deir el-Baharî. Amenôthes II. and Thûtmosis IV. could doubtless have found room in this crowded necropolis,[1] although the space was becoming limited, but the pride of the Pharaohs began to rebel against this promiscuous burial side by side with their subjects. Amenôthes III. sought for a site, therefore, where he would have ample room to display his magnificence, far from the vulgar crowd, and found what he

[1] The generally received opinion is that these sovereigns of the XVIIIth dynasty were buried in the Bibân el-Molûk, but I have made several examinations of this valley, and cannot think that this was the case. On the contrary, the scattered notices in the fragments of papyrus preserved at Turin seem to me to indicate that Amenôthes II. and Thûtmosis IV. must have been buried in the neighbourhood of the Assassîf or of Deir el-Baharî.

desired at the further end of the valley which opens out behind the village of Qûrnah. Here, an hour's journey from the bank of the Nile, he cut for himself a magnificent rock-tomb with galleries, halls, and deep pits, the walls being decorated with representations of the Voyage of the Sun through the regions which he traverses during the twelve hours of his nocturnal course. A sarcophagus of red granite received his mummy, and *Ushabti's* of extraordinary dimensions and admirable workmanship mounted guard around him, so as to release him from the *corvée* in the fields of Ialû. The chapel usually attached to such tombs is not to be found in the neighbourhood. As the road to the funeral valley was a difficult one, and as it would be unreasonable to condemn an entire priesthood to live in solitude, the king decided to separate the component parts which had hitherto been united in every tomb since the Memphite period, and to place the vault for the mummy and the passages leading to it some distance away in the mountains, while the necessary buildings for the cultus of the statue and the accommodation of the priests were transferred to the plain, and were built at the southern extremity of the lands which were at that time held by private persons. The divine character of Amenôthes, ascribed to him on account of his solar origin and the co-operation of Amon-Râ at his birth, was, owing to this separation of the funerary constituents, brought into further prominence. When once the body which he had animated while on earth was removed and hidden from sight, the people soon became accustomed to think only of his Double enthroned in the recesses of the sanctuary:

seeing him receive there the same honours as the gods themselves, they came naturally to regard him as a deity himself. The arrangement of his temple differed in no way from those in which Amon, Maût, and Montû were worshipped, while it surpassed in size and splendour most

THE TWO COLOSSI OF MEMNON IN THE PLAIN OF THEBES.[1]

of the sanctuaries dedicated to the patron gods of the chief towns of the nomes. It contained, moreover, colossal statues, objects which are never found associated with the heavenly gods. Several of these figures have been broken to pieces, and only a few scattered fragments of them remain, but two of them still maintain their positions on

[1] Drawn by Faucher-Gudin, from a photograph by Beato. The "Vocal Statue of Memon" is that on the right-hand side of the illustration.

each side of the entrance, with their faces towards the east. They are each formed of a single block of red breccia from Syenê,[1] and are fifty-three feet high, but the more northerly one was shattered in the earthquake which completed the ruin of Thebes in the year 27 B.C. The upper part toppled over with the shock, and was dashed to pieces on the floor of the court, while the lower half remained in its place. Soon after the disaster it began to be rumoured that sounds like those produced by the breaking of a harp-string proceeded from the pedestal at sunrise, whereupon travellers flocked to witness the miracle, and legend soon began to take possession of the giant who spoke in this marvellous way. In vain did the Egyptians of the neighbourhood declare that the statue represented the Pharaoh Amenôthes; the Greeks refused to believe them, and forthwith recognised in the colossus an image of Memnon the Ethiopian, son of Tithonus and Aurora, slain by their own Achilles beneath the walls of Troy—maintaining that the music heard every morning was the clear and harmonious voice of the hero saluting his mother. Towards the middle of the second century of our era, Hadrian undertook a journey to Upper Egypt, and heard the wonderful song; sixty years later, Septimus Severus restored the statue by the employment of courses of stones, which were so arranged as to form a rough representation of a human

[1] It is often asserted that they are made of rose granite, but Jollois and Devilliers describe them as being of "a species of sandstone breccia, composed of a mass of agate flint, conglomerated together by a remarkably hard cement. This material, being very dense and of a heterogeneous composition, presents to the sculptor perhaps greater difficulties than even granite."

head and shoulders. His piety, however, was not rewarded as he expected, for Memnon became silent, and his oracle fell into oblivion.[1] The temple no longer exists, and a few ridges alone mark the spot where it rose; but the two colossi remain at their post, in the same condition in which they were left by the Roman Cæsar: the features are quite obliterated, and the legs and the supporting female figures on either side are scored all over with Greek and Latin inscriptions expressing the appreciation of ancient tourists. Although the statues tower high above the fields of corn and *bersim* which surround them, our first view of them, owing to the scale of proportion observed in their construction, so different from that to which we are accustomed, gives us the impression that they are smaller than they really are, and it is only when we stand close to one of them and notice the insignificant appearance of the crowd of sightseers clustered on its pedestal that we realize the immensity of the colossi.

The descendants of Âhmosis had by their energy won for Thebes not only the supremacy over the peoples of Egypt and of the known world, but had also secured for the Theban deities pre-eminence over all their rivals. The booty collected both in Syria and Ethiopia went to enrich the god Amon as much as it did the kings themselves; every victory brought him the tenth part of the spoil gathered on the field of battle, of the tribute levied on vassals, and of the prisoners taken as slaves. When Thûtmosis III., after having reduced Megiddo, organised a systematic plundering of the surrounding country, it was for the benefit of Amon-Râ that he reaped the fields and sent their harvest into Egypt; if during his journeys he collected useful plants or rare animals, it was that he might dispose of them in the groves or gardens of Amon as well as in his own, and he never retained for his personal use the whole of what he won by arms, but always reserved some portion for the sacred treasury. His successors acted in a simi-

A PARTY OF TOURISTS AT THE FOOT OF THE VOCAL STATUE OF MEMNON.[1]

lar manner, and in the reigns of Amenôthes II., Thûtmosis IV., and Amenôthes III., the patrimony of the Theban priesthood continued to increase. The Pharaohs, perpetually called upon as they were to recompense one or other of their servants, were never able to retain for

[1] Drawn by Boudier, from a photograph by Insinger.

THE INCREASING GREATNESS OF AMON

long their share of the spoils of war. Gold and silver, lands, jewels, and slaves passed as quickly out of their hands as they had fallen into them, and although their fortune was continually having additions made to it in every fresh campaign, yet the increase was rarely in proportion to the trouble expended. The god, on the contrary, received what he got for all time, and gave back nothing in return : fresh accumulations of precious metals were continually being added to his store, his meadows were enriched by the addition of vineyards, and with his palm forests he combined fish-ponds full of fish ; he added farms and villages to those he already possessed, and each reign saw the list of his possessions increase. He had his own labourers, his own tradespeople, his own fishermen, soldiers, and scribes, and, presiding over all these, a learned hierarchy of divines, priests, and prophets, who administered everything. This immense domain, which was a kind of State within the State, was ruled over by a single high priest, chosen by the sovereign from among the prophets. He was the irresponsible head of it, and his spiritual ambition had increased step by step with the extension of his material resources. As the human Pharaoh showed himself entitled to homage from the lords of the earth, the priests came at length to the conclusion that Amon had a right to the allegiance of the lords of heaven, and that he was the Supreme Being, in respect of whom the others were of little or no account, and as he was the only god who was everywhere victorious, he came at length to be regarded by them as the only god in existence. It was impossible that the kings could see this rapid development of sacerdotal power without anxiety, and with all their devotion to the patron of their city, solicitude for their own authority compelled them to seek elsewhere for another divinity, whose influence might in some degree counterbalance that of Amon. The only one who could vie with him at Thebes, either for the antiquity of his worship or for the rank which he occupied in the public esteem, was the Sun-lord of Heliopolis, head of the first Ennead. Thûtmosis IV. owed his crown to him, and displayed his gratitude in clearing away the sand from the Sphinx, in which the spirit of Harmakhis was considered to dwell; and Amenôthes III., although claiming to be the son of Amon himself, inherited the disposition shown by Thûtmosis in favour of the Heliopolitan religions, but instead of attaching himself to the forms most venerated by theologians, he bestowed his affection on a more popular deity—Atonû, the fiery disk. He may have been influenced in his choice by private reasons. Like his predecessors, he had taken, while still very young, wives from among his own family, but neither these reasonable ties, nor his numerous diplomatic alliances with foreign princesses, were enough for him. From the very beginning of his reign he had loved a maiden who was not of the blood of the Pharaohs, Tîi, the daughter of Iûia and his wife Tûia.[1]

[1] For the last thirty years Queen Tîi has been the subject of many hypotheses and of much confusion. The scarabæi engraved under Amenôthes III. say explicitly that she was the daughter of two personages, Iûia and Tûia, but these names are not accompanied by any of the signs which are characteristic of foreign names, and were considered Egyptian by contemporaries. Hincks was the first who seems to have believed her to be a Syrian; he compares her father's name with that of Levi,

MARRIAGE OF AMENÔTHES III. WITH TÎI.

Connexions of this kind had been frequently formed by his ancestors, but the Egyptian women of inferior rank whom they had brought into their harems had always remained in the background, and if the sons of these concubines were ever fortunate enough to come to the throne, it was in default of heirs of pure blood. Amenôthes III. married Tii, gave her for her dowry the town of Zâlû in Lower Egypt, and raised her to the position of queen, in spite of her low extraction. She busied herself in the affairs of State, took precedence of the princesses of the solar family, and appeared at her husband's side in public ceremonies, and was so figured on the monuments. If, as there is reason to believe, she was born near Heliopolis, it is easy to understand how her influence may have led Amenôthes to pay special honour to a Heliopolitan

MARRIAGE SCARABÆUS.[1]

and attributes the religious revolution which followed to the influence of her foreign education. This theory has continued to predominate; some prefer a Libyan origin to the Asiatic one, and latterly there has been an attempt to recognise in Tii one of the princesses of Mitanni mentioned in the correspondence of Tel el-Amarna. As long ago as 1877, I showed that Tii was an Egyptian of middle rank, probably of Heliopolitan origin.

[1] Drawn by Faucher-Gudin, from a photograph of the scarabæus preserved at Gizeh.

divinity. He had built, at an early period of his reign, a sanctuary to Atonû at Memphis, and in the Xth year he constructed for him a chapel at Thebes itself,[1] to the south of the last pylon of Thûtmosis III., and endowed this deity with property at the expense of Amon.

He had several sons;[2] but the one who succeeded him, and who, like him, was named Amenôthes, was the most paradoxical of all the Egyptian sovereigns of ancient times.[3] He made up for the inferiority of his birth on

[1] This temple seems to have been raised on the site of the building which is usually attributed to Amenôthes II. and Amenôthes III. The blocks bearing the name of Amenôthes II. had been used previously, like most of those which bear the cartouches of Amenôthes III. The temple of Atonû, which was demolished by Harmhabî or one of the Ramses, was subsequently rebuilt with the remains of earlier edifices, and dedicated to Amon.

[2] One of them, Thûtmosis, was high priest of Phtah, and we possess several monuments erected by him in the temple of Memphis; another, Tûtonkhamon, subsequently became king. He also had several daughters by Tii—Sîtamon.

[3] The absence of any cartouches of Amenôthes IV. or his successors in the table of Abydos prevented Champollion and Rosellini from classifying these sovereigns with any precision. Nestor L'hôte tried to recognise in the first of them, whom he called *Bakhen-Bakhnan*, a king belonging to the very ancient dynasties, perhaps the Hyksôs Apakhnan, but Lepsius and Hincks showed that he must be placed between Amenôthes III. and Harmhabî, that he was first called Amenôthes like his father, but that he afterwards took the name of Baknaten, which is now read Khûnaten or Khûniaton. His singular aspect made it difficult to decide at first whether a man or a woman was represented. Mariette, while pronouncing him to be a man, thought that he had perhaps been taken prisoner in the Sûdân and mutilated, which would have explained his effeminate appearance, almost like that of an eunuch. Recent attempts have been made to prove that Amenôthes IV. and Khûniaton were two distinct persons, or that Khûniaton was a queen; but they have hitherto been rejected by Egyptologists.

BEGINNING OF THE REIGN OF AMENÔTHES IV. 81

account of the plebeian origin of his mother Tîi,[1] by his marriage with Nofrîtîti, a princess of the pure solar race.[2] Tîi, long accustomed to the management of affairs, exerted her influence over him even more than she had done over her husband. Without officially assuming the rank, she certainly for several years possessed the power, of regent, and gave a definite Oriental impress to her son's religious policy. No outward changes were made at first; Amenôthes, although showing his preference for Heliopolis by inscribing in his protocol the title of prophet of Harmakhis, which he may, however, have borne before his accession, maintained his residence at Thebes, as his father had done before him, continued to sacrifice to the Theban divinities, and to follow the ancient paths and the conventional practices.[3] He either built a temple to the

---

[1] The filiation of Amenôthes IV. and Tîi has given rise to more than one controversy. The Egyptian texts do not define it explicitly, and the title borne by Tîi has been considered by some to prove that Amenôthes IV. was her son, and by others that she was the mother of Queen Nofrîtîti. The Tel el-Amarna correspondence solves the question, however, as it gives a letter from Dushratta to Khûniaton, in which Tii is called "thy mother."

[2] Nofrîtîti, the wife of Amenôthes IV., like all the princesses of that time, has been supposed to be of Syrian origin, and to have changed her name on her arrival in Egypt. The place which she holds beside her husband is the same as that which belongs to legitimate queens, like Nofrîtari, Âhmosis, and Hâtshopsîtû, and the example of these princesses is enough to show us what was her real position; she was most probably a daughter of one of the princesses of the solar blood, perhaps of one of the sisters of Amenôthes III., and Amenôthes IV. married her so as to obtain through her the rights which were wanting to him through his mother Tîi.

[3] The tomb of Ramses, governor of Thebes and priest of Mâit, shows us in one part of it the king, still faithful to his name of Amenôthes, paying homage to the god Amon, lord of Karnak, while everywhere else the worship

Theban god, or enlarged the one which his father had constructed at Karnak, and even opened new quarries at Syene and Silsileh for providing granite and sandstone for the adornment of this monument. His devotion to the invincible Disk, however, soon began to assert itself, and rendered more and more irksome to him the religious observances which he had constrained himself to follow. There was nothing and no one to hinder him from giving free course to his inclinations, and the nobles and priests were too well trained in obedience to venture to censure anything he might do, even were it to result in putting the whole population into motion, from Elephantinê to the sea-coast, to prepare for the intruded deity a dwelling which should eclipse in magnificence the splendour of the great temple. A few of those around him had become converted of their own accord to his favourite worship, but these formed a very small minority. Thebes had belonged to Amon so long that the king could never hope to bring it to regard Atonû as anything but a being of inferior rank. Each city belonged to some god, to whom was attributed its origin, its development, and its prosperity, and whom it could not forsake without renouncing its very existence. If Thebes became separated from Amon it would be Thebes no longer, and of this Amenôthes was so well aware that he never attempted to induce it to renounce its patron. His

of Atonû predominates. The cartouches on the tomb of Pâri, read by Bouriant Âkhopîrûri, and by Scheil more correctly Nofirkhopîrûri, seem to me to represent a transitional form of the protocol of Amenôthes IV., and not the name of a new Pharaoh; the inscription in which they are to be found bears the date of his third year.

residence among surroundings which he detested at length became so intolerable, that he resolved to leave the place and create a new capital elsewhere. The choice of a new abode would have presented no difficulty to him had he been able to make up his mind to relegate Atonû to the second rank of divinities; Memphis, Heracleopolis, Siût, Khmûnû, and, in fact, all the towns of the valley would have deemed themselves fortunate in securing the inheritance of their rival, but not one of them would be false to its convictions or accept the degradation of its own divine founder, whether Phtah, Harshafîtû, Anubis, or Thot. A newly promoted god demanded a new city; Amenôthes, therefore, made selection of a broad plain extending on the right bank of the Nile, in the eastern part of the Hermopolitan nome, to which he removed with all his court about the fourth or fifth year of his reign.[1] He found here several obscure villages without any historical or religious traditions, and but thinly populated; Amenôthes chose one of them, the Et-Tel of the present day, and built there a palace for himself and a temple for his god. The temple, like that of Râ at Heliopolis, was named *Haît-Banbonû*, the Mansion of the Obelisk. It covered an immense area, of which the sanctuary, however, occupied an inconsiderable part; it was flanked by brick

---

[1] The last date with the name of Amenôthes is that of the year V., on a papyrus from the Fayûm; elsewhere we find from the year VI. the name of Khûniaton, by the side of monuments with the cartouche of Amenôthes; we may conclude from this that the foundation of the town dates from the year IV. or V. at the latest, when the prince, having renounced the worship of Amon, left Thebes that he might be able to celebrate freely that of Atonû.

storehouses, and the whole was surrounded by a thick wall. The remains show that the temple was built of white limestone, of fine quality, but that it was almost devoid of ornament, for there was no time to cover it with the usual decorations.[1] The palace was built of brick; it was

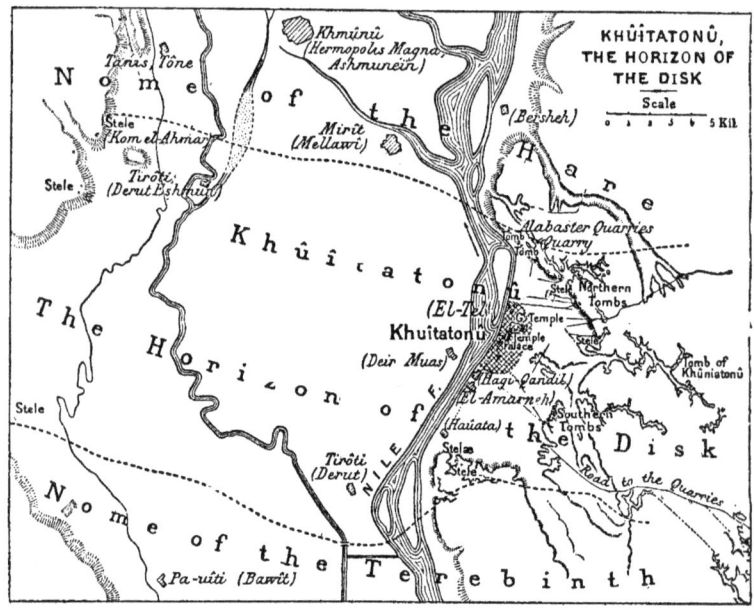

approached by a colossal gateway, and contained vast halls, interspersed with small apartments for the accommodation of the household, and storehouses for the necessary provisions, besides gardens which had been hastily planted with rare

[1] The opinion of Brugsch, that the arrangement of the various parts differed from that of other temples, and was the effect of foreign influence, has not been borne out by the excavations of Prof. Petrie, the little which he has brought to light being entirely of Egyptian character. The temple is represented on the tomb of the high priest Mariri.

shrubs and sycamores. Fragments of furniture and of the roughest of the utensils contained in the different chambers are still unearthed from among the heaps of rubbish, and the cellars especially are full of potsherds and cracked jars, on which we can still see written an indication of the reign and the year when the wine they once contained was made. Altars of massive masonry rose in the midst of the courts, on which the king or one of his ministers heaped offerings and burnt incense morning, noon, and evening, in honour of the three decisive moments in the life of Atonû.[1] A few painted and gilded columns supported the roofs of the principal apartments in which the Pharaoh held his audiences, but elsewhere the walls and pillars were coated with cream-coloured stucco or whitewash, on which scenes of private life were depicted in colours. The pavement, like the walls, was also decorated. In one of the halls which seems to have belonged to the harem, there is still to be seen distinctly the picture of a rectangular piece of water containing fish and lotus-flowers in full bloom; the edge is adorned with water-plants and flowering shrubs, among which birds fly and calves graze and gambol; on the right and left were depicted rows of stands laden with fruit, while at each end of the room were seen the grinning faces of a gang of negro and Syrian prisoners, separated from each other by gigantic arches. The tone of colouring is bright and cheerful, and the animals are treated with

[1] Naville discovered at Deir el-Bahari a similar altar, nearly intact. No other example was before known in any of the ruined towns or temples, and no one had any idea of the dimensions to which these altars attained.

great freedom and facility. The Pharaoh had collected about him several of the best artists then to be found at Thebes, placing them under the direction of Baûki, the chief of the corporation of sculptors,[1] and probably others subsequently joined these from provincial studios. Work for them was not lacking, for houses had to be built for all the courtiers and government officials who had been obliged to follow the king, and in a few years a large town had sprung up, which was called Khûîtatonû, or the "Horizon of the Disk." It was built on a regular plan, with straight streets and open spaces, and divided into two separate quarters, interspersed with orchards and shady trellises. Workmen soon began to flock to the new city— metal-founders, glass-founders, weavers; in fine, all who followed any trade indispensable to the luxury of a capital. The king appropriated a territory for it from the ancient nome of the Hare, thus compelling the god Thot to contribute to the fortune of Atonû; he fixed its limits by means of stelæ placed in the mountains, from Gebel-Tûnah to Deshlûît on the west, and from Sheîkh-Saîd to El-Haûata on the eastern bank;[2] it was a new nome improvised for the divine *parvenu*.

Atonû was one of the forms of the Sun, and perhaps the most material one of all those devised by the Egyptians. He was defined as "the good god who rejoices in truth,

[1] Baûki belonged to a family of artists, and his father Mani had filled before him the post of chief of the sculptors. The part played by these personages was first defined by Brugsch, with perhaps some exaggeration of their artistic merit and originality of talent.

[2] We know at present of fourteen of these stelæ. A certain number must still remain to be discovered on both banks of the Nile.

the lord of the solar course, the lord of the disk, the lord of heaven, the lord of earth, the living disk which lights up the two worlds, the living Harmakhis who rises on the horizon bearing his name of Shû, which is disk, the eternal infuser of life." His priests exercised the same functions as those of Heliopolis, and his high priest was called "Oirimaû," like the high priest of Râ in Aunû. This functionary was a certain Marirî, upon whom the king showered his favours, and he was for some time the chief authority in the State after the Pharaoh himself. Atonû was represented sometimes by the ordinary figure of Horus,[1] sometimes by the solar disk, but a disk whose rays were prolonged towards the earth, like so many arms ready to lay hold with their little hands of the offerings of the faithful, or to distribute to mortals the *crux ansata*, the symbol of life. The other gods, except Amon, were sharers with humanity in his benefits. Atonû proscribed him, and tolerated him only at Thebes; he required, moreover, that the name of Amon should be effaced wherever it occurred, but he respected Râ and Horus and Harmakhis—all, in fact, but Amon: he was content with being regarded as their king, and he strove rather to become their chief than their destroyer.[2] His nature, moreover, had nothing in it of the mysterious or ambiguous; he was the glorious torch which gave light to humanity, and which was seen every day to flame in

---

[1] It was probably this form of Horus which had, in the temple at Thebes, the statue called "the red image of Atonû in Paatonû."

[2] Prisse d'Avennes has found at Karnak, on fragments of the temple, the names of other divinities than Atonû worshipped by Khûniatonû.

the heavens without ever losing its brilliance or becoming weaker. When he hides himself "the world rests in darkness, like those dead who lie in their rock-tombs, with their heads swathed, their nostrils stuffed up, their eyes sightless, and whose whole property might be stolen from them, even that which they have under their head, without their knowing it; the lion issues from his lair, the serpent roams ready to bite, it is as obscure as in a dark room, the earth is silent whilst he who creates everything dwells in his horizon." He has hardly arisen when "Egypt becomes festal, one awakens, one rises on one's feet; when thou hast caused men to clothe themselves, they adore thee with outstretched hands, and the whole earth attends to its work, the animals betake themselves to their herbage, trees and green crops abound, birds fly to their marshy thickets with wings outstretched in adoration of thy double, the cattle skip, all the birds which were in their nests shake themselves when thou risest for them; the boats come and go, for every way is open at thy appearance, the fish of the river leap before thee as soon as thy rays descend upon the ocean." It is not without reason that all living things thus rejoice at his advent; all of them owe their existence to him, for "he creates the female germ, he gives virility to men, and furnishes life to the infant in its mother's womb; he calms and stills its weeping, he nourishes it in the maternal womb, giving forth the breathings which animate all that he creates, and when the infant escapes from the womb on the day of its birth, thou openest his mouth for speech, and thou satisfiest his necessities. When the chick is in the egg, a cackle in a stone, thou givest to it air while within to keep it alive; when thou hast caused it to be developed in the egg to the point of being able to break it, it goes forth proclaiming its existence by its cackling, and walks on its feet from the moment of its leaving the egg." Atonû presides over the universe and arranges within it the lot of human beings, both Egyptians and foreigners. The celestial Nile springs up in Hades far away in the north; he makes its current run down to earth, and spreads its waters over the fields during the inundation in order to nourish his creatures. He rules the seasons, winter and summer; he constructed the far-off sky in order to display himself therein, and to look down upon his works below. From the moment that he reveals himself there, " cities, towns, tribes, routes, rivers—all eyes are lifted to him, for he is the disk of the day upon the earth."[1] The sanctuary in which he is invoked contains only his divine shadow;[2] for he himself never leaves the firmament. His worship assumes none of the severe and gloomy forms of the Theban cults: songs resound therein, and hymns accompanied by the harp or flute; bread, cakes, vegetables, fruits, and flowers are associated with his rites, and only on very rare

[1] These extracts are taken from the hymns of Tel el-Amarna.
[2] In one of the tombs at Tel el-Amarna the king is depicted leading his mother Tii to the temple of Atonû in order to see " the Shadow of Râ,"·and it was thought with some reason that " the Shadow of Râ " was one of the names of the temple. I think that this designation applied also to the statue or symbol of the god; the *shadow* of a god was attached to the statue in the same manner as the " double," and transformed it into an animated body.

occasions one of those bloody sacrifices in which the other gods delight. The king made himself supreme pontiff of Atonû, and took precedence of the high priest. He himself celebrated the rites at the altar of the god, and we see him there standing erect, his hands outstretched, offering incense and invoking blessings from on high.[1] Like the Caliph Hakim of a later age, he formed a school to propagate his new doctrines, and preached them before his courtiers: if they wished to please him, they had to accept his teaching, and show that they had profited by it. The renunciation of the traditional religious observances of the solar house involved also the rejection of such personal names as implied an ardent devotion to the banished god; in place of Amenôthes, "he to whom Amon is united," the king assumed after a time the name of Khûniatonû, "the Glory of the Disk," and all the members of his family, as well as his adherents at court, whose appellations involved the name of the same god, soon followed his example. The proscription of Amon extended to inscriptions, so that while his name or figure, wherever either could be got at, was chiselled out, the vulture, the emblem of Mût, which expressed the idea of mother, was also avoided.[2] The king would have nothing about him to suggest to eye or ear the

[1] The altar on which the king stands upright is one of those cubes of masonry of which Naville discovered such a fine example in the temple of Hâtshopsîtû at Deir el-Bahari.

[2] We find, however, some instances where the draughtsman, either from custom or design, had used the vulture to express the word *maût*, "the mother," without troubling himself to think whether it answered to the name of the goddess.

remembrance of the gods or doctrines of Thebes. It would consequently have been fatal to them and their pretensions to the primacy of Egypt if the reign of the young king had continued as long as might naturally have been expected. After having been for nearly two centuries almost the national head of Africa, Amon was degraded by a single blow to the secondary rank and languishing existence in which he had lived before the expulsion of the Hyksôs. He had surrendered his sceptre as king of heaven and earth, not to any of his rivals who in old times had enjoyed the highest rank, but to an individual of a lower order, a sort of demigod, while he himself had thus become merely a local deity, confined to the corner of the Saîd in which he had had his origin. There was not even left to him the peaceful possession of this restricted domain, for he was obliged to act as host to the enemy who had deposed him: the temple of Atonû was erected at the door of his own sanctuary, and without leaving their courts the priests of Amon could hear at the hours of worship the chants intoned by hundreds of heretics in the temple of the Disk. Amon's priests saw, moreover, the royal gifts flowing into other treasuries, and the gold of Syria and Ethiopia no longer came into their hands. Should they stifle their complaints, and bow to this insulting oppression, or should they raise a protest against the action which had condemned them to obscurity and a restricted existence? If they had given indications of resistance, they would have been obliged to submit to prompt repression, but we see no sign of this. The bulk of the people—clerical as well as lay—accepted the deposition with complacency, and the nobles hastened to offer their adherence to that which afterwards became the official confession of faith of the Lord King.[1] The lord of Thebes itself, a certain Ramses, bowed his head to the new cult, and the bas-reliefs of his tomb display to our eyes the proofs of his apostasy: on the right-hand side Amon is the only subject of his devotion, while on the left he declares himself an adherent of Atonû. Religious formularies, divine appellations, the representations of the costume, expression, and demeanour of the figures are at issue with each other in the scenes on the two sides of the door, and if we were to trust to appearances only, one would think that the two pictures belonged to two separate reigns, and were concerned with two individuals strangers to each other.[2]

The rupture between the past and the present was so complete, in fact, that the sovereign was obliged to change, if not his face and expression, at least the mode in which they were represented. The name and personality of an Egyptian were so closely allied that interference with one implied interference with the other. Khûniatonû could not continue to be such as he was when Amenôthes, and, in fact, their respective portraits differ from each other to that degree that there is some doubt at moments as to their identity. Amenôthes is hardly to be distinguished

---

[1] The political character of this reaction against the growing power of the high priests and the town of Amon was pointed out for the first time by Maspero in 1878. Ed. Meyer and Tiele blend with the political idea a monotheistic conception which does not seem to me to be fully justified, at least at present, by anything in the materials we possess.

[2] His tomb was discovered in 1878 by Villiers-Stuart.

from his father : he has the same regular and somewhat heavy features, the same idealised body and conventional

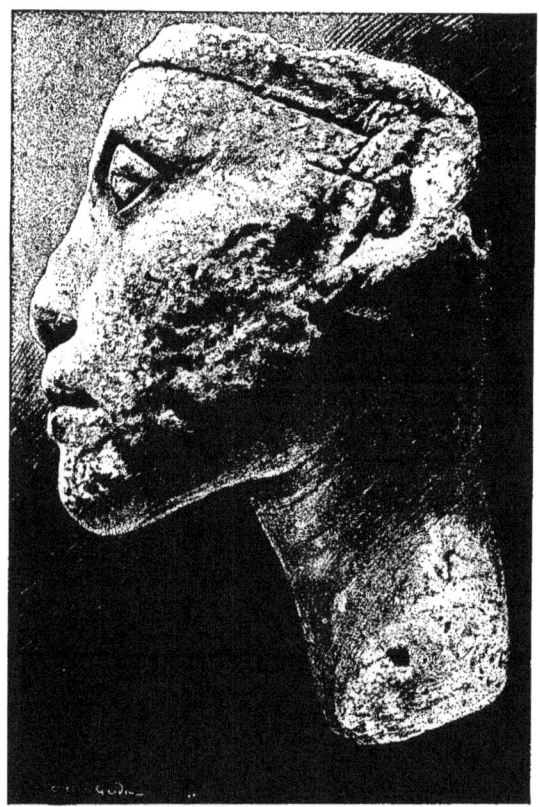

THE MASK OF KHÛNIATONÛ.[1]

shape as those which we find in the orthodox Pharaohs. Khûniatonû affects a long and narrow head, conical at

[1] Drawn by Faucher-Gudin, from a photograph by Petrie. Petrie thinks that the monument discovered by him, which is of fine plaster, is a cast of the dead king, executed possibly to enable the sculptors to make *Ushabtiu*, "Respondents," for him.

the top, with a retreating forehead, a large aquiline and pointed nose, a small mouth, an enormous chin projecting in front, the whole being supported by a long, thin neck.

AMENÔTHES IV., FROM THE STATUETTE IN THE LOUVRE.[1]

His shoulders are narrow, with little display of muscle, but his breasts are so full, his abdomen so prominent, and his hips so large, that one would think they belonged to a woman. Etiquette required the attendants upon the king, and those who aspired to his favour, to be portrayed in the bas-reliefs of temples or tombs in all points, both as regards face and demeanour, like the king himself. Hence it is that the majority of his contemporaries, after having borne the likeness of Amenôthes, came to adopt, without a break, that of Khûniatonû. The scenes at Tel el-Amarna contain, therefore, nothing but angular profiles, pointed skulls, ample breasts, flowing figures, and swelling stomachs. The outline of these is one that lends itself

[1] Drawn by Boudier, from a photograph by Faucher-Gudin.

readily to caricature, and the artists have exaggerated the various details with the intention, it may be, of rendering the representations grotesque. There was nothing ridiculous, however, in the king, their model, and several of his statues attribute to him a languid, almost valetudinarian grace, which is by no means lacking in dignity. He was a good and affectionate man, and was passionately fond of his wife, Nofrîtîti, associating her with himself in his sovereign acts. If he set out to visit the temple, she followed him in a chariot; if he was about to reward one of his faithful subjects, she stood beside him and helped to distribute the golden necklaces. She joined him in his prayers to the Solar Disk; she ministered to him in domestic life, when, having broken away from the worries of his public duties, he sought relaxation in his harem; and their union was so tender, that we find her on one occasion, at least, seated in a coaxing attitude on her husband's knees—a unique instance of such affection among all the representations on the monuments of Egypt. They had six daughters, whom they brought up to live with them on terms of the closest intimacy: they accompanied their father and mother everywhere, and are

KHÛNIATONÛ WITH HIS WIFE UPON HIS KNEES.

[1] Drawn by Faucher-Gudin, from a drawing by Petrie.

exhibited as playing around the throne while their parents are engaged in performing the duties of their office. The gentleness and gaiety of the king were reflected in the life of his subjects: all the scenes which they have left us consist entirely of processions, cavalcades, banquets,

KHÛNIATONÛ AND HIS WIFE REWARDING ONE OF THE GREAT OFFICERS OF THE COURT.[1]

and entertainments. Khûniatonû was prodigal in the gifts of gold and the eulogies which he bestowed on Marirî, the chief priest: the people dance around him while he is receiving from the king the just recompense of his activity. When Hûia, who came back from Syria in the XIIth year of the king's reign, brought solemnly before him the tribute he had collected, the king, borne in his jolting palanquin

[1] Drawn by Faucher-Gudin, from a photograph by Insinger.

on the shoulders of his officers, proceeded to the temple to return thanks to his god, to the accompaniment of chants and the waving of the great fans. When the divine father Aî had married the governess of one of the king's daughters, the whole city gave itself up to enjoyment, and wine flowed freely during the wedding feast. Notwithstanding the frequent festivals, the king found time to watch jealously over the ordinary progress of government and foreign affairs. The architects, too, were not allowed to stand idle, and without taking into account the repairs of existing buildings, had plenty to do in constructing edifices in honour of Atonû in the principal towns of the Nile valley, at Memphis, Heliopolis, Hermopolis, Hermonthis, and in the Fayûm. The provinces in Ethiopia remained practically in the same condition as in the time of Amenôthes III.;[1] Kûsh was pacified, notwithstanding the raids which the tribes of the desert were accustomed to make from time to time, only to receive on each occasion rigorous chastisement from the king's viceroy. The sudden degradation of Amon had not brought about any coldness between the Pharaoh and his princely allies in Asia. The aged Amenôthes had, towards the end of his reign, asked the hand of Dushratta's daughter in marriage, and the Mitannian king, highly flattered by the request, saw his opportunity and took advantage of it in the interest of his treasury. He discussed the amount of the dowry, demanded a considerable sum of gold, and

---

[1] The name and the figure of Khûniatonû are met with on the gate of the temple of Soleb, and he received in his XIIth year the tributes of Kûsh, as well as those of Syria.

when the affair had been finally arranged to his satisfaction, he despatched the princess to the banks of the Nile. On her arrival she found her affianced husband was dead, or, at all events, dying. Amenôthes IV., however, stepped into his father's place, and inherited his bride with his

THE DOOR OF A TOMB AT TEL EL-AMARNA.[1]

crown. The new king's relations with other foreign princes were no less friendly; the chief of the Khâti (Hittites) complimented him on his accession, the King of Alasia wrote to him to express his earnest desire for a continuance of peace between the two states. Burnaburiash of Babylon had, it is true, hoped to obtain an Egyptian

[1] Drawn by Faucher-Gudin, from a photograph by Insinger.

princess in marriage for his son, and being disappointed, had endeavoured to pick a quarrel over the value of the presents which had been sent him, together with the notice of the accession of the new sovereign. But his kingdom lay too far away to make his ill-will of much consequence, and his complaints passed unheeded. In Cœle-Syria and Phœnicia the situation remained unchanged. The vassal cities were in a perpetual state of disturbance, though not more so than in the past. Azîru, son of Abdashirti, chief of the country of the Amorites, had always, even during the lifetime of Amenôthes III., been the most turbulent of vassals. The smaller states of the Orontes and of the coast about Arvad had been laid waste by his repeated incursions and troubled by his intrigues. He had taken and pillaged twenty towns, among which were Simyra, Sini, Irqata, and Qodshû, and he was already threatening Byblos, Berytus, and Sidon. It was useless to complain of him, for he always managed to exculpate himself to the royal messengers. Khaî, Dûdû, Amenemaûpît had in turn all pronounced him innocent. Pharaoh himself, after citing him to appear in Egypt to give an explanation of his conduct, had allowed himself to be won over by his fair speaking, and had dismissed him uncondemned. Other princes, who lacked his cleverness and power, tried to imitate him, and from north to south the whole of Syria could only be compared to some great arena, in which fighting was continually carried on between one tribe or town and another—Tyre against Sidon, Sidon against Byblos, Jerusalem against Lachish. All of them appealed to Khûniatonû, and endeavoured to enlist him on their side. Their despatches arrived by scores, and the perusal of them at the present day would lead us to imagine that Egypt had all but lost her supremacy. The Egyptian ministers, however, were entirely unmoved by them, and continued to refuse material support to any of the numerous rivals, except in a few rare cases, where a too prolonged indifference would have provoked an open revolt in some part of the country.

Khûniatonû died young, about the XVIIIth year of his reign.[1] He was buried in the depths of a ravine in the mountain-side to the east of the town, and his tomb remained unknown till within the last few years. Although one of his daughters who died before her father had been interred there, the place seems to have been entirely unprepared for the reception of the king's body. The funeral chamber and the passages are scarcely even rough-hewn, and the reception halls show a mere commencement of decoration.[2] The other tombs of the locality are divided into two groups, separated by the ravine reserved for the burying-place of the royal house. The noble families possessed each their own tomb on the slopes of the hillside; the common people were laid to rest in pits lower down, almost on the level of the plain. The cutting and

[1] The length of Khûniatonû's reign was fixed by Griffith with almost absolute certainty by means of the dates written in ink on the jars of wine and preserves found in the ruins of the palace.

[2] The tomb has been found, as I anticipated, in the ravine which separates the northern after the southern group of burying-places. The Arabs opened it in 1891, and Grébaut has since completely excavated it. The scenes depicted in it are connected with the death and funeral of the Princess Mâqîtatonû.

decoration of all these tombs had been entrusted to a company of contractors, who had executed them according to two or three stereotyped plans, without any variation, except in size. Nearly all the walls are bare, or present but few inscriptions; those tombs only are completed

INTERIOR OF A TOMB AT TEL-AMARNA.[1]

whose occupants died before the Pharaoh. The façades of the tombs are cut in the rock, and contain, for the most part, but one door, the jambs of which are covered on both sides by several lines of hieroglyphs; and it is just possible to distinguish traces of the adoration of the radiant Disk on the lintels, together with the cartouches containing the

[1] Drawn by Boudier, after a photograph by Insinger.

names of the king and god. The chapel is a large rectangular chamber, from one end of which opens the inclined passage leading to the coffin. The roof is sometimes supported by columns, having capitals decorated with designs of flowers or of geese hung from the abacus by their feet with their heads turned upwards.

The religious teaching at Tel el-Amarna presents no difference in the main from that which prevailed in other parts of Egypt.[1] The Double of Osiris was supposed to reside in the tomb, or else to take wing to heaven and embark with Atonû, as elsewhere he would embark with Râ. The same funerary furniture is needed for the deceased as in other local cults—ornaments of vitreous paste, amulets, and *Ushabtiu*, or "Respondents," to labour for the dead man in the fields of Ialû. Those of Khûniatonû were, like those of Amenôthes III., actual statuettes in granite of admirable workmanship. The dead who reached the divine abode, retained the same rank in life that they had possessed here below, and in order to ensure the enjoyment of it, they related, or caused to be depicted in their tombs, the events of their earthly career. A citizen of Khûîtatonû would naturally represent the manners and customs of his native town, and this would account for the local colouring of the scenes in which we see him taking

[1] The peculiar treatment of the two extremities of the sign for the sky, which surmounts the great scene on the tomb of Âhmosis, shows that there had been no change in the ideas concerning the two horizons or the divine tree found in them: the aspirations for the soul of Mariri, the high priest of Atonû, or for that of the sculptor Baûkû, are the same as those usually found, and the formula on the funerary stelæ differs only in the name of the god from that on the ordinary stelæ of the same kind.

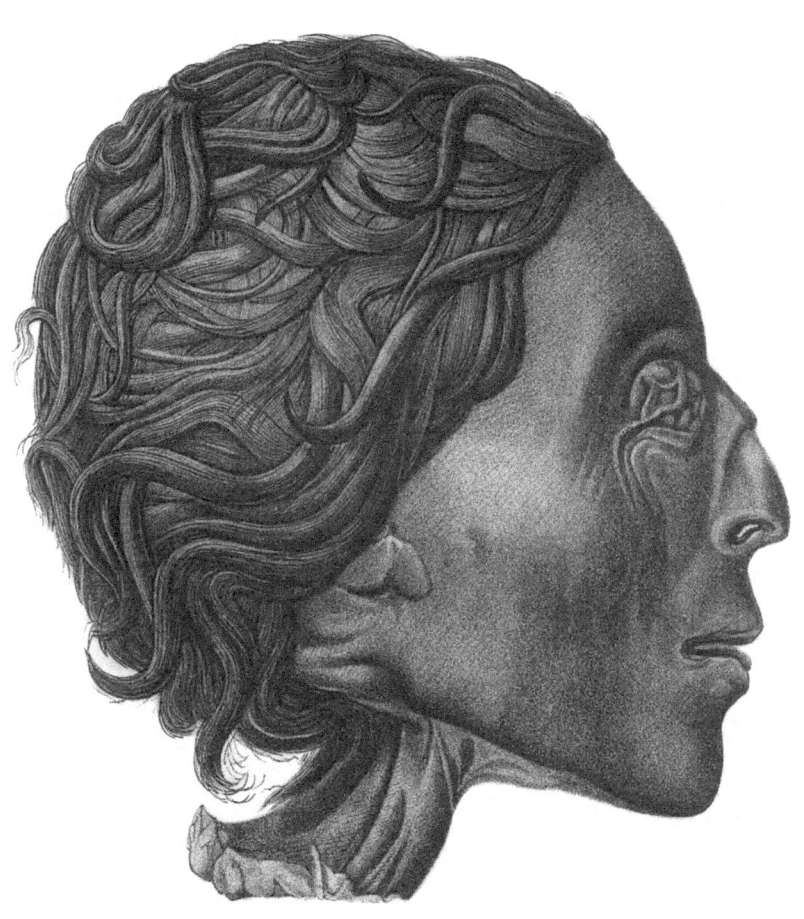

PROFILE OF HEAD OF A MUMMY (FEMALE). (THEBES TOMBS.)

part. They bear no resemblance to the traditional pictures of the buildings and gardens of Thebes with which we are familiar; we have instead the palaces, colonnades, and pylons of the rising city, its courts planted with sycomores, its treasuries, and its storehouses. The sun's disk hovers above and darts its prehensile rays over every object; its hands present the *crux ansata* to the nostrils of the various members of the family, they touch caressingly the queen and her daughters, they handle the offerings of bread and cakes, they extend even into the government warehouses to pilfer or to bless. Throughout all these scenes Khûniatonû and the ladies of his harem seem to be ubiquitous: here he visits one of the officers, there he repairs to the temple for the dedication of its sanctuary. His chariot, followed at a little distance by that of the princesses, makes its way peaceably through the streets. The police of the city and the soldiers of the guard, whether Egyptians or foreigners, run before him and clear a path among the crowd, the high priest Marirî stands at the gate to receive him, and the ceremony is brought to a close by a distribution of gold necklaces or rings, while the populace dance with delight before the sovereign. Meantime the slaves have cooked the repast, the dancers and musicians within their chambers have rehearsed for the evening's festival, and the inmates of the house carry on animated dialogues during their meal. The style and the technique of these wall-paintings differ in no way from those in the necropolis of the preceding period, and there can be no doubt that the artists who decorated these monuments were trained in the schools of Thebes. Their drawing is often very refined, and there is great freedom in their composition; the perspective of some of the bas-reliefs almost comes up to our own, and the movement of animated crowds is indicated with perfect accuracy. It is, however, not safe to conclude from these examples that the

TWO OF THE DAUGHTERS OF KHÛNIATONÛ.[1]

artists who executed them would have developed Egyptian art in a new direction, had not subsequent events caused a reaction against the worship of Atonû and his followers. Although the tombs in which they worked differ from the generality of Egyptian burying-places, their originality does not arise from any effort, either conscious or other-

[1] Drawn by Faucher-Gudin, from a photograph by Petrie.

THE ART OF THE TIME OF KHÛNIATONÛ

wise, to break through the ordinary routine of the art of the time; it is rather the result of the extraordinary appearance of the sovereign whose features they were called on to portray, and the novelty of several of the subjects which they had to treat. That artist among them who first gave concrete form to the ideas circulated by the priests of Atonû, and drew the model cartoons, evidently possessed a master-hand, and was endowed with undeniable originality and power. No other Egyptian draughtsman ever expressed a child's grace as he did, and the portraits which he sketched of the daughters of Khûniatonû playing undressed at their mother's side, are examples of a reserved and delicate grace. But these models, when once composed and finished even to the smallest details, were entrusted for execution to workmen of mediocre powers, who were recruited not only from Thebes, but from the neighbouring cities of Hermopolis and Siût. These estimable people, with a praiseworthy patience, traced bit by bit the cartoons confided to them, omitting or adding individuals or groups according to the extent of the wall-space they had to cover, or to the number of relatives and servants whom the proprietor of the tomb desired should share in his future happiness. The style of these draughtsmen betrays the influence of the second-rate schools in which they had learned their craft, and the clumsiness of their work would often repel us, were it not that the interest of the episodes portrayed redeems it in the eyes of the Egyptologist.

Khûniatonû left no son to succeed him; two of his sons-in-law successively occupied the throne—Sâakerî, who had married his eldest daughter Marîtatonû, and Tûtankhamon, the husband of Ankhnasaton. The first had been associated in the sovereignty by his father-in-law;[1] he showed himself a zealous partisan of the "Disk," and he continued to reside in.the new capital during the few years of his sole reign.[2] The second son-in-law was a son of Amenôthes III., probably by a concubine. He returned to the religion of Amon, and his wife, abjuring the creed of her father, changed her name from Ankhnasaton to that of Ânkhnasamon. Her husband abandoned Khûitatonû[3] at the end of two or three years, and after his departure the town fell into decadence as quickly as it had arisen. The streets were unfrequented, the palaces and temples stood empty, the tombs remained unfinished and unoccupied, and its patron god returned to his former state, and was relegated to the third or fourth rank in the Egyptian Pantheon. The town struggled for a short time against its adverse fate, which was no doubt retarded owing to the various industries founded in it by Khûniatonû, the

[1] He and his wife are represented by the side of Khûniatonû, with the protocol and the attributes of royalty. Petrie assigns to this double reign those minor objects on which the king's prenomen Ankhkhopîrûri is followed by the epithet *beloved of Uânirâ*, which formed part of the name of Khûniatonû.

[2] Petrie thinks, on the testimony of the lists of Manetho, which give twelve years to Akenkheres, daughter of Horos, that Sâakerî reigned twelve years, and only two or three years as sole monarch without his father-in-law. I think these two or three years a probable maximum length of his reign, whatever may be the value we should here assign to the lists of Manetho.

[3] Petrie, judging from the number of minor objects which he has found in his excavations at Tel el-Amarna, believes that he can fix the length of Tûtankhamon's sojourn at Khûitatonû at six years, and that of his whole reign at nine years.

manufactories of enamel and coloured glass requiring the presence of many workmen; but the latter emigrated ere long to Thebes or the neighbouring city of Hermopolis, and the "Horizon of Atonû" disappeared from the list of nomes, leaving of what might have been the capital of the Egyptian empire, merely a mound of crumbling bricks with two or three fellahîn villages scattered on the eastern bank of the Nile.[1] Thebes, whose influence and population had meanwhile never lessened, resumed her supremacy undisturbed. If, out of respect for the past, Tûtankhamon continued the decoration of the temple of Atonû at Karnak, he placed in every other locality the name and figure of Amon; a little stucco spread over the parts which had been mutilated, enabled the outlines to be restored to their original purity, and the alteration was rendered invisible by a few coats of colour. Tûtankhamon was succeeded by the divine father Aî, whom Khûniatonû had assigned as husband to one of his relatives named Tîi, so called after the widow of Amenôthes III. Aî laboured no less diligently than his predecessor to keep up the traditions which had been temporarily interrupted. He had been a faithful worshipper of the Disk, and had given orders for the construction of two funerary chapels for himself in the mountain-side above Tel el-Amarna, the paintings in which indicate a complete adherence to the

---

[1] Petrie thinks that the temples and palaces were systematically destroyed by Harmhabî, and the ruins used by him in the buildings which he erected at different places in Egypt. But there is no need for this theory: the beauty of the limestone which Khûniatonû had used sufficiently accounts for the rapid disappearance of the deserted edifices.

faith of the reigning king. But on becoming Pharaoh, he was proportionally zealous in his submission to the gods of Thebes, and in order to mark more fully his return to the ancient belief, he chose for his royal burying-place a site close to that in which rested the body of Amenôthes III.[1] His sarcophagus, a large oblong of carved rose

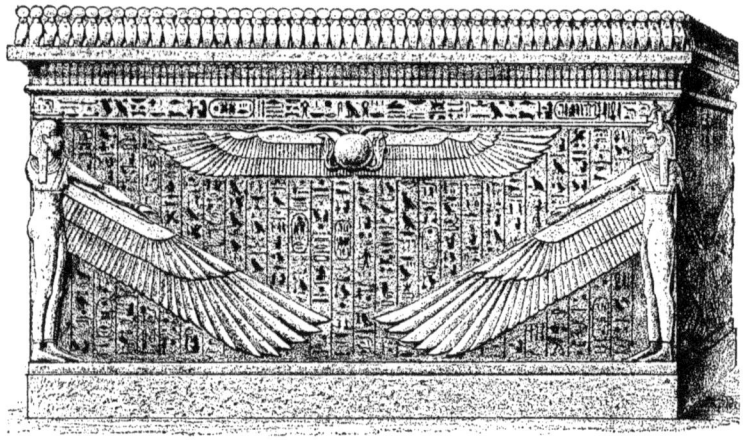

SARCOPHAGUS OF THE PHARAOH AÎ.[2]

granite, still lies open and broken on the spot. Figures of goddesses stand at the four angles and extend their winged arms along its sides, as if to embrace the mummy of the sovereign. Tûtankhamon and Aî were obeyed from one end of Egypt to the other, from Napata to the shores of the Mediterranean. The peoples of Syria raised no disturbances during their reigns, and

[1] The first tomb seems to have been dug before his marriage, at the time when he had no definite ambitions; the second was prepared for him and his wife Tii.
[2] Drawn by Faucher-Gudin, after the drawing of Prisse d'Avennes.

THE END OF THE DYNASTY 111

paid their accustomed tribute regularly;[1] if their rule was short, it was at least happy. It would appear, however, that after their deaths, troubles arose in the state. The lists of Manetho give two or three princes—Râthôtis, Khebres, and Akherres—whose names are not found on the monuments.[2] It is possible that we ought not to regard them as historical personages, but merely as heroes of popular romance, of the same type as those introduced so freely into the history of the preceding dynasties by the chroniclers of the Saite and Greek periods. They were, perhaps, merely short-lived pretenders who were overthrown one by the other before either had succeeded in establishing himself on the seat of Horus. Be that as it may, the XVIIIth dynasty drew to its close amid strife and quarreling, without our being able to discover the cause of its overthrow, or the name of the last of its sovereigns.[3]

Scarcely half a century had elapsed between the moment when the XVIIIth dynasty reached the height of its power under Amenôthes III. and that of its downfall. It is impossible to introduce with impunity changes of any kind into the constitution or working of so complicated a machine as an empire founded on conquest. When the parts of the mechanism have been once put together and

---

[1] Tûtankhamon receives the tribute of the Kûshites as well as that of the Syrians; Aî is represented at Shataûi in Nubia as accompanied by Paûirû, the prince of Kûsh.

[2] Wiedemann has collected six royal names which, with much hesitation, he places about this time.

[3] The list of kings who make up the XVIIIth dynasty can be established with certainty, with the exception of the order of the three last sovereigns who succeed Khûniatonû. It is here given in its authentic form, as the

set in motion, and have become accustomed to work harmoniously at a proper pace, interference with it must not be attempted except to replace such parts as are broken or worn out, by others exactly like them. To make alterations while the machine is in motion, or to introduce

monuments have permitted us to reconstruct it, and in its Greek form as it is found in the lists of Manetho:

ACCORDING TO THE MONUMENTS.

I. ÂHMÔSI I. NIBPAHÎTIRÎ.
II. AMENHOTPÛ I. ZOSIRKERÎ.
III. THÛTMÔSI I. ÂKHPIRKERÎ.
IV. THÛTMÔSI II. ÂKHPIRNIRÎ.
V. TḤÛTMOSI III. MANAKHPIRRÎ.
VI. AMƱNHOTPÛ II. ÂKHPÎRÛRÎ.
VII. THÛTMÔSI IV. MANAKHPÎRÛRÎ.
VIII. AMENHOTPÛ III. NIBMÂÛRÎ.
IX. {AMENHOTPÛ IV.} NAFIRKHOPÎRÛ-
    {KHÛNIATONÛ} RÎ-ÛÂNIRÎ.
X. SÂḲERÎ SOZÎRKHOPÎRÛ ÂNKHKHO-
   PÎRÛRÎ.
XI. TÛTÂNKHAMONÛ HAQ - ON - RÎSÎT NIBKHOPÎRÛRÎ.
XII. IÔTNÛTIR AÎ NÛTIR - HIQ - OÎSÎT KHOPIRKHOPÎRÛRÎ IRI-MÂÎT.

ACCORDING TO MANETHO.

I. AMÔSIS.
II. KHEBRÔS.
III. AMENÔPHTHIS.
IV. AMENSIS.
V. MISAPHRIS.
VI. MISPHRAGMOUTHÔSIS.
VII. THOUTMOSIS.
VIII. AMENÔPHIS.
IX. HÔROS.
X. AKHERRES I.
XI. RATHÔS.
XII. KKEBRES.
XIII. AKHERRES II.

Manetho's list, as we have it, is a very ill-made extract, wherein the official kings are mixed up with the legitimate queens, as well as, at least towards the end, with persons of doubtful authenticity. Several kings, between Khûniatonû and Harmhabî, are sometimes added at the end of the list; some of these I think, belonged to previous dynasties, e.g. Teti to the VIth, Râhotpû to the XVIIth; several are heroes of romance, as Mernebphtah or Merkhopirphtah, while the names of the others are either variants from the cartouche names of known princes, or else are nicknames, such as was Sesû, Sestûrî for Ramses II. Dr. Mahler believes that he can fix, within a few days, the date of the kings of whom the list is composed, from Âhmosis I. to Aî. I hold to the approximate date which I have given in vol. iv. p. 153 of this History, and I give the years 1600 to 1350 as the period of the dynasty, with a possible error of about fifty years, more or less.

THE END OF THE DYNASTY

new combinations, however ingenious, into any part of the original plan, might produce an accident or a breakage of the gearing when perhaps it would be least expected. When the devout Khûniatonû exchanged one city and one god for another, he thought that he was merely transposing equivalents, and that the safety of the commonwealth was not concerned in the operation. Whether it was Amon or Atonû who presided over the destinies of his people, or whether Thebes or Tel el-Amarna were the centre of impulse, was, in his opinion, merely a question of internal arrangement which could not affect the economy of the whole. But events soon showed that he was mistaken in his calculations. It is probable that if, on the expulsion of the Hyksôs, the earlier princes of the dynasty had attempted an alteration in the national religion, or had moved the capital to any other city they might select, the remainder of the kingdom would not have been affected by the change. But after several centuries of faithful adherence to Amon in his city of Thebes, the governing power would find it no easy matter to accomplish such a resolution. During three centuries the dynasty had become wedded to the city and to its patron deity, and the locality had become so closely associated with the dynasty, that any blow aimed at the god could not fail to destroy the dynasty with it; indeed, had the experiment of Khûniatonû been prolonged beyond a few years, it might have entailed the ruin of the whole country. All who came into contact with Egypt, or were under her rule, whether Asiatics or Africans, were quick to detect any change in her administration, and to remark a falling away from the traditional systems of the times of Thûtmosis III. and Amenôthes II. The successors of the heretic king had the sense to perceive at once the first symptoms of disorder, and to refrain from persevering in his errors; but however quick they were to undo his work, they could not foresee its serious consequences. His immediate followers were powerless to maintain their dynasty, and their posterity had to make way for a family who had not incurred the hatred of Amon, or rather that of his priests. If those who followed them were able by their tact and energy to set Egypt on her feet again, they were at the same time unable to restore her former prosperity or her boundless confidence in herself.

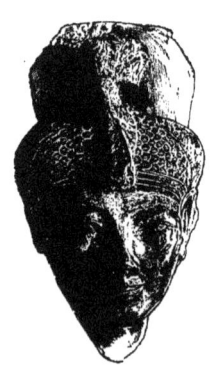

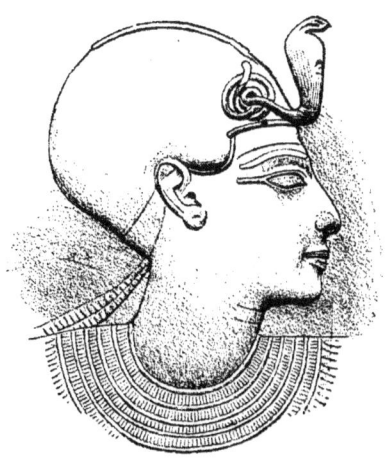

THE REACTION AGAINST EGYPT

THE XIXTH DYNASTY: HARMHABÎ—THE HITTITE EMPIRE IN SYRIA AND IN ASIA MINOR—SETI I. AND RAMSES II.—THE PEOPLE OF THE SEA: MÎNEPHTAH AND THE ISRAELITE EXODUS.

The birth and antecedents of Harmhabî, his youth, his enthronement—The final triumph of Amon and his priests—Harmhabî infuses order into the government: his wars against the Ethiopians and Asiatics—The Khâti, their civilization, religion; their political and military constitution; the extension of their empire towards the north—The countries and populations of Asia Minor; commercial routes between the Euphrates and the Ægean Sea—The treaty concluded between Harmhabî and Sapalulu.

Ramses I. and the uncertainties as to his origin—Seti I. and the campaign against Syria in the 1ˢᵗ year of his reign; the re-establishment of the Egyptian empire—Working of the gold-mines at Etbaï—The monuments constructed by Seti I. in Nubia, at Karnak, Luxor, and Abydos—The valley of the kings and tomb of Seti I. at Thebes.

(116)

Ramses II., his infancy, his association in the Government, his début in Ethiopia : he builds a residence in the Delta—His campaign against the Khâti in the 5th year of his reign—The taking of Qodshû, the victory of Ramses II. and the truce established with Khâtusaru : the poem of Pentaûîrît—His treaty with the Khâti in the 21st year of his reign : the balance of power in Syria : the marriage of Ramses II. with a Hittite princess—Public works : the Speos at Abu-Simbel ; Luxor, Karnak, the Ramesseum, the monuments in the Delta— The regency of Khamoîsît and Minephtah, the legend of Sesostris, the coffin and mummy of Ramses II.

Minephtah—The kinjdom of Libya, the people of the sea—The first invasion of Libya : the Egyptian victory at Piriû ; the triumph of Minephtah— Seti II., Amenmeses, Siphtah-Minephtah—The foreign captives in Egypt ; the Exodus of the Hebrews and their march to Sinai—An Egyptian romance of the Exodus : Amenophis, son of Pa-apis.

THE GREAT HYPOSTYLE HALL AT KARNAK, SEEN FROM THE SOUTHERN SIDE OF THE SACRED LAKE.[1]

CHAPTER II

THE REACTION AGAINST EGYPT

The XIXth dynasty : Harmhabî—The Hittite empire in Syria and in Asia Minor—Seti I. and Ramses II.—The people of the sea : Mînephtah and the Israelite Exodus.

WHILE none of these ephemeral Pharaohs left behind them a son, either legitimate or illegitimate, there was no lack of princesses, any of which, having on her accession to the throne to choose a consort after her own heart, might thus become the founder of a new dynasty. By such a chance alliance Harmhabî, who

[1] Drawn by Boudier, from a photograph by Émil Brugsch-Bey. The vignette, which is by Faucher-Gudin, represents a photograph by Petrie of Amonrâ and Harmhabî, a group now in the Turin Museum.

118   THE REACTION AGAINST EGYPT

was himself descended from Thûtmosis III., was raised to the kingly office.[1] His mother, Mûtnozmît, was of the royal line, and one of the most beautiful statues in the Gîzeh Museum probably represents her. The body is mutilated, but the head is charming in its intelligent and animated expression, in its full eyes and somewhat large, but finely modelled, mouth. The material of the statue is a fine-grained limestone, and its milky whiteness tends to soften the malign character of her look and smile. It is possible that Mûtnozmît was the daughter of Amenôthes III. by his marriage with one of his sisters: it was from her, at any rate, and not from his great-grandfather, that Harmhabî derived his indisputable claims to royalty.[2] He was born, probably, in the last years of Amenôthes, when Tîi was the exclusive favourite of the sovereign; but it was alleged later on, when Harmhabî had emerged from obscurity, that Amon, destining him for the throne, had condescended to become his father by Mûtnozmît—a customary procedure with the god when his race on earth threatened to become

[1] A fragment of an inscription at Karnak calls Thûtmosis III. "the father of his fathers." Champollion called him Hornemneb, Rosellini, Hôr-hemheb, Hôr-em-hbai, and both identified him with the Hôros of Manetho, hence the custom among Egyptologists for a long time to designate him by the name Horus. Dévéria was the first to show that the name corresponded with the Armais of the lists of Manetho, and, in fact, Armais is the Greek transcription of the group Harmhabî in the bilingual texts of the Ptolemaic period.

[2] Mûtnozmît was at first considered the daughter and successor of Harmhabî, or his wife. Birch showed that the monuments did not confirm these hypotheses, and he was inclined to think that she was Harmhabî's mother. As far as I can see for the present, it is the only solution which agrees with the evidence on the principal monument which has made known her existence.

debased.¹ It was he who had rocked the newly born infant to sleep, and, while Harsiesis was strengthening his limbs with protective amulets, had spread over the child's skin the freshness and brilliance which are the peculiar privilege of the immortals. While still in the nursery, the great and the insignificant alike prostrated themselves before Harmhabî, making him liberal offerings. Every one recognised in him, even when still a lad and incapable of reflection, the carriage and complexion of a god, and Horus of Cynopolis was accustomed to follow his steps, knowing that the time of his advancement was near. After having called the attention of the Egyptians to Harmhabî, Amon was anxious, in fact, to hasten the coming of the day when he might confer upon him supreme rank, and for this purpose inclined the heart of the reigning Pharaoh towards him. Aï proclaimed him his heir over the whole land.²
He never gave cause for any dissatisfaction when called to

¹ All that we know of the youth of Harmhabî is contained in the texts on a group preserved in the Turin Museum, and pointed out by Champollion, translated and published subsequently by Birch and by Brugsch. The first lines of the inscription seem to me to contain an account of the union of Amon with the queen, analogous to those at Deir el-Bahari treating of the birth of Hâtshopsîtû, and to those at Luxor bearing upon Amenôthes III. (cf. vol. iv. pp. 342, 343 ; and p. 51 of the present volume), and to prove for certain that Harmhabî's mother was a princess of the royal line by right.

² The king is not named in the inscription. It cannot have been Amenôthes IV., for an individual of the importance of Harmhabî, living alongside this king, would at least have had a tomb begun for him at Tel el-Amarna. We may hesitate between Ai and Tûtankhamon ; but the inscription seems to say definitely that Harmhabî succeeded directly to the king under whom he had held important offices for many years, and this compels us to fix upon Ai, who, as we have said at p. 108, et seq., of the present volume, was, to all appearances, the last of the so-called heretical sovereigns.

court, and when he was asked questions by the monarch he replied always in fit terms, in such words as were calculated to produce serenity, and thus gained for himself a reputation as the incarnation of wisdom, all his plans and intentions appearing to have been conceived by Thot the Ibis himself. For many years he held a place of confidence with the sovereign. The nobles, from the moment he appeared at the gate of the palace, bowed their backs before him; the barbaric chiefs from the north or south stretched out their arms as soon as they approached him, and gave him the adoration they would bestow upon a god. His favourite residence was Memphis, his preference for it arising from his having possibly been born there, or from its having been assigned to him for his abode. Here he constructed for himself a magnificent tomb, the bas-reliefs of which exhibit him as already king, with the sceptre in his hand and the uræus on his brow, while the adjoining cartouche does not as yet contain his name.[1] He was the mighty of the mighty, the great among the great, the

[1] This part of the account is based upon a study of a certain number of texts and representations all coming from Harmhabî's tomb at Saqqârah, and now scattered among the various museums—at Gizeh, Leyden, London, and Alexandria. Birch was the first to assign these monuments to the Pharaoh Harmhabî, supposing at the same time that he had been dethroned by Ramses I., and had lived at Mêmphis in an intermediate position between that of a prince and that of a private individual; this opinion was adopted by Ed. Meyer, rejected by Wiedemann and by myself. After full examination, I think the Harmhabî of the tomb at Saqqârah and the Pharaoh Harmhabî are one and the same person; Harmhabi, sufficiently high placed to warrant his wearing the uræus, but not high enough to have his name inscribed in a cartouche, must have had his tomb constructed at Saqqârah, as Aï and possibly Ramses I. had theirs built for them at Tel el-Amarna.

general of generals, the messenger who ran to convey orders to the people of Asia and Ethiopia, the indispensable companion in council or on the field of battle,[1] at the time when Horus of Cynopolis resolved to seat him upon his eternal throne. Aî no longer occupied it. Horus took Harmhabî with him to Thebes, escorted him thither amid expressions of general joy, and led him to Amon in order that the god might bestow upon him the right to reign. The reception took place in the temple of Luxor, which served as a kind of private chapel for the descendants of Amenôthes. Amon rejoiced to see Harmhabî, the heir of the two worlds; he took him with him to the royal palace, introduced him into the apartments of his august daughter, Mûtnozmît; then, after she had recognised her child and had pressed him to her bosom, all the gods broke out into acclamations, and their cries ascended up to heaven.[2] "Behold, Amon arrives with his son before him, at the

---

[1] The fragments of the tomb preserved at Leyden show him leading to the Pharaoh Asiatics and Ethiopians, burthened with tribute. The expressions and titles given above are borrowed from the fragments at Gizeh.

[2] Owing to a gap, the text cannot be accurately translated at this point. The reading can be made out that Amon "betook himself to the palace, placing the prince before him, as far as the sanctuary of his (Amon's) daughter, the very august . . .; she poured water on his hands, she embraced the beauties (of the prince), she placed herself before him." It will be seen that the name of the daughter of Amon is wanting, and Birch thought that a terrestrial princess whom Harmhabî had married was in question, Mûtnozmît, according to Brugsch. If the reference is not to a goddess, who along with Amon took part in the ceremonies, but to Mûtnozmit, we must come to the conclusion that she, as heir and queen by birth, must have ceded her rights by some ritual to her son before he could be crowned.

palace, in order to put upon his head the diadem, and to prolong the length of his life ! We install him, therefore, in his office, we give to him the insignia of Râ, we pray Amon for him whom he has brought as our protector : may he as king have the festivals of Râ and the years of Horus; may he accomplish his good pleasure in Thebes, in Heliopolis, in Memphis, and may he add to the veneration with which these cities are invested." And they immediately decided that the new Pharaoh should be called Horus-sturdy-bull, mighty in wise projects, lord of the Vulture and of the very marvellous Uræus in Thebes, the conquering Horus who takes pleasure in the truth, and who maintains the two lands, the lord of the south and north, Sozir Khopîrûrî chosen of Râ, the offspring of the Sun, Harmhabî Mîamûn, giver of life. The *cortége* came afterwards to the palace, the king walking before Amon : there the god embraced his son, placed the diadems upon his head, delivered to him the rule of the whole world, over foreign populations as well as those of Egypt, inasmuch as he possessed this power as the sovereign of the universe.

This is the customary subject of the records of enthronement. Pharaoh is the son of a god, chosen by his father, from among all those who might have a claim to it, to occupy for a time the throne of Horus; and as he became king only by a divine decree, he had publicly to express, at the moment of his elevation, his debt of gratitude to, and his boundless respect for, the deity, who had made him what he was. In this case, however, the protocol embodied something more than the traditional formality, and its hackneyed phrases borrowed a special meaning from the circumstances of the moment. Amon, who had been insulted and proscribed by Khûniatonû, had not fully recovered his prestige under the rule of the immediate successors of his enemy. They had restored to him his privileges and his worship, they had become reconciled to him, and avowed themselves his faithful ones,

THE FIRST PYLON OF HARMHABÎ AT KARNAK.[1]

but all this was as much an act of political necessity as a matter of religion : they still continued to tolerate, if not to favour, the rival doctrinal system, and the temple of the hateful Disk still dishonoured by its vicinity the sanctuary of Karnak. Harmhabî, on the other hand, was devoted to Amon, who had moulded him in embryo, and

[1] Drawn by Faucher-Gudin, from a photograph taken by Beato.

had trained him from his birth to worship none but him. Harmhabî's triumph marked the end of the evil days, and inaugurated a new era, in which Amon saw himself again master of Thebes and of the world. Immediately after his enthronement Harmhabî rivalled the first Amenôthes in his zeal for the interests of his divine father: he overturned the obelisks of Atonû and the building before which they stood; then, that no trace of them might remain, he worked up the stones into the masonry of two pylons, which he set up upon the site, to the south of the gates of Thûtmosis III. They remained concealed in the new fabric for centuries, but in the year 27 B.C. a great earthquake brought them abruptly to light. We find everywhere among the ruins, at the foot of the dislocated gates, or at the bases of the headless colossal figures, heaps of blocks detached from the structure, on which can be made out remnants of prayers addressed to the Disk, scenes of worship, and cartouches of Amenôthes IV., Aî, and Tûtankhamon. The work begun by Harmhabî at Thebes was continued with unabated zeal through the length of the whole river-valley. "He restored the sanctuaries from the marshes of Athû even to Nubia; he repaired their sculptures so that they were better than before, not to speak of the fine things he did in them, rejoicing the eyes of Râ. That which he had found injured he put into its original condition, erecting a hundred statues, carefully formed of valuable stone, for every one which was lacking. He inspected the ruined towns of the gods in the land, and made them such as they had been in the time of the first Ennead, and he allotted to them estates and offerings for every day, as well as a set of sacred vessels entirely of gold and silver; he settled priests in them, bookmen, carefully chosen soldiers, and assigned to them fields, cattle, all the necessary material to make prayers to Râ every morning." These measures were inspired by consideration for the ancient deities; but he added to them others, which tended to secure the welfare of the people and the stability of the government. Up to this time the officials and the Egyptian soldiers had displayed a tendency to oppress the fellahin, without taking into consideration the injury to the treasury occasioned by their rapacity. Constant supervision was the only means of restraining them, for even the best-served Pharaohs, Thûtmosis, and Amenôthes III. themselves, were obliged to have frequent recourse to the rigour of the law to keep the scandalous depredations of the officials within bounds.[1] The religious disputes of the preceding years, in enfeebling the authority of the central power, had given a free hand to these oppressors. The scribes and tax-collectors were accustomed to exact contributions for the public service from the ships, whether laden or not, of those who were in a small way of business, and once they had laid their hands upon them, they did not readily let them go. The poor fellow falling into their clutches lost his cargo, and he was at his wits' end to know how to deliver at the royal storehouses the various wares with which he calculated to pay his taxes. No sooner had the Court arrived at some place than the servants scoured the neighbourhood, confiscating the land produce, and seizing upon slaves, under pretence that they

[1] Harmhabî refers to the edicts of Thûtmosis III.

were acting for the king, while they had only their personal ends in view. Soldiers appropriated all the hides of animals with the object, doubtless, of making from them leather jackets and helmets, or of duplicating their shields, with the result that when the treasury made its claim for leather, none was to be found. It was hardly possible, moreover, to bring the culprits to justice, for the chief men of the towns and villages, the prophets, and all those who ought to have looked after the interests of the taxpayer, took money from the criminals for protecting them from justice, and compelled the innocent victims also to purchase their protection. Harmhabî, who was continually looking for opportunities to put down injustice and to punish deceit, at length decided to promulgate a very severe edict against the magistrates and the double-dealing officials: any of them who was found to have neglected his duty was to have his nose cut off, and was to be sent into perpetual exile to Zalu, on the eastern frontier. His commands, faithfully carried out, soon produced a salutary effect, and as he would on no account relax the severity of the sentence, exactions were no longer heard of, to the advantage of the revenue of the State. On the last day of each month the gates of his palace were open to every one. Any one on giving his name to the guard could

AMENÔTHES IV., FROM A FRAGMENT USED AGAIN BY HARMHABÎ.[1]

[1] Drawn by Faucher-Gudin, from a sketch by Prisse d'Avennes.

enter the court of honour, where he would find food in abundance to satisfy his hunger while he was awaiting an audience. The king all the while was seated in the sight of all at the tribune, whence he would throw among his faithful friends necklaces and bracelets of gold: he inquired into complaints one after another, heard every case, announced his judgments in brief words, and dismissed his subjects, who went away proud and happy at having had their affairs dealt with by the sovereign himself.[1]

The portraits of Harmhabî which have come down to us give us the impression of a character at once energetic and agreeable. The most beautiful of these is little more than a fragment broken off a black granite statue. Its mournful expression is not pleasing to the spectator, and at the first view alienates his sympathy. The face, which is still youthful, breathes an air of melancholy, an expression which is somewhat rare among the Pharaohs of the best period: the thin and straight nose is well set on the face, the elongated eyes have somewhat heavy lids; the large, fleshy lips, slightly contracted at the corners of the mouth, are cut with a sharpness that gives them singular vigour, and the firm and finely modelled chin loses little of its form from the false beard depending from it. Every detail is treated with such freedom that one would think the sculptor must have had some soft material to work upon, rather than a rock almost hard enough to defy the chisel;

---

[1] All these details are taken from a stele discovered in 1882. The text is so mutilated that it is impossible to give a literal rendering of it in all its parts, but the sense is sufficiently clear to warrant our filling up the whole with considerable certainty.

the command over it is so complete that the difficulty of the work is forgotten in the perfection of the result. The dreamy expression of his face, however, did not prevent Harmhabî from displaying beyond Egypt, as within it, singular activity. Although Egypt had never given up its claims to dominion over the whole river-valley, as far as the plains of Sennar, yet since the time of Amenôthes III. no sovereign had condescended, it would appear, to conduct in person the expeditions directed against the tribes of the Upper Nile. Harmhabi was anxious to revive the custom which imposed upon the Pharaohs the obligation to make their first essay in arms in Ethiopia, as Horus, son of Isis, had done of yore, and he seized the pretext of the occurrence of certain raids there to lead a body of troops himself into the heart of the negro country. He had just

HARMHABÎ.[1]

[1] Drawn by Faucher-Gudin, from a photograph by Émil Brugsch-Bey.

THE VAULTED PASSAGE OF THE ROCK-TOMB AT GEBEL SILSILEH.[1]

ordered at this time the construction of the two southern pylons at Karnak, and there was great activity in the

[1] Drawn by Faucher-Gudin, from a photograph by Insinger.

quarries of Silsileh. A commemorative chapel also was in course of excavation here in the sandstone rock, and he had dedicated it to his father, Amon-Râ of Thebes, coupling with him the local divinities, Hapî the Nile, and Sobkû the patron of Ombos. The sanctuary is excavated somewhat deeply into the hillside, and the dark rooms within it are decorated with the usual scenes of worship, but the vaulted approach to them displays upon its western wall the victory of the king. We see here a figure receiving from Amon the assurance of a long and happy life, and another letting fly his arrows at a host of fleeing enemies; Ethiopians raise their heads to him in suppliant gesture; soldiers march past with their captives; above one of the doors we see twelve military leaders marching and carrying the king aloft upon their shoulders, while a group of priests and nobles salute him, offering incense.[1] At this period Egyptian ships were ploughing the Red Sea, and their captains were renewing official relations with Pûanît. Somali chiefs were paying visits to the palace, as in the time of Thûtmosis III. The wars of Amon had, in fact, begun again. The god, having suffered neglect for half a century, had a greater need than ever of gold and silver to fill his coffers; he required masons for his buildings, slaves and cattle for his farms, perfumed essences and incense for his daily rites. His resources had gradually become exhausted, and his treasury would soon be empty if he did

---

[1] The significance of the monument was pointed out first by Champollion. The series of races conquered was represented at Karnak on the internal face of one of the pylons built by Harmhabî; it appears to have been "usurped" by Ramses II.

not employ the usual means to replenish it. He incited Harmhabî to proceed against the countries from which in olden times he had enriched himself—to the south in the first place, and then, having decreed victory there, and having naturally taken for himself the greater part of the

THE TRIUMPH OF HARMHABÎ IN THE SANCTUARY OF GEBEL SILSILEH.[1]

spoils, he turned his attention to Asia. In the latter campaign the Egyptian troops took once more the route through Cœle-Syria, and if the expedition experienced here more difficulties than on the banks of the Upper Nile, it

[1] Drawn by Faucher-Gudin, from a photograph by Daniel Heron. The black spots are due to the torches of the fellahin of the neighbourhood who have visited the rock-tomb in bygone years.

was, nevertheless, brought to an equally triumphant conclusion. Those of their adversaries who had offered an obstinate resistance were transported into other lands, and the rebel cities were either razed to the ground or given to the flames: the inhabitants having taken refuge in the mountains, where they were in danger of perishing from hunger, made supplications for peace, which was granted to them on the usual conditions of doing homage and paying tribute.[1] We do not exactly know how far he penetrated into the country; the list of the towns and nations over which he boasts of having triumphed contains, along with names unknown to us, some already famous or soon to become so—Arvad, Pibukhu, the Khâti, and possibly Alasia. The Haui-Nibu themselves must have felt the effects of the campaign, for several of their chiefs associated, doubtless, with the Phœnicians, presented themselves before the Pharaoh at Thebes. Egypt was maintaining, therefore, its ascendency, or at least appearing to maintain it in those regions where the kings of the XVIIIth dynasty had ruled after the campaigns of Thûtmosis I., Thûtmosis III., and Amenôthes II. Its influence, nevertheless, was not so undisputed as in former days; not that the Egyptian soldiers were less valiant, but owing to the fact that another power had risen up alongside them whose armies were strong enough to encounter them on the field of battle and to obtain a victory over them.

[1] These details are taken from the fragment of an inscription now in the museum at Vienna; Bergmann, and also Erman, think that we have in this text the indication of an immigration into Egypt of a tribe of the Monâtiu.

Beyond Naharaim, in the deep recesses of the Amanus and Taurus, there had lived, for no one knows how many centuries, the rude and warlike tribes of the Khâti, related not so much to the Semites of the Syrian plain as to the populations of doubtful race and language who occupied the upper basins of the Halys and Euphrates.[1] The Chaldæan conquest had barely touched them; the Egyptian campaign had not more effect, and Thûtmosis III. himself, after having crossed their frontiers and sacked several of their towns, made no serious pretence to reckon them among his subjects. Their chiefs were accustomed, like their neighbours, to use, for correspondence with other countries, the cuneiform mode of writing; they had among them, therefore, for this purpose, a host of scribes, interpreters, and official registrars of events, such as we find to have accompanied the sovereigns of Assyria and Babylon.[2] These chiefs were accustomed to send from time to time a present to the Pharaoh, which the latter was pleased to regard as a tribute,[3] or they would offer,

[1] Halévy asserts that the Khâti were Semites, and bases his assertion on materials of the Assyrian period. The Khâti, absorbed in Syria by the Semites, with whom they were blended, appear to have been by origin a non-Semitic people.

[2] A letter from the King of the Khâti to the Pharaoh Amenôthes IV. is written in cuneiform writing and in a Semitic language. It has been thought that other documents, drawn up in a non-Semitic language and coming from Mitanni and Arzapi, contain a dialect of the Hittite speech or that language itself. A "writer of books," attached to the person of the Hittite King Khâtusaru, is named amongst the dead found on the field of battle at Qodshû.

[3] It is thus perhaps we must understand the mention of tribute from the Khâti in the *Annals of Thútmosis III.*, l. 26, in the year XXXIII., also in the year XL. One of the Tel el-Amarna letters refers to presents of this

perhaps, one of their daughters in marriage to the king at Thebes, and after the marriage show themselves anxious to maintain good faith with their son-in-law. They had, moreover, commercial relations with Egypt, and furnished it with cattle, chariots, and those splendid Cappadocian horses whose breed was celebrated down to the Greek period.[1] They were already, indeed, people of consideration; their territory was so extensive that the contemporaries of Thûtmosis III. called them the Greater Khâti; and the epithet "vile," which the chancellors of the Pharaohs added to their name, only shows by its virulence the impression which they had produced upon the mind of their adversaries.[2] Their type of face distinguishes them clearly from the nations conterminous with them on the south. The Egyptian draughtsmen represented them as squat and short in stature, though

kind, which the King of Khâti addresses to Amenôthes IV. to celebrate his enthronement, and to ask him to maintain with himself the traditional good relations of their two families.

[1] The horses of the Khâti were called *abarî*, strong, vigorous, as also their bulls. The King of Alasia, while offering to Amenôthes III. a profitable speculation, advises him to have nothing to do with the King of the Khâti or with the King of Sangar, and thus furnishes proof that the Egyptians held constant commercial relations with the Khâti.

[2] M. de Rougé suggested that Khâti "the Little" was the name of the Hittites of Hebron. The expression, "Khâti the Great," has been compared with that of Khanirabbat, "Khani the Great," which in the Assyrian texts would seem to designate a part of Cappadocia, in which the province of Miliddi occurs, and the identification of the two has found an ardent defender in W. Max Muller. Until further light is thrown upon it, the most probable reading of the word is not Khani-ra*b*bat, but Khani-*ga*lbat. The name Khani-Galbat is possibly preserved in Julbat, which the Arab geographers applied in the Middle Ages to a province situated in Lesser Armenia.

vigorous, strong-limbed, and with broad and full shoulders in youth, but as inclined frequently to obesity in old age. The head is long and heavy, the forehead flattened, the chin moderate in size, the nose prominent, the eyebrows and cheeks projecting, the eyes small, oblique, and deep-set, the mouth fleshy, and usually framed in by two deep wrinkles; the flesh colour is a yellowish or reddish white,

THREE HEADS OF HITTITE SOLDIERS [1]

but clearer than that of the Phœnicians or the Amurru. Their ordinary costume consisted, sometimes of a shirt with short sleeves, sometimes of a sort of loin-cloth, more or less ample according to the rank of the individual wearing it, and bound round the waist by a belt. To these they added a scanty mantle, red or blue, fringed like that of the Chaldæans, which they passed over the left shoulder and brought back under the right, so as to leave the latter exposed. They wore shoes with thick soles, turning

[1] Drawn by Faucher-Gudin, from a photograph by Insinger.

up distinctly at the toes,[1] and they encased their hands in gloves, reaching halfway up the arm. They shaved off both moustache and beard, but gave free growth to their hair, which they divided into two or three locks, and allowed to fall upon their backs and breasts. The king's head-dress, which was distinctive of royalty, was a tall pointed hat, resembling to some extent the white crown of the Pharaohs. The dress of the people, taken all together, was of better and thicker material than that of the Syrians or Egyptians. The mountains and elevated plateaus which they inhabited were subject to extraordinary vicissitudes of heat and cold. If the summer burnt up everything, the winter reigned here with an extreme rigour, and dragged on for months: clothing and foot-gear had to be seen to, if the snow and the icy winds of December were to be resisted. The character of their towns, and the domestic life of their nobles and the common people, can only be guessed at. Some, at least, of the peasants must have sheltered themselves in villages half underground, similar to those which are still to be found in this region. The town-folk and the nobles had adopted for the most part the Chaldæan or Egyptian manners and customs in use among the Semites of Syria. As to their religion, they reverenced a number of secondary deities who had their abode in the tempest, in the clouds,

---

[1] This characteristic is found on the majority of the monuments which the peoples of Asia Minor have left to us, and it is one of the most striking indications of the northern origin of the Khâti. The Egyptian artists and modern draughtsmen have often neglected it, and the majority of them have represented the Khâti without shoes.

the sea, the rivers, the springs, the mountains, and the forests. Above this crowd there were several sovereign divinities of the thunder or the air, sun-gods and moon-gods, of which the chief was called Khâti, and was considered to be the father of the nation. They ascribed to all their deities a warlike and savage character. The Egyptians pictured some of them as a kind of Râ,[1] others as representing Sit, or rather Sûtkhû, that patron of the Hyksôs which was identified by them with Sît: every town had its tutelary heroes, of whom they were accustomed to speak as if of its Sûtkhû—Sûtkhû of Paliqa, Sûtkhû of Khissapa, Sûtkhû of Sarsu, Sûtkhû of Salpina. The goddesses in their eyes also became Astartés, and this one fact suggests that these deities were, like their Phœnician and Canaanite sisters, of a double nature—in one aspect chaste, fierce, and warlike, and in another lascivious and pacific. One god was called Mauru, another Targu, others Qaui and Khepa.[2] Tishubu, the Rammân of the Assyrians,

---

[1] The Cilician inscriptions of the Græco-Roman period reveal the existence in this region of a god, Rho, Rhos. Did this god exist among the Khâti, and did the similarity of the pronunciation of it to that of the god Râ suggest to the Egyptians the existence of a similar god among these people, or did they simply translate into their language the name of the Hittite god representing the sun?

[2] The names Mauru and Qaui are deduced from the forms Maurusaru and Qauisaru, which were borne by the Khâti: Qaui was probably the eponymous hero of the Qui people, as Khâti was of the Khâti. Tarku and Tisubu appear to me to be contained in the names Targanunasa, Targazatas, and Tartisubu; Tisubu is probably the Têssupas mentioned in the letter from Dushratta written in Mitannian, and identical with the Tushupu of another letter from the same king, and in a despatch from Tarkondaraush. Targu, Targa, Targanu, resemble the god Tarkhu, which is known to us from the proper names of these regions preserved in

138 THE REACTION AGAINST EGYPT

was doubtless lord of the tempest and of the atmosphere; Shausbe answered to Shala and to Ishtar the queen of love;[1] but we are frequently in ignorance as to the

A HITTITE KING.[2]

attributes covered by each of these divine names, and as to the forms with which they were invested. The majority of them, both male and female, were of gigantic stature, and were arrayed in the vesture of earthly kings and queens: they brandished their arms, displayed the insignia of their authority, such as a flower or bunch of grapes, and while receiving the offerings of the people were seated on a chair before an altar, or stood each on the animal representing him —such as a lion, a stag, or wild goat. The temples of their towns have disappeared, but they could never have been, it would seem, either large or magnificent: the favourite places of worship were the tops of mountains, in the vicinity of springs, or the depths of mysterious grottoes,

Assyrian and Greek inscriptions. Kheba, Khepa, Khîpa, is said to be a denomination of Rammân; we find it in the names of the princesses Tadu-khîpa, Gilu-khîpa, Puu-khîpa.

[1] The association of Tushupu, Tessupas, Tisubu, with Rammânu is made out from an Assyrian tablet published by Bezold: it was reserved for Sayce and Jensen to determine the nature of the god. Shausbe has been identified with Ishtar or Shala by Jensen.

[2] Drawn by Faucher-Gudin, from a picture in Lepsius. Khatusaru, King of the Khâti, who was for thirty years a contemporary of Ramses II.

MILITARY ORGANISATION OF THE KHÂTI   139

where the deity revealed himself to his priests, and received the faithful at the solemn festivals celebrated several times a year.[1]

We know as little about their political organisation as about their religion. We may believe, however, that it was feudal in character, and that every clan had its hereditary chief and its proper gods: the clans collectively rendered obedience to a common king, whose effective authority depended upon his character and age.[2] The various contingents which the sovereign could collect together and lead would, if he were an incapable general, be of little avail against the well-officered and veteran troops of Egypt. Still they were not to be despised, and contained the elements of an excellent army, superior both in quality and quantity to any which Syria had ever been able to put into the field. The infantry consisted of a limited number of archers or slingers. They had usually neither shield nor cuirass, but merely, in the way of protective armour, a padded head-dress, ornamented with a tuft. The bulk of the army carried short lances and broad-bladed choppers, or more generally, short thin-

---

[1] The religious cities and the festivals of the Greek epoch are described by Strabo; these festivals were very ancient, and their institution, if not the method of celebrating them, may go back to the time of the Hittite empire.

[2] The description of the battle of Qodshû in the time of Ramses II. shows us the King of the Khâti surrounded by his vassals. The evidence of the existence of a similar feudal organisation from the time of the XVIIIth dynasty is furnished by a letter of Dushratta, King of Mitanni, where he relates to Amenôthes IV. the revolt of his brother Artassumara, and speaks of the help which one of the neighbouring chiefs, Pirkhi, and all the Khâti had given to the rebel.

handled swords with flat two-edged blades, very broad at the base and terminating in a point. Their mode of attack was in close phalanxes, whose shock must have been hard to bear, for the soldiers forming them were in part at least recruited from among the strong and hardy mountaineers of the Taurus. The chariotry comprised the nobles and the *élite* of the army, but it was differently constituted from that of the Egyptians, and employed other tactics.

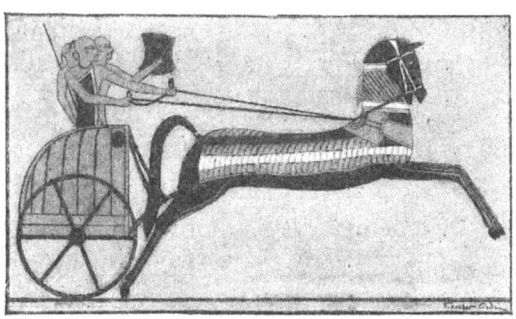

A HITTITE CHARIOT WITH ITS THREE OCCUPANTS.[1]

The Hittite chariots were heavier, and the framework, instead of being a mere skeleton, was pannelled on the sides, the contour at the top being sometimes quite square, at other times rudely curved. It was bound together in the front by two disks of metal, and strengthened by strips of copper or bronze, which were sometimes plated with silver or gold. There were no quiver-cases as in Egyptian chariots, for the Hittite charioteers rarely resorted to the bow and arrow. The occupants of a chariot were three in number—the driver; the shield-bearer, whose office it

[1] Drawn by Faucher-Gudin, from Champollion.

was to protect his companions by means of a shield, sometimes of a round form, with a segment taken out on each side, and sometimes square; and finally, the warrior, with his sword and lance. The Hittite princes whom fortune had brought into relations with Thûtmosis III. and Amenôthes II. were not able to avail themselves properly of the latent forces around them. It was owing probably to the feebleness of their character or to the turbulence of their barons that we must ascribe the poor part they played in the revolutions of the Eastern world at this time. The establishment of a strong military power on their southern frontier was certain, moreover, to be anything but pleasing to them; if they preferred not to risk everything by entering into a great struggle with the invaders, they could, without compromising themselves too much, harass them with sudden attacks, and intrigue in an underhand way against them to their own profit. Pharaoh's generals were accustomed to punish, one after the other, these bands of invading tribes, and the sculptors duly recorded their names on a pylon at Thebes among those of the conquered nations, but these disasters had little effect in restraining the Hittites. They continued, in spite of them, to march southward, and the letters from the Egyptian governors record their progress year after year. They had a hand in all the plots which were being hatched among the Syrians, and all the disaffected who wished to be free from foreign oppression—such as Abdashirti and his son Azîru—addressed themselves to them for help in the way of chariots and men.[1] Even in

[1] Azîru defends himself in one of his letters against the accusation

the time of Amenôthes III. they had endeavoured to reap profit from the discords of Mitanni, and had asserted their supremacy over it. Dushratta, however, was able to defeat one of their chiefs. Repulsed on this side, they fell back upon that part of Naharaim lying between the Euphrates and Orontes, and made themselves masters of one town after another in spite of the despairing appeals of the conquered to the Theban king. From the accession of Khûniatonû, they set to work to annex the countries of Nukhassi, Nîi, Tunipa, and Zinzauru: they looked with covetous eyes upon Phœnicia, and were already menacing Cœle-Syria. The religious confusion in Egypt under Tûtankhamon and Aî left them a free field for their ambitions, and when Harmhabî ventured to cross to the east of the isthmus, he found them definitely installed in the region stretching from the Mediterranean and the Lebanon to the Euphrates. Their then reigning prince, Sapalulu, appeared to have been the founder of a new dynasty: he united the forces of the country in a solid body, and was within a little of making a single state out of all Northern Syria.[1] All Naharaim had submitted to

of having received four messengers from the King of the Khâti, while he refused to receive those from Egypt. The complicity of Azîru with the Khâti is denounced in an appeal from the inhabitants of Tunipa. In a mutilated letter, an unknown person calls attention to the negotiations which a petty-Syrian prince had entered into with the King of the Khâti.

[1] Sapalulu has the same name as that we meet with later on in the country of Patin, in the time of Salmanasar III., viz. Sapalulme. It is known to us only from a treaty with the Khâti, which makes him coeval with Ramses I.: it was with him probably that Harmhabî had to deal in his Syrian campaigns. The limit of his empire towards the south is gathered in a measure from what we know of the wars of Seti I. with the Khâti.

him: Zahi, Alasia, and the Amurru had passed under his government from that of the Pharaohs; Carchemish, Tunipa, Nîi, Hamath, figured among his royal cities, and Qodshû was the defence of his southern frontier. His progress towards the east was not less considerable. Mitanni, Arzapi, and the principalities of the Euphrates as far as the Balikh, possibly even to the Khabur,[1] paid him homage: beyond this, Assyria and Chaldæa barred his way. Here, as on his other frontiers, fortune brought him face to face with the most formidable powers of the Asiatic world.

Had he sufficient forces at his disposal to triumph over them, or only enough to hold his ground? Both hypotheses could have been answered in the affirmative if each one of these great powers, confiding in its own resources, had attacked him separately. The Amorites, the people of Zahi, Alasia, and Naharaim, together with recruits from Hittite tribes, would then have put him in a position to resist, and even to carry off victory with a high hand in the final struggle. But an alliance between Assyria or Babylon and Thebes was always possible. There had been such things before, in the time of Thûtmosis IV. and in that of Amenôthes III., but they were

The latter prince was obliged to capture Qodshû, and to conquer the people of the Lebanon.

[1] The text of the poem of Pentaûirît mentions, among the countries confederate with the Khâti, all Naharaim; that is to say, the country on either side of the Euphrates, embracing Mitanni and the principalities named in the Amarna correspondence, and in addition some provinces whose sites have not yet been discovered, but which may be placed without much risk of error to the north of the Taurus.

lukewarm agreements, and their effect was not much to boast of, for the two parties to the covenant had then no common enemy to deal with, and their mutual interests were not, therefore, bound up with their united action. The circumstances were very different now. The rapid growth of a nascent kingdom, the restless spirit of its people, its trespasses on domains in which the older powers had been accustomed to hold the upper hand,—did not all this tend to transform the convention, more commercial than military, with which up to this time they had been content, into an offensive and defensive treaty? If they decided to act in concert, how could Sapalulu or his successors, seeing that he was obliged to defend himself on two frontiers at the same moment, muster sufficient resources to withstand the double assault? The Hittites, as we know them more especially from the hieroglyphic inscriptions, might be regarded as the lords only of Northern Syria, and their power be measured merely by the extent of territory which they occupied to the south of the Taurus and on the two banks of the Middle Euphrates. But this does not by any means represent the real facts. This was but the half of their empire; the rest extended to the westward and northward, beyond the mountains into that region, known afterwards as Asia Minor, in which Egyptian tradition had from ancient times confused some twenty nations under the common vague epithet of Haûî-nîbû. Official language still employed it as a convenient and comprehensive term, but the voyages of the Phœnicians and the travels of the "Royal Messengers," as well as, probably, the maritime commerce of the merchants of the Delta, had taught the scribes for more than a century and a half to make distinctions among these nations which they had previously summed up in one. The Luku[1] were to be found there, as well as the Danauna,[2] the Shardana,[3] and others besides, who lay behind one another on the coast. Of the second line of populations behind the region of the coast tribes, we have up to the present no means of knowing anything with certainty. Asia Minor, furthermore, is divided into two regions, so distinctly separated by nature as well as by races that one would be almost inclined to regard them as two countries foreign to each other. In its centre it consists of a well-defined undulating plain, having a gentle slope towards the Black Sea, and of the shape of a kind

[1] The Luku, Luka, are mentioned in the Amarna correspondence under the form Lukki as pirates and highway robbers. The identity of these people with the Lycians I hold as well established.

[2] The Danauna are mentioned along with the Luku in the Amarna correspondence. The termination, -auna, -ôna of this word appears to be the ending in -aon found in Asiatic names like Lykaôn by the side of Lykos, Kataôn by the side of Kêtis and Kat-patuka; while the form of the name Danaos is preserved in Greek legend, Danaôn is found only on Oriental monuments. The Danauna came "from their islands," that is to say, from the coasts of Asia Minor, or from Greece, the term not being pressed too literally, as the Egyptians were inclined to call all distant lands situated to the north beyond the Mediterranean Sea "islands."

[3] E. de Rougé and Chabas were inclined to identify the Shardana with the Sardes and the island of Sardinia. Unger made them out to be the Khartanoi of Libya, and was followed by Brugsch. W. Max Muller revived the hypotheses of De Rougé and Chabas, and saw in them bands from the Italian island. I am still persuaded, as I was twenty-five years ago, that they were Asiatics—the Mæonian tribe which gave its name to Sardis. The Serdani or Shardana are mentioned as serving in the Egyptian Army in the Tel el-Amarna tablets.

of convex trapezium, clearly bounded towards the north by the highlands of Pontus, and on the south by the tortuous chain of the Taurus. A line of low hills fringes the country on the west, from the Olympus of Mysia to the Taurus of Pisidia. Towards the east it is bounded by broken chains of mountains of unequal height, to which the name Anti-Taurus is not very appropriately applied. An immense volcanic cone, Mount Argæus, looks down from a height of some 13,000 feet over the wide isthmus which connects the country with the lands of the Euphrates. This volcano is now extinct, but it still preserved in old days something of its languishing energy, throwing out flames at intervals above the sacred forests which clothed its slopes. The rivers having their sources in the region just described, have not all succeeded in piercing the obstacles which separate them from the sea, but the Pyramus and the Sarus find their way into the Mediterranean and the Iris, Halys and Sangarios into the Euxine. The others flow into the lowlands, forming meres, marshes, and lakes of fluctuating extent. The largest of these lakes, called Tatta, is salt, and its superficial extent varies with the season. In brief, the plateau of this region is nothing but an extension of the highlands of Central Asia, and has the same vegetation, fauna, and climate, the same extremes of temperature, the same aridity, and the same wretched and poverty-stricken character as the latter. The maritime portions are of an entirely different aspect. The western coast which stretches into the Ægean is furrowed by deep valleys, opening out as they reach the sea, and the rivers—the Caicus, the Hermos, the Cayster,

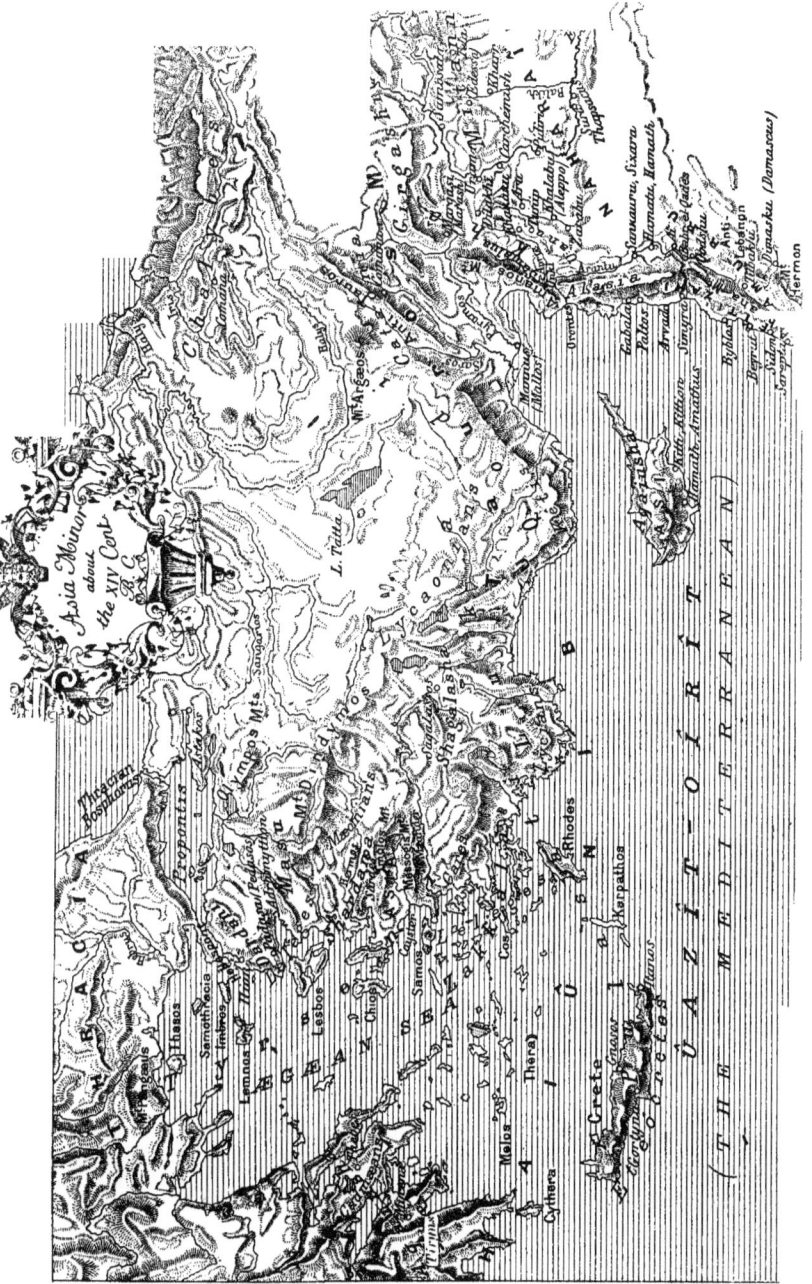

and Meander—which flow through them are effective makers of soil, bringing down with them, as they do, a continual supply of alluvium, which, deposited at their mouths, causes the land to encroach there upon the sea. The littoral is penetrated here and there by deep creeks, and is fringed with beautiful islands—Lesbos, Chios, Samos, Cos, Rhodes—of which the majority are near enough to the continent to act as defences of the seaboard, and to guard the mouths of the rivers, while they are far enough away to be secure from the effects of any violent disturbances which might arise in the mainland. The Cyclades, distributed in two lines, are scattered, as it were, at hazard between Asia and Europe, like great blocks which have fallen around the piers of a broken bridge. The passage from one to the other is an easy matter, and owing to them, the sea rather serves to bring together the two continents than to divide them. Two groups of heights, imperfectly connected with the central plateau, tower above the Ægean slope—wooded Ida on the north, veiled in cloud, rich in the flocks and herds upon its sides, and in the metals within its bosom; and on the south, the volcanic bastions of Lycia, where tradition was wont to place the fire-breathing Chimæra. A rocky and irregularly broken coast stretches to the west of Lycia, in a line almost parallel with the Taurus, through which, at intervals, torrents leaping from the heights make their way into the sea. At the extreme eastern point of the coast, almost at the angle where the Cilician littoral meets that of Syria, the Pyramus and the Sarus have brought down between them sufficient material to form an alluvial plain, which the classical geographers designated by the name of the Level Cilicia, to distinguish it from the rough region of the interior, Cilicia Trachea.

The populations dwelling in this peninsula belong to very varied races. On the south and south-west certain Semites had found an abode—the mysterious inhabitants of Solyma, and especially the Phœnicians in their scattered trading-stations. On the north-east, beside the Khâti, distributed throughout the valleys of the Anti-Taurus, between the Euphrates and Mount Argæus, there were tribes allied to the Khâti [1]—possibly at this time the Tabal and the Mushkâ—and, on the shores of the Black Sea, those workers in metal, which, following the Greeks, we may call, for want of a better designation, the Chalybes. We are at a loss to know the distribution of tribes in the centre and in the north-west, but the Bosphorus and the Hellespont, we may rest assured, never formed an ethnographical frontier. The continents on either side of them appear at this point to form the banks of a river, or the two slopes of a single valley, whose bottom lies buried beneath the waters. The barbarians of the Balkans had forced their way across at several points. Dardanians were to be encountered in the neighbourhood of Mount Ida, as well as on the banks of the Axios, from early times, and the Kebrenes of Macedonia had colonised a district of the Troad near Ilion, while the great nation of the Mysians had issued, like them, from the European populations of the Hebrus and the Strymon. The hero

[1] A certain number of these tribes or of their towns are to be found in the list contained in the treaty of Ramses II. with the Khâti.

Dardanos, according to legend, had at first founded, under the auspices of the Idæan Zeus, the town of Dardania; and afterwards a portion of his progeny followed the course of the Scamander, and entrenched themselves upon a precipitous hill, from the top of which they could look far and wide over the plain and sea. The most ancient Ilion, at first a village, abandoned on more than one occasion in the course of centuries, was rebuilt and transformed, earlier than the XVth century before Christ, into an important citadel, the capital of a warlike and prosperous kingdom. The ruins on the spot prove the existence of a primitive civilization analogous to that of the islands of the Archipelago before the arrival of the Phœnician navigators. We find that among both, at the outset, flint and bone, clay, baked and unbaked, formed the only materials for their utensils and furniture; metals were afterwards introduced, and we can trace their progressive employment to the gradual exclusion of the older implements. These ancient Trojans used copper, and we encounter only rarely a kind of bronze, in which the proportion of tin was too slight to give the requisite hardness to the alloy, and we find still fewer examples of iron and lead. They were fairly adroit workers in silver, electrum, and especially in gold. The amulets, cups, necklaces, and jewellery discovered in their tombs or in the ruins of their houses, are sometimes of a not ungraceful form. Their pottery was made by hand, and was not painted or varnished, but they often gave to it a fine lustre by means of a stone-polisher. Other peoples of uncertain origin, but who had attained a civilization as advanced as that of the

Trojans, were the Mæonians, the Leleges, and the Carians who had their abode to the south of Troy and of the Mysians. The Mæonians held sway in the fertile valleys of the Hermos, Cayster, and Mæander. They were divided into several branches, such as the Lydians, the Tyrseni, the Torrhebi, and the Shardana, but their most ancient traditions looked back with pride to a flourishing state to which, as they alleged, they had all belonged long ago on the slopes of Mount Sipylos, between the valley of the Hermos and the Gulf of Smyrna. The traditional capital of this kingdom was Magnesia, the most ancient of cities, the residence of Tantalus, the father of Niobe and the Pelopidæ. The Leleges rise up before us from many points at the same time, but always connected with the most ancient memories of Greece and Asia. The majority of the strongholds on the Trojan coast belonged to them—such as Antandros and Gargara—and Pedasos on the Satniois boasted of having been one of their colonies, while several other towns of the same name, but very distant from each other, enable us to form some idea of the extent of their migrations.[1] In the time of Strabo, ruined tombs and deserted sites of cities were shown in Caria which the natives regarded as Lelegia—that is, abode of the Leleges. The Carians were dominant in the southern angle of the peninsula and in the Ægean Islands;

[1] According to the scholiast on Nicander, the word "Pedasos" signified "mountain," probably in the language of the Leleges. We know up to the present of four Pedasi, or Pedasa: the first in Messenia, which later on took the name of Methône; the second in the Troad, on the banks of the Satniois; the third in the neighbourhood of Cyzicus; and the fourth in Caria.

THE LYCIANS, CARIANS, AND LELEGES 153

and the Lycians lay next them on the east, and were sometimes confounded with them. One of the most powerful tribes of the Carians, the Tremilæ, were in the eyes of the Greeks hardly to be separated from the mountainous district which they knew as Lycia proper; while other tribes extended as far as the Halys. A district of the Troad, to the south of Mount Ida, was called Lycia, and there was a Lycaonia on both sides of the Middle Taurus; while Attica had its Lycia, and Crete its Lycians. These three nations—the Lycians, Carians, and Leleges— were so entangled together from their origin, that no one would venture now to trace the lines of demarcation between them, and we are often obliged to apply to them collectively what can be appropriately ascribed to only one.

How far the Hittite power extended in the first years of its expansion we have now hardly the means of knowing. It would appear that it took within its scope, on the south-west, the Cilician plain, and the undulating region bordering on it—that of Qodi: the prince of the latter district, if not his vassal, was at least the colleague of the King of the Khâti, and he acted in concert with him in peace as well as in war.[1] It embraced also the upper basin of the Pyramos and its affluents, as well as the regions situated between the Euphrates and the Halys,

---

[1] The country of Qidi, Qadi, Qodi, has been connected by Chabas with Galilee, and Brugsch adopted the identification. W. Max Muller identified it with Phœnicia. I think the name served to designate the Cilician coast and plain from the mouth of the Orontes, and the country which was known in the Græco-Roman period by the name Kêtis and Kataonia.

but its frontier in this direction was continually fluctuating, and our researches fail to follow it. It is somewhat probable that it extended considerably towards the west and north-west in the direction of the Ægean Sea. The forests and escarpments of Lycaonia, and the desolate steppes of the central plateau, have always presented a barrier difficult to surmount by any invader from the east. If the Khâti at that period attacked it in front, or by a flank movement, the assault must rather have been of the nature of a hurried reconnaissance, or of a raid, than of a methodically conducted campaign.[1] They must have preferred to obtain possession of the valleys of the Thermodon and the Iris, which were rich in mineral wealth, and from which they could have secured an inexhaustible revenue. The extraction and working of metals in this region had attracted thither from time immemorial merchants from neighbouring and distant countries—at first from the south to supply the needs of Syria, Chaldæa, and Egypt, then from the west for the necessities of the countries on the Ægean. The roads, which, starting from the archipelago on the one hand, or the Euphrates on the other, met at this point, fell naturally into one, and thus formed a continuous route, along which the caravans of commerce, as well as warlike expeditions, might henceforward pass. Starting from the cultivated regions of Mæonia, the road proceeded up the valley of the Hermos from west to east; then, scaling the heights of the central plateau and taking a direction

[1] The idea of a Hittite empire extending over almost all Asia Minor was advanced by Sayce.

more and more to the north-east, it reached the fords of the Halys. Crossing this river twice—for the first time at a point about two-thirds the length of its course, and for the second at a short distance from its source—it made an abrupt turn towards the Taurus, and joined, at Melitene, the routes leading to the Upper Tigris, to Nisibis, to Singara, and to Old Assur, and connecting further down beyond the mountainous region, under the walls of Carchemish, with the roads which led to the Nile and to the river-side cities on the Persian Gulf.[1] There were other and shorter routes, if we think only of the number of miles, from the Hermos in Pisidia or Lycaonia, across the central steppe and through the Cilician Gates, to the meeting of the ways at Carchemish; but they led through wretched regions, without industries, almost without tillage, and inhospitable alike to man and beast, and they were ventured on only by those who aimed at trafficking among the populations who lived in their neighbourhood. The Khâti, from the time even when they were enclosed among the fastnesses of the Taurus, had within their control the most important section of the great land route which served to maintain regular relations between the ancient kingdoms of the east and the rising states of the Ægean, and whosoever would pass through their country had to pay them toll. The conquest of Naharaim, in giving them control of a new section, placed almost at their discretion the whole traffic between Chaldæa and Egypt. From the time of Thûtmosis III. caravans employed in this traffic

[1] The very early existence of this road, which partly coincides with the royal route of the Persian Achemenids, was proved by Kiepert.

accomplished the greater part of their journey in territories depending upon Babylon, Assyria, or Memphis, and enjoyed thus a relative security; the terror of the Pharaoh protected the travellers even when they were no longer in his domains, and he saved them from the flagrant exactions made upon them by princes who called themselves his brothers, or were actually his vassals. But the time had now come when merchants had to encounter, between Qodshû and the banks of the Khabur, a sovereign owing no allegiance to any one, and who would tolerate no foreign interference in his territory. From the outbreak of hostilities with the Khâti, Egypt could communicate with the cities of the Lower Euphrates only by the Wadys of the Arabian Desert, which were always dangerous and difficult for large convoys; and its commercial relations with Chaldæa were practically brought thus to a standstill, and, as a consequence, the manufactures which fed this trade being reduced to a limited production, the fiscal receipts arising from it experienced a sensible diminution. When peace was restored, matters fell again into their old groove, with certain reservations to the Khâti of some common privileges: Egypt, which had formerly possessed these to her own advantage, now bore the burden of them, and the indirect tribute which she paid in this manner to her rivals furnished them with arms to fight her in case she should endeavour to free herself from the imposition. All the semi-barbaric peoples of the peninsula of Asia Minor were of an adventurous and warlike temperament. They were always willing to set out on an expedition, under the leadership of some chief of noble family or renowned for valour; sometimes by sea in their light craft, which would bring them unexpectedly to the nearest point of the Syrian coast, sometimes by land in companies of foot-soldiers and charioteers. They were frequently fortunate enough to secure plenty of booty, and return with it to their homes safe and sound; but as frequently they would meet with reverses by falling into some ambuscade: in such a case their conqueror would not put them to the sword or sell them as slaves, but would promptly incorporate them into his army, thus making his captives into his soldiers. The King of the Khâti was able to make use of them without difficulty, for his empire was conterminous on the west and north with some of their native lands, and he had often whole regiments of them in his army—Mysians, Lycians, people of Augarît,[1] of Ilion,[2] and of Pedasos.[3] The revenue of the provinces taken from Egypt, and the products of his tolls, furnished

[1] The country of Augarît, Ugarit, is mentioned on several occasions in the Tel el-Amarna correspondence. The name has been wrongly associated with Caria; it has been placed by W. Max Müller well within Naharaim, to the east of the Orontes, between Khalybôn (Aleppo) and Apamæa, the writer confusing it with Akaîti, named in the campaign of Amenôthes II. I am not sure about the site, but its association in the Amarna letters with Gugu and Khanigalbat inclines me to place it beyond the northern slopes of the Taurus, possibly on the banks of the Halys or of the Upper Euphrates.

[2] The name of this people was read Eiûna by Champollion, who identified it with the Ionians; this reading and identification were adopted by Lenormant and by W. Max Müller. Chabas hesitates between Eiûna and Maiûna, Ionia and Mæonia and Brugsch read it Malunna. The reading Iriûna, Iliûna, seems to me the only possible one, and the identification with Ilion as well.

[3] Owing to its association with the Dardanians, Mysians, and Ilion, I think it answers to the Pedasos on the Satniois near Troy.

him with abundance of means for obtaining recruits from among them.[1]

All these things contributed to make the power of the Khâti so considerable, that Harmhabî, when he had once tested it, judged it prudent not to join issues with them. He concluded with Sapalulu a treaty of peace and friendship, which, leaving the two powers in possession respectively of the territory each then occupied, gave legal sanction to the extension of the sphere of the Khâti at the expense of Egypt.[2] Syria continued to consist of two almost equal parts, stretching from Byblos to the sources of the Jordan and Damascus: the northern portion, formerly tributary to Egypt, became a Hittite possession; while the southern, consisting of Phœnicia and Canaan,[3] which the

[1] E. de Rougé and the Egyptologists who followed him thought at first that the troops designated in the Egyptian texts as Lycians, Mysians, Dardanians, were the national armies of these nations, each one commanded by its king, who had hastened from Asia Minor to succour their ally the King of the Khâti. I now think that these were bands of adventurers, consisting of soldiers belonging to these nations, who came to put themselves at the service of civilized monarchs, as the Carians, Ionians, and the Greeks of various cities did later on: the individuals whom the texts mention as their princes were not the kings of these nations, but the warrior chiefs to which each band gave obedience.

[2] It is not certain that Harmhabî was the Pharaoh with whom Sapalulu entered into treaty, and it might be insisted with some reason that Ramses I. was the party to it on the side of Egypt; but this hypothesis is rendered less probable by the fact of the extremely short reign of the latter Pharaoh. I am inclined to think, as W. Max Muller has supposed, that the passage in the *Treaty of Ramses II. with the Prince of the Khâti*, which speaks of a treaty concluded with Sapalulu, looks back to the time of Ramses II.'s predecessor, Harmhabî.

[3] This follows from the situation of the two empires, as indicated in the account of the campaign of Seti I. in his first year. The king, after having defeated the nomads of the Arabian desert, passed on without further

Pharaoh had held for a long time with a more effective authority, and had more fully occupied, was retained for Egypt. This could have been but a provisional arrangement: if Thebes had not altogether renounced the hope of repossessing some day the lost conquests of Thûtmosis III., the Khâti, drawn by the same instinct which had urged them to cross their frontiers towards the south, were not likely to be content with less than the expulsion of the Egyptians from Syria, and the absorption of the whole country into the Hittite dominion. Peace was maintained during Harmhabî's lifetime. We know nothing of Egyptian affairs during the last years of his reign. His rule may have come to an end owing to some court intrigue, or he may have had no male heir to follow him.[1] Ramses, who succeeded him, did not belong to the royal line, or was only remotely connected with it.[2] He was already an old man when he ascended the throne, and we ought perhaps to

fighting into the country of the Amûrrû and the regions of the Lebanon, which fact seems to imply the submission of Kharû. W. Max Muller was the first to discern clearly this part of the history of Egyptian conquest; he appears, however, to have circumscribed somewhat too strictly the dominion of Harmhabî in assigning Carmel as its limit. The list of the nations of the north who yielded, or are alleged to have yielded, submission to Harmhabî, were traced on the first pylon of this monarch at Karnak, and on its adjoining walls. Among others, the names of the Khâti and of Arvad are to be read there.

[1] It would appear, from an Ostracon in the British Museum, that the year XXI. follows after the year VII. of Harmhabî's reign; it is possible that the year XXI. may belong to one of Harmhabî's successors, Seti I. or Ramses II., for example.

[2] The efforts to connect Ramses I. with a family of Semitic origin, possibly the Shepherd-kings themselves, have not been successful. Everything goes to prove that the Ramses family was, and considered itself to be, of Egyptian origin. Brugsch and Ed. Meyer were inclined to see in

identify him with one or other of the Ramses who flourished under the last Pharaohs of the XVIIIth dynasty, perhaps the one who governed Thebes under Khûniatonû, or another, who began but never finished his tomb in the

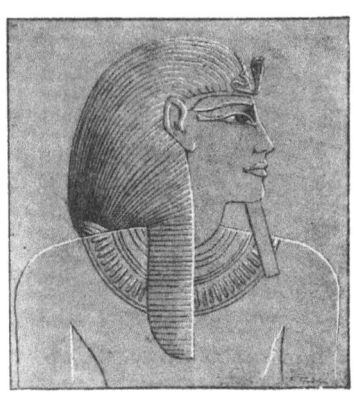

RAMSES I.[³]

hillside above Tel el-Amarna, in the burying-place of the worshippers of the Disk. He had held important offices under Harmhabî,[1] and had obtained in marriage for his son Seti the hand of Tuîa, who, of all the royal family, possessed the strongest rights to the crown.[2] Ramses reigned only six or seven years, and associated Seti with himself in the government from his second year. He undertook a short military expedition into Ethiopia, and perhaps

Ramses I. a younger brother of Harmhabî. This hypothesis has nothing either for or against it up to the present.

[1] This Tel el-Amarna Ramses is, perhaps, identical with the Theban one: he may have followed his master to his new capital, and have had a tomb dug for himself there, which he subsequently abandoned, on the death of Khûniatonû, in order to return to Thebes with Tûtankhamon and Ai.

[2] The fact that the marriage was celebrated under the auspices of Harmhabî, and that, consequently, Ramses must have occupied an important position at the court of that prince, is proved by the appearance of Ramses II., son of Tuia, as early as the first year of Seti, among the ranks of the combatants in the war carried on by that prince against the Tihonû; even granting that he was then ten years old, we are forced to admit that he must have been born before his grandfather came to the throne. There is in the Vatican a statue of Tuia; other statues have been discovered at Sân.

[3] Drawn by Faucher-Gudin, from a sketch in Rosellini.

a raid into Syria; and we find remains of his monuments in Nubia, at Bohani near Wady Halfa, and at Thebes, in the temple of Amon.[1] He displayed little activity, his advanced age preventing him from entering on any serious undertaking: but his accession nevertheless marks an important date in the history of Egypt. Although Harmhabî was distantly connected with the line of the Ahmessides, it is difficult at the present day to know what position to assign him in the Pharaonic lists: while some regard him as the last of the XVIIIth dynasty, others prefer to place him at the head of the XIXth. No such hesitation, however, exists with regard to Ramses I., who was undoubtedly the founder of a new family. The old familiar names of Thûtmosis and Amenôthes henceforward disappear from the royal lists, and are replaced by others, such as Seti, Mînephtah, and, especially, Ramses, which now figure in them for the first time. The princes who bore these names showed themselves worthy successors of those who had raised Egypt to the zenith of her power; like them they were successful on the battle-field, and like them they devoted the best of the spoil to building innumerable monuments. No sooner had Seti celebrated his father's obsequies, than he assembled his army and set out for war.

It would appear that Southern Syria was then in open revolt. "Word had been brought to His Majesty: 'The vile Shaûsû have plotted rebellion; the chiefs of their

---

[1] He began the great Hypostyle Hall at Karnak; E. de Rougé thinks that the idea of building this was first conceived under the XVIIIth dynasty.

tribes, assembled in one place on the confines of Kharû, have been smitten with blindness and with the spirit of violence; every one cutteth his neighbour's throat."[1] It was imperative to send succour to the few tribes who remained faithful, to prevent them from succumbing to the repeated attacks of the insurgents. Seti crossed the frontier at Zalû, but instead of pursuing his way along the coast, he marched due east in order to attack the Shaûsû in the very heart of the desert. The road ran through wide wadys, tolerably well supplied with water, and the length of the stages necessarily depended on the distances between the wells. This route was one frequented in early times, and its security was ensured by a number of fortresses and isolated towers built along it, such as "The House of the Lion"—*ta aît pa maû*—near the pool of the same name, the Migdol of the springs of Huzîna, the fortress of Uazît, the Tower of the Brave, and the Migdol of Seti at the pools of Absakaba. The Bedawin, disconcerted by the rapidity of this movement, offered no serious resistance. Their flocks were carried off, their trees cut down, their harvests destroyed, and they surrendered their strongholds at discretion. Pushing on from one halting-place to another, the conqueror soon reached Rabbîti, and finally Pakanâna.[2] The latter town occupied

[1] The pictures of this campaign and the inscriptions which explain them were engraved by Seti I., on the outside of the north wall of the great hypostyle hall at Karnak.

[2] The site of Pakanâna has, with much probability, been fixed at El-Kenân or Khurbet-Kanâan, to the south of Hebron. Brugsch had previously taken this name to indicate the country of Canaan, but Chabas rightly contested this view. W. Max Müller took up the matter afresh: he perceived

a splendid position on the slope of a rocky hill, close to a small lake, and defended the approaches to the vale of Hebron. It surrendered at the first attack, and by its fall the Egyptians became possessed of one of the richest provinces in the southern part of Kharû. This result

THE RETURN OF THE NORTH WALL OF THE HYPOSTYLE HALL AT KARNAK, WHERE SETI I. REPRESENTS SOME EPISODES IN HIS FIRST CAMPAIGN.[1]

having been achieved, Seti took the caravan road to his left, on the further side of Gaza, and pushed forward at full speed towards the Hittite frontier. It was probably

that we have here an allusion to the first town encountered by Seti I. in the country of Canaan to the south-west of Raphia, the name of which is not mentioned by the Egyptian sculptor; it seems to me that this name should be **Pakanâna**, and that the town bore the same name as the country.

[1] Drawn by Boudier, from a photograph, by Émil Brugsch-Bey.

unprotected by any troops, and the Hittite king was absent in some other part of his empire. Seti pillaged the Amurru, seized Ianuâmu and Qodshû by a sudden attack, marched in an oblique direction towards the Mediterranean, forcing the inhabitants of the Lebanon to cut timber from their mountains for the additions which he was premeditating in the temple of the Theban Amon, and finally returned by the coast road, receiving, as he passed through their territory, the homage of the Phœnicians. His entry into Egypt was celebrated by solemn festivities. The nobles, priests, and princes of both south and north hastened to meet him at the bridge of Zalû, and welcomed, with their chants, both the king and the troops of captives whom he was bringing back for the service of his father Amon at Karnak. The delight of his subjects was but natural, since for many years the Egyptians had not witnessed such a triumph, and they no doubt believed that the prosperous era of Thûtmosis III. was about to return, and that the wealth of Naharaim would once more flow into Thebes as of old. Their illusion was short-lived, for this initial victory was followed by no other. Maurusaru, King of the Khâti, and subsequently his son Mautallu, withstood the Pharaoh with such resolution that he was forced to treat with them. A new alliance was concluded on the same conditions as the old one, and the boundaries of the two kingdoms remained the same as under Harmhabî, a proof that neither sovereign had gained any advantage over his rival. Hence the campaign did not in any way restore Egyptian supremacy, as had been hoped at the moment; it merely served to strengthen her authority in those provinces which the

Khâti had failed to take from Egypt. The Phœnicians of Tyre and Sidon had too many commercial interests on the banks of the Nile to dream of breaking the slender tie which held them to the Pharaoh, since independence, or submission to another sovereign, might have ruined their trade. The Kharû and the Bedawîn, vanquished wherever they had ventured to oppose the Pharaoh's troops, were less than ever capable of throwing off the Egyptian yoke. Syria fell back into its former state. The local princes once more resumed their intrigues and quarrels, varied at intervals by appeals to their suzerain for justice or succour. The "Royal Messengers" appeared from time to time with their escorts of archers and chariots to claim tribute, levy taxes, to make peace between quarrelsome vassals, or, if the case required it, to supersede some insubordinate chief by a governor of undoubted loyalty; in fine, the entire administration of the empire was a continuation of that of the preceding century. The peoples of Kûsh meanwhile had remained quiet during the campaign in Syria, and on the western frontier the Tihonû had suffered so severe a defeat that they were not likely to recover from it for some time.[1] The bands of pirates, Shardana and others, who infested the Delta, were hunted down, and the prisoners taken from among them were incorporated into the royal guard.[2] Seti, however, does not appear to have had a

[1] This war is represented at Karnak, and Ramses II. figures there among the children of Seti I.
[2] We gather this from passages in the inscriptions from the year V. onwards, in which Ramses II. boasts that he has a number of Shardana prisoners in his guard; Rougé was, perhaps, mistaken in magnifying these piratical raids into a war of invasion.

confirmed taste for war. He showed energy when occasion required it, and he knew how to lead his soldiers, as the expedition of his first year amply proved; but when the necessity was over, he remained on the defensive, and made

REPRESENTATION OF SETI I. VANQUISHING THE LIBYANS AND ASIATICS ON THE WALLS, KARNAK [1]

no further attempt at conquest. By his own choice he was "the jackal who prowls about the country to protect it," rather than "the wizard lion marauding abroad by hidden paths,"[2] and Egypt enjoyed a profound peace in consequence of his ceaseless vigilance.

[1] Drawn by Boudier, from a photograph by Émil Brugsch-Bey.
[2] These phrases are taken direct from the inscriptions of Seti I.

A peaceful policy of this kind did not, of course, produce the amount of spoil and the endless relays of captives which had enabled his predecessors to raise temples and live in great luxury without overburdening their subjects with taxes. Seti was, therefore, the more anxious to do all in his power to develop the internal wealth of the country. The mining colonies of the Sinaitic Peninsula had never ceased working since operations had been resumed there under Hâtshopsîtû and Thûtmosis III., but the output had lessened during the troubles under the heretic kings. Seti sent inspectors thither, and endeavoured to stimulate the workmen to their former activity, but apparently with no great success. We are not able to ascertain if he continued the revival of trade with Pûanît inaugurated by Harmhabî; but at any rate he concentrated his attention on the regions bordering the Red Sea and the gold-mines which they contained. Those of Etbaï, which had been worked as early as the XIIth dynasty, did not yield as much as they had done formerly; not that they were exhausted, but owing to the lack of water in their neighbourhood and along the routes leading to them, they were nearly deserted. It was well known that they contained great wealth, but operations could not be carried on, as the workmen were in danger of dying of thirst. Seti despatched engineers to the spot to explore the surrounding wadys, to clear the ancient cisterns or cut others, and to establish victualling stations at regular intervals for the use of merchants supplying the gangs of miners with commodities. These stations generally consisted of square or rectangular enclosures, built of stones without mortar, and capable of resisting a prolonged attack. The entrance was by a narrow doorway of stone slabs, and in the interior were a few huts and one or two reservoirs for catching rain or storing the water of neighbouring springs. Sometimes a chapel was built close at hand, consecrated to the divinities of the desert, or to their compeers, Mînû of Coptos, Horus, Maut, or Isis. One of these, founded by Seti, still exists near the modern town of Redesieh, at the entrance to one of the valleys which

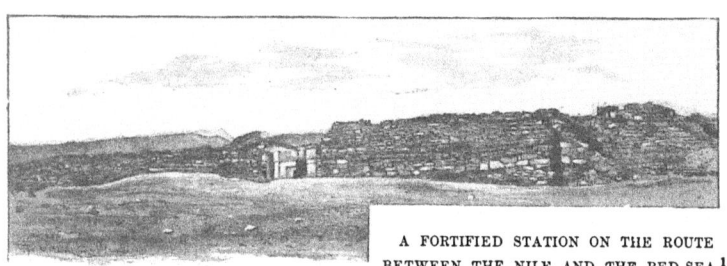

A FORTIFIED STATION ON THE ROUTE BETWEEN THE NILE AND THE RED SEA.[1]

furrow this gold region. It is built against, and partly excavated in, a wall of rock, the face of which has been roughly squared, and it is entered through a four-columned portico, giving access to two dark chambers, whose walls are covered with scenes of adoration and a lengthy inscription. In this latter the sovereign relates how, in the IXth year of his reign, he was moved to inspect the roads of the desert; he completed the work in honour of Amon-Râ, of Phtah of Memphis, and of Harmakhis, and he states that travellers were at a loss to express their gratitude and thanks for what he had done. "They

[1] Drawn by Faucher-Gudin, from a photograph by M. de Bock.

THE WORKING OF THE GOLD-MINES

repeated from mouth to mouth: 'May Amon give him an endless existence, and may he prolong for him the length of eternity!' O ye gods of fountains, attribute to him your life, for he has rendered back to us accessible roads, and he has opened that which was closed to us. Henceforth we can take our way in peace, and reach our destination alive; now that the difficult paths are open and the road has become good, gold can be brought back, as our lord and master has commanded." Plans were drawn on papyrus of the configuration of the district, of the beds of precious metal, and of the position of the stations. One of these plans has come down to us, in which the districts are coloured bright red, the mountains dull ochre, the roads dotted over with footmarks to show the direction to be taken, while the superscriptions give the local names, and inform us that the

THE TEMPLE OF SETI I. AT REDESIEH.[1]

[1] Drawn by Faucher-Gudin, from a photograph by Golénischeff.

map represents the Bukhni mountain and a fortress and stele of Seti. The whole thing is executed in a rough and naïve manner, with an almost childish minuteness

FRAGMENT OF THE MAP OF THE GOLD-MINES.[1]

which provokes a smile; we should, however, not despise it, for it is the oldest map in the world.

The gold extracted from these regions, together with that brought from Ethiopia, and, better still, the regular payment of taxes and custom-house duties, went to make up for the lack of foreign spoil all the more

[1] Facsimile by Faucher-Gudin of coloured chalk-drawing by Chabas.

opportunely, for, although the sovereign did not share the military enthusiasm of Thûtmosis III., he had inherited from him the passion for expensive temple-building. He did not neglect Nubia in this respect, but repaired several of the monuments at which the XVIIIth dynasty had

THE THREE STANDING COLUMNS OF THE TEMPLE OF SESEBI.[1]

worked—among others, Kalabsheh, Dakkeh, and Amada, besides founding a temple at Sesebi, of which three columns are still standing.[2] The outline of these columns is not graceful, and the decoration of them is very poor, for art degenerated rapidly in these distant provinces of

[1] Drawn by Boudier, from a photograph by Insinger.
[2] In Lepsius's time there were still four columns standing; Insinger shows us only three.

the empire, and only succeeded in maintaining its vigour and spirit in the immediate neighbourhood of the Pharaoh, as at Abydos, Memphis, and above all at Thebes. Seti's predecessor Ramses, desirous of obliterating all traces of the misfortunes lately brought about by the changes effected by the heretic kings, had contemplated building at Karnak, in front of the pylon of Amenôthes III., an enormous hall for the ceremonies connected with the cult of Amon, where the immense numbers of priests and worshippers at festival times could be accommodated without inconvenience. It devolved on Seti to carry out what had been merely an ambitious dream of his father's.[1] We long to know who was the architect possessed of such confidence in his powers that he ventured to design, and was able to carry out, this almost superhuman undertaking. His name would be held up to almost universal admiration beside those of the greatest masters that we are familiar with, for no one in Greece or Italy has left us any work which surpasses it, or which with such simple means could produce a similar impression of boldness and immensity. It is almost impossible to convey by words to those who have not seen it, the impression which it makes on the spectator. Failing description, the dimensions speak for themselves. The hall measures one hundred and sixty-two feet in length, by three hundred and twenty-five in breadth. A row of twelve columns, the largest ever placed inside a building,

[1] The great hypostyle hall was cleared and the columns were strengthened in the winter of 1895-6, as far, at least, as it was possible to carry out the work of restoration without imperilling the stability of the whole.

runs up the centre, having capitals in the form of inverted bells. One hundred and twenty-two columns with lotiform capitals fill the aisles, in rows of nine each. The roof

AN AVENUE OF ONE OF THE AISLES OF THE HYPOSTYLE HALL AT KARNAK.[1]

of the central bay is seventy-four feet above the ground, and the cornice of the two towers rises sixty-three feet higher. The building was dimly lighted from the roof of the central colonnade by means of stone gratings,

[1] Drawn by Faucher-Gudin, from a photograph by Beato.

through which the air and the sun's rays entered sparingly. The daylight, as it penetrated into the hall, was rendered more and more obscure by the rows of columns; indeed,

THE GRATINGS OF THE CENTRAL COLONNADE IN THE HYPOSTYLE HALL AT KARNAK.[1]

at the further end a perpetual twilight must have reigned, pierced by narrow shafts of light falling from the ventilation

[1] Drawn by Faucher-Gudin, from a photograph by Beato. In the background, on the right, may be seen a column which for several centuries has been retained in a half-fallen position by the weight of its architrave.

holes which were placed at intervals in the roof. The whole building now lies open to the sky, and the sunshine which floods it, pitilessly reveals the mutilations which it has suffered in the course of ages; but the general effect, though less mysterious, is none the less overwhelming. It is the only monument in which the first *coup d'œil* surpasses the expectations of the spectator instead of disappointing him. The size is immense, and we realise its immensity the more fully as we search our memory in vain to find anything with which to compare it. Seti may have entertained the project of building a *replica* of this hall in Southern Thebes. Amenôthes III. had left his temple at Luxor unfinished. The sanctuary and its surrounding buildings were used for purposes of worship, but the court of the customary pylon was wanting, and merely a thin wall concealed the mysteries from the sight of the vulgar. Seti resolved to extend the building in a northerly direction, without interfering with the thin screen which had satisfied his predecessors. Starting from the entrance in this wall, he planned an avenue of giant columns rivalling those of Karnak, which he destined to become the central colonnade of a hypostyle hall as vast as that of the sister temple. Either money or time was lacking to carry out his intention. He died before the aisles on either side were even begun. At Abydos, however, he was more successful. We do not know the reason of Seti's particular affection for this town; it is possible that his family held some fief there, or it may be that he desired to show the peculiar estimation in which he held its local god, and intended, by the homage that he lavished on him, to cause the fact to be forgotten that he bore the name of Sît the accursed. The king selected a favourable site for his temple to the south of the town, on the slope of a sandhill bordering

ONE OF THE COLONNADES OF THE HYPOSTYLE HALL IN THE TEMPLE OF SETI I. AT ABYDOS.[1]

the canal, and he marked out in the hardened soil a ground plan of considerable originality. The building was approached through two pylons, the remains of which are now hidden under the houses of Aarabat el-Madfûneh. A fairly large courtyard, bordered by two crumbling walls, lies between the second pylon and the temple façade,

[1] Drawn by Faucher-Gudin, from a photograph by Beato.

THE FAÇADE OF THE TEMPLE OF SETI I. AT ABYDOS.
Drawn by Faucher-Gudin, from a photograph by Beato.

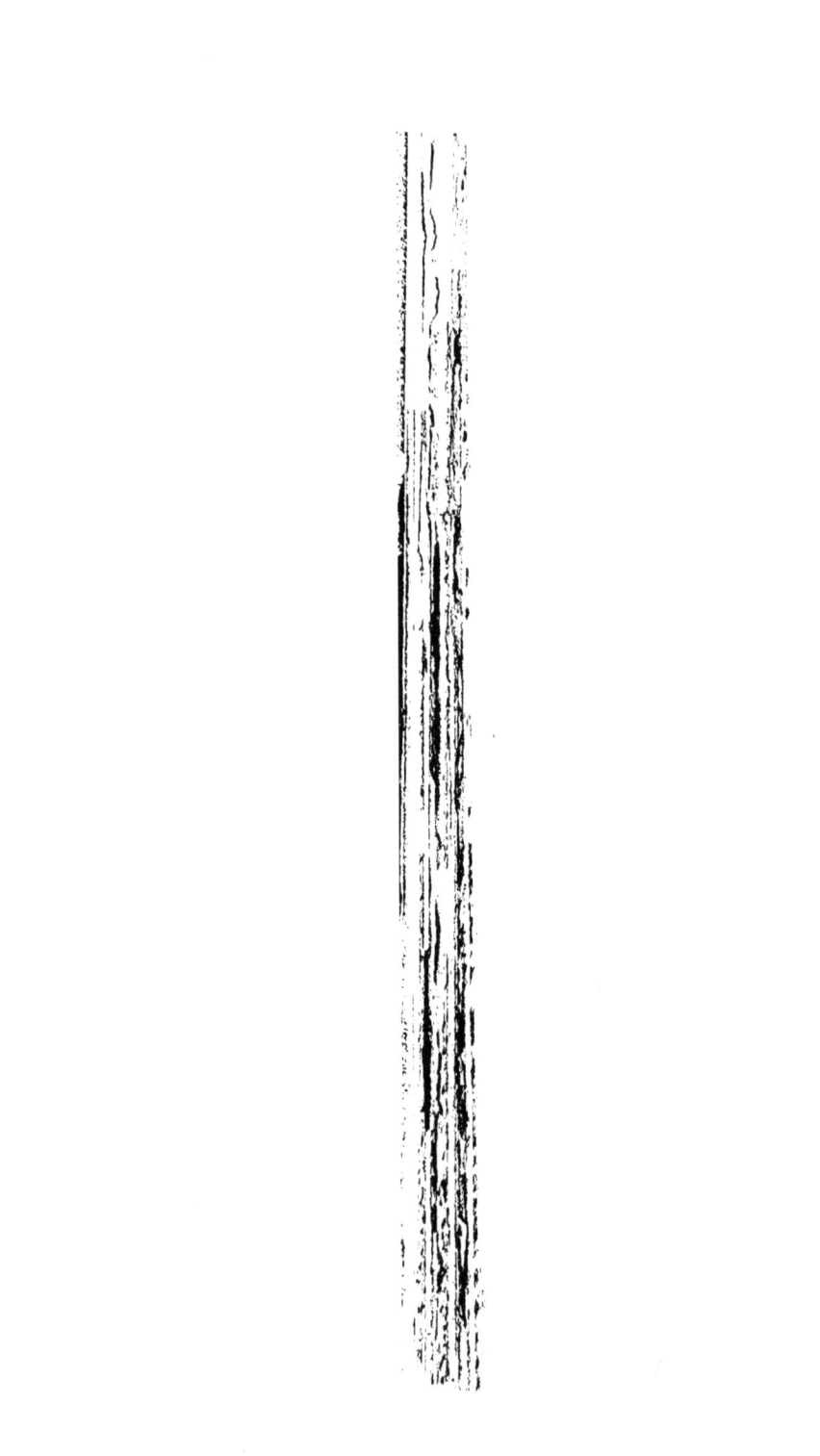

THE DECORATION OF THE TEMPLE 179

which was composed of a portico resting on square pillars. Passing between these, we reach two halls supported by columns of graceful outline, beyond which are eight chapels arranged in a line, side by side, in front of two chambers built in to the hillside, and destined for the reception of Osiris. The holy of holies in ordinary temples is surrounded by chambers of lesser importance, but here it is concealed behind them. The building-material mainly employed here was the white limestone of Tûrah, but of a most beautiful quality, which lent itself to the execution of bas-reliefs of great delicacy, perhaps the finest in ancient Egypt. The artists who carved and painted them belonged to the Theban school, and while their subjects betray a remarkable similarity to those of the monuments dedicated by Amenôthes III., the execution surpasses them in freedom and perfection of modelling; we can, in fact, trace in them the influence of the artists who furnished the drawings for the scenes at Tel el-Amarna. They have represented the gods and goddesses with the same type of profile as that of the king—a type of face of much purity and gentleness, with its aquiline nose, its decided mouth, almond-shaped eyes, and melancholy smile. When the decoration of the temple was completed, Seti regarded the building as too small for its divine inmate, and accordingly added to it a new wing, which he built along the whole length of the southern wall; but he was unable to finish it completely. Several parts of it are lined with religious representations, but in others the subjects have been merely sketched out in black ink with corrections in red, while elsewhere the walls are bare, except for a few inscriptions, scribbled over them after an interval of twenty centuries by the monks who turned the temple chambers into a convent. This new wing was connected with the second hypostyle hall of the original building by a passage, on one of the walls of which is a list of seventy-five royal names, representing the ancestors of the sovereign traced back to Mîni. The whole temple must be regarded as a vast funerary chapel, and no one who has studied the religion of Egypt can entertain a doubt as to its purpose. Abydos was the place where the dead assembled before passing into the other world. It was here, at the mouth of the "Cleft," that they received the provisions and offerings of their relatives and friends who remained on this earth. As the dead flocked hither from all quarters of the world, they collected round the tomb of Osiris, and there waited till the moment came to embark on the Boat of the Sun. Seti did not wish his soul to associate with those of the common crowd of his vassals, and prepared this temple for himself, as a separate resting-place, close to the mouth of Hades. After having dwelt within it for a short time subsequent to his funeral, his soul could repair thither whenever it desired, certain of always finding within it the incense and the nourishment of which it stood in need.

Thebes possessed this king's actual tomb. The chapel was at Qurnah, a little to the north of the group of pyramids in which the Pharaohs of the XIth dynasty lay side by side with those of the XIIIth and XVIIth. Ramses had begun to build it, and Seti continued the work, dedicating it to the cult of his father and of himself. Its pylon has altogether disappeared, but the façade with lotus-bud columns is nearly perfect, together with several of the chambers in front of the sanctuary. The decoration is as carefully carried out and the execution as delicate as that in the work at Abydos; we are tempted to believe

THE TEMPLE OF QURNAH.[1]

from one or two examples of it that the same hands have worked at both buildings. The rock-cut tomb is some distance away up in the mountain, but not in the same ravine as that in which Amenôthes III., Aî, and probably Tûtankhamon and Harmhabî, are buried.[2] There then

[1] Drawn by Faucher-Gudin, from a photograph by Beato.
[2] There are, in fact, close to those of Ai and Amenôthes III., three other tombs, two at least of which have been decorated with paintings, now completely obliterated, and which may have served as the burying-places of Tûtankhamon and Harmhabî: the earlier Egyptologists believed them to have been dug by the first kings of the XVIIIth dynasty.

existed, behind the rock amphitheatre of Deîr el-Baharî, a kind of enclosed basin, which could be reached from the plain only by dangerous paths above the temple of Hâtshopsîtû. This basin is divided into two parts, one of which runs in a south-easterly direction, while the other trends to the south-west, and is subdivided into minor branches. To the east rises a barren peak, the outline of which is not unlike that of the step-pyramid of Saqqâra, reproduced on a colossal scale. No spot could be more appropriate to serve as a cemetery for a family of kings. The difficulty of reaching it and of conveying thither the heavy accessories and of providing for the endless processions of the Pharaonic funerals, prevented any attempt being made to cut tombs in it during the Ancient and Middle Empires. About the beginning of the XIXth dynasty, however, some engineers, in search of suitable burial sites, at length noticed that this basin was only separated from the wady issuing to the north of Qurnah by a rocky barrier barely five hundred cubits in width. This presented no formidable obstacle to such skilful engineers as the Egyptians. They cut a trench into the living rock some fifty or sixty cubits in depth, at the bottom of which they tunnelled a narrow passage giving access to the valley.[1] It is not known whether this herculean work was accomplished during the reign of Harmhabî or in that of Ramses I. The latter was the

[1] French scholars recognised from the beginning of this century that the passage in question had been made by human agency. I attribute the execution of this work to Ramses I., as I believe Harmhabî to have been buried in the eastern valley, near Amenôthes III.

first of the Pharaohs to honour the spot by his presence. His tomb is simple, almost coarse in its workmanship, and comprises a gentle inclined passage, a vault and a sarcophagus of rough stone. That of Seti, on the contrary, is a veritable palace, extending to a distance of 325 feet into the mountain-side. It is entered by a wide and lofty door, which opens on to a staircase of twenty-seven steps, leading to an inclined corridor; other staircases of shallow steps follow with their landings; then come successively a hypostyle hall, and, at the extreme end, a vaulted chamber, all of which are decorated with mysterious scenes and covered with inscriptions. This is, however, but the first storey, containing the antechambers of the dead, but not their living-rooms. A passage and steps, concealed under a slab to the left of the hall, lead to the real vault, which held the mummy and its funerary furniture. As we penetrate further and further by the light of torches into this subterranean abode, we see that the walls are covered with pictures and formulæ, setting forth the voyages of the soul through the twelve hours of the night, its trials, its judgment, its reception by the departed, and its apotheosis—all depicted on the rock with the same perfection as that which characterises the bas-reliefs on the finest slabs of Tûrah stone at Qurnah and Abydos. A gallery leading out of the last of these chambers extends a few feet further and then stops abruptly; the engineers had contemplated the excavation of a third storey to the tomb, when the death of their master obliged them to suspend their task. The king's sarcophagus consists of a block of alabaster, hollowed out,

184   THE REACTION AGAINST EGYPT

polished, and carved with figures and hieroglyphs, with all the minuteness which we associate with the cutting

ONE OF THE PILLARS OF THE TOMB OF SETI I.[1]

of a gem. It contained a wooden coffin, shaped to the human figure and painted white, the features picked out

[1] Drawn by Boudier, from a photograph by Insinger, taken in 1884.

THE CHILDHOOD OF RAMSES II.

in black, and enamel eyes inserted in a mounting of bronze. The mummy is that of a thin elderly man, well preserved; the face was covered by a mask made of linen smeared with pitch, but when this was raised by means of a chisel, the fine kingly head was exposed to view. It was a masterpiece of the art of the embalmer, and the expression of the face was that of one who had only a few hours previously breathed his last. Death had slightly drawn the nostrils and contracted the lips, the pressure of the bandages had flattened the nose a little, and the skin was darkened by the pitch; but a calm and gentle smile still played over the mouth, and the half-opened eyelids allowed a glimpse to be seen from under their lashes of an apparently moist and glistening line,—the reflection from the white porcelain eyes let in to the orbit at the time of burial.

Seti had had several children by his wife Tuia, and the eldest had already reached manhood when his father ascended the throne, for he had accompanied him on his Syrian campaign. The young prince died, however, soon after his return, and his right to the crown devolved on his younger brother, who, like his grandfather, bore the name of Ramses. The prince was still very young,[1] but Seti did not on that account delay enthroning with great pomp this son who had a better right to the throne than himself. "From the time that I was in the egg," Ramses writes

[1] The history of the youth and the accession of Ramses II. is known to us from the narrative given by himself in the temple of Seti I. at Abydos. The bulk of the narrative is confirmed by the evidence of the Kubân inscription, especially as to the extreme youth of Ramses at the time when he was first associated with the crown.

later on, "the great ones sniffed the earth before me; when I attained to the rank of eldest son and heir upon the throne of Sibû, I dealt with affairs, I commanded as chief the foot-soldiers and the chariots. My father having appeared before the people, when I was but a very little boy in his arms, said to me: 'I shall have him crowned king, that I may see him in all his splendour while I am still on this earth!' The nobles of the court having drawn near to place the pschent upon my head: 'Place the diadem upon his forehead!' said he." As Ramses increased in years, Seti delighted to confer upon him, one after the other, the principal attributes of power; "while he was still upon this earth, regulating everything in the land, defending its frontiers, and watching over the welfare of its inhabitants, he cried: 'Let him reign!' because of the love he had for me." Seti also chose for him wives, beautiful "as are those of his palace," and he gave him in marriage his sisters Nofrîtari II. Mîmût and Isîtnofrît, who, like Ramses himself, had claims to the throne. Ramses was allowed to attend the State councils at the age of ten; he commanded armies, and he administered justice under the direction of his father and his viziers. Seti, however, although making use of his son's youth and activity, did not in any sense retire in his favour; if he permitted Ramses to adopt the insignia of royalty—the cartouches, the pschent, the bulbous-shaped helmet, and the various sceptres—he still remained to the day of his death the principal State official, and he reckoned all the years of this dual sovereignty as those of his sole reign.[1] Ramses

[1] Brugsch is wrong in reckoning the reign of Ramses II. from the time

repulsed the incursions of the Tihonû, and put to the sword such of their hordes as had ventured to invade Egyptian territory. He exercised the functions of viceroy of Ethiopia, and had on several occasions to chastise the pillaging negroes. We see him at Beit-Wally and at Abu

RAMSES II. PUTS THE NEGROES TO FLIGHT.[1]

Simbel charging them in his chariot: in vain they flee in confusion before him; their flight, however swift, cannot save them from captivity and destruction. He was engaged in Ethiopia when the death of Seti recalled him to

of his association in the crown; the great inscription of Abydos, which has been translated by Brugsch himself, dates events which immediately followed the death of Seti I. as belonging to the first year of Ramses II.

[1] Drawn by Faucher-Gudin, from a photograph by Insinger.

Thebes.[1] He at once returned to the capital, celebrated the king's funeral obsequies with suitable pomp, and after keeping the festival of Amon, set out for the north in order to make his authority felt in that part of his domains. He stopped on his way at Abydos to give the necessary orders for completing the decoration of the principal chambers of the resting-place built by his father, and chose a site some 320 feet to the north-west of it for a similar Memnonium for himself. He granted cultivated fields and meadows in the Thinite nome for the maintenance of these two mausolea, founded a college of priests and soothsayers in connexion with them, for which he provided endowments, and also assigned them considerable fiefs in all parts of the valley of the Nile. The Delta next occupied his attention. The increasing importance of the Syrian provinces in the eyes of Egypt, the growth of the Hittite monarchy, and the migrations of the peoples of the Mediterranean, had obliged the last princes of the preceding dynasty to reside more frequently at Memphis than Amenôthes I. or Thûtmosis III. had done. Amenôthes III. had set to work to restore certain cities which had been abandoned since the days of the Shepherds, and Bubastis, Athribis, and perhaps Tanis, had, thanks to his efforts, revived from their decayed condition. The

---

[1] We do not know how long Seti I. reigned; the last date is that of his IXth year at Redesieh and at Aswân, and that of the year XXVII. sometimes attributed to him belongs to one of the later Ramessides. I had at first supposed his reign to have been a long one, merely on the evidence afforded by Manetho's lists, but the presence of Ramses II. as a stripling, in the campaign of Seti's I[st] year, forces us to limit its duration to fifteen or twenty years at most, possibly to only twelve or fifteen.

Pharaohs, indeed, felt that at Thebes they were too far removed from the battle-fields of Asia; distance made it difficult for them to counteract the intrigues in which their vassals in Kharû and the lords of Naharaim were perpetually implicated, and a revolt which might have been easily anticipated or crushed had they been advised of it within a few days, gained time to increase and extend during the interval occupied by the couriers in travelling to and from the capital. Ramses felt the importance of possessing a town close to the Isthmus where he could reside in security, and he therefore built close to Zahî, in a fertile and healthy locality, a stronghold to which he gave his own name,[1] and of which the poets of the time have left us an enthusiastic description. "It extends," they say, "between Zahi and Egypt—and is filled with provisions and victuals.—It resembles Hermonthis,—it is strong like Memphis,—and the sun rises—and sets in it— so that men quit their villages and establish themselves in its territory."—"The dwellers on the coasts bring conger eels and fish in homage,—they pay it the tribute of their marshes.—The inhabitants don their festal garments every day,—perfumed oil is on their heads and new wigs;—they stand at their doors, their hands full of bunches of flowers, —green branches from the village of Pihâthor,—garlands of Pahûrû,—on the day when Pharaoh makes his entry.— Joy then reigns and spreads, and nothing can stay it,—O Usirmarî-sotpûnirî, thou who art Montû in the two lands,— Ramses-Mîamûn, the god." The town acted as an advance

[1] An allusion to the foundation of this residence occurs in an inscription at Abu Simbel, dated in his XXVth year.

190   THE REACTION AGAINST EGYPT

post, from whence the king could keep watch against all intriguing adversaries,—whether on the banks of the Orontes or the coast of the Mediterranean.

Nothing appeared for the moment to threaten the peace of the empire. The Asiatic vassals had raised no disturbance on hearing of the king's accession, and Mautallu continued to observe the conditions of the treaty which he had signed with Seti. Two military expeditions undertaken beyond the isthmus in the IInd and IVth years of the new sovereign were accomplished almost without fighting. He repressed by the way the marauding Shaûsû, and on reaching the Nahr el-Kelb, which then formed the northern frontier of his empire, he inscribed at the turn of the road, on the rocks which overhang the mouth of the river, two triumphal stelæ in which he related his successes.[1] Towards the end of his IVth year a rebellion broke out among the Khâti, which caused a rupture of relations between the two kingdoms and led to some irregular fighting. Khâtusaru, a younger brother of Maurusaru, murdered the latter and made himself king in his stead.[2] It is not certain whether the Egyptians took up arms against him, or whether he judged it wise to oppose them in order to divert the attention of his

---

[1] The stelæ are all in a very bad condition; in the last of them the date is no longer legible.

[2] In the *Treaty of Ramses II. with the Prince of Khâti*, the writer is content to use a discreet euphemism, and states that Mautallu succumbed "to his destiny." The name of the Prince of the Khâti is found later on under the form Khatusharu, in that of a chief defeated by Tiglath-pileser I. in the country of Kummukh, though this name has generally been read Khatukhi.

THE CAMPAIGN OF THE YEAR V.

subjects from his crime. At all events, he convoked his Syrian vassals and collected his mercenaries; the whole of Naharaim, Khalupu, Carchemish, and Arvad sent their quota, while bands of Dardanians, Mysians, Trojans, and Lycians, together with the people of Pedasos and Girgasha,[1] furnished further contingents, drawn from an area extending from the most distant coasts of the Mediterranean to the mountains of Cilicia. Ramses, informed of the enemy's movement by his generals and the governors of places on the frontier, resolved to anticipate the attack. He assembled an army almost as incongruous in its component elements as that of his adversary: besides Egyptians of unmixed race, divided into four corps bearing the names of Amon, Phtah, Harmakhis and Sûtkhû, it contained Ethiopian auxiliaries, Libyans, Mazaiû, and Shardana.[2] When preparations were completed, the force crossed the canal

[1] The name of this nation is written Karkisha, Kalkisha, or Kashkisha, by one of those changes of *sh* into *r-l* which occur so frequently in Assyro-Chaldæan before a dental; the two different spellings seem to show that the writers of the inscriptions bearing on this war had before them a list of the allies of Khâtusaru, written in cuneiform characters. If we may identify the nation with the Kashki or Kashku of the Assyrian texts, the ancestors of the people of Colchis of classical times, the termination *-isha* of the Egyptian word would be the inflexion *-ash* or *-ush* of the Eastern-Asiatic tongues which we find in so many race-names, *e.g.* Adaush, Saradaush, Ammaush. Rougé and Brugsch identified them with the Girgashites of the Bible. Brugsch, adopting the spelling Kashki, endeavoured to connect them with Casiotis; later on he identified them with the people of Gergis in Troas. Ramsay recognises in them the Kiskisos of Cilicia.

[2] In the account of the campaign the Shardana only are mentioned; but we learn from a list in the *Anastasi Papyrus I.*, that the army of Ramses II. included, in ordinary circumstances, in addition to the Shardana, a contingent of Mashauasha, Kahaka, and other Libyan and negro mercenaries.

at Zalû, on the 9th of Payni in his V^{th} year, marched rapidly across Canaan till they reached the valley of the Litâny, along which they took their way, and then followed up that of the Orontes. They encamped for a few days at Shabtuna, to the south-west of Qodshû,[1] in the midst of the Amorite country, sending out scouts and endeavouring to discover the position of the enemy, of whose movements they possessed but vague information. Khâtusaru lay concealed in the wooded valleys of the Lebanon; he was kept well posted by his spies, and only waited an opportunity to take the field; as an occasion did not immediately present itself, he had recourse to a ruse with which the generals of the time were familiar. Ramses, at length uneasy at not falling in with the enemy, advanced to the south of Shabtuna, where he endeavoured to obtain information from two Bedawîn. " Our brethren," said they, " who are the chiefs of the tribes united under the vile Prince of Khâti, send us to give information to your Majesty: We desire to serve the Pharaoh. We are deserting the vile Prince of the Khâti; he is close to Khalupu (Aleppo), to the north of the city of Tunipa, whither he has rapidly retired from fear of the Pharaoh." This story had every appearance of probability; and the distance—Khalupu was at least forty leagues away—

[1] Shabtuna had been placed on the Nahr es-Sebta, on the site now occupied by Kalaat el-Hosn, a conjecture approved by Mariette; it was more probably a town situated in the plain, to the south of Bahr el-Kades, a little to the south-west of Tell Keby Mindoh which represents Qodshû, and close to some forests which at that time covered the slopes of Lebanon, and, extending as they did to the bottom of the valley, concealed the position of the Khâti from the Egyptians.

THE CAMPAIGN OF THE YEAR V.

explained why the reconnoitring parties of the Egyptians had not fallen in with any of the enemy. The Pharaoh, with this information, could not decide whether to lay siege to Qodshû and wait until the Hittites were forced to succour the town, or to push on towards the Euphrates

THE SHARDANA GUARD OF RAMSES II.[1]

and there seek the engagement which his adversary seemed anxious to avoid. He chose the latter of the two alternatives. He sent forward the legions of Amon, Phrâ, Phtah, and Sûtkhû, which constituted the main body of his troops, and prepared to follow them with his household chariotry. At the very moment when this division was being effected, the Hittites, who had been represented by the spies as

[1] Drawn by Faucher-Gudin, from a photograph by Insinger.

being far distant, were secretly massing their forces to the north-east of Qodshû, ready to make an attack upon the Pharaoh's flank as soon as he should set out on his march towards Khalupu. The enemy had considerable forces at their disposal, and on the day of the engagement they placed 18,000 to 20,000 picked soldiers in the field.[1] Besides a well-disciplined infantry, they possessed 2500 to 3000 chariots, containing, as was the Asiatic custom, three men in each.[2]

The Egyptian camp was not entirely broken up, when the scouts brought in two spies whom they had seized —Asiatics in long blue robes arranged diagonally over one shoulder, leaving the other bare. The king, who was seated on his throne delivering his final commands, ordered them to be beaten till the truth should be extracted from them. They at last confessed that they had been despatched to watch the departure of the Egyptians, and admitted that the enemy was concealed in ambush behind the town. Ramses hastily called a council of war and laid the situation before his generals, not without severely reprimanding them for the bad organisation of the intelligence department. The officers excused themselves as best they could, and threw the blame on the provincial governors,

[1] An army corps is reckoned as containing 9000 men on the wall scenes at Luxor, and 8000 at the Ramesseum; the 3000 chariots were manned by 9000 men. In allowing four to five thousand men for the rest of the soldiers engaged, we are not likely to be far wrong, and shall thus obtain the modest total mentioned in the text, contrary to the opinion current among historians.

[2] The mercenaries are included in these figures, as is shown by the reckoning of the Lycian, Dardanian, and Pedasian chiefs who were in command of the chariots during the charges against Ramses II.

who had not been able to discover what was going on. The king cut short these useless recriminations, sent swift messengers to recall the divisions which had started early that morning, and gave orders that all those remaining in camp should hold themselves in readiness to attack. The council were still deliberating when news was brought that

TWO HITTITE SPIES BEATEN BY THE EGYPTIAN SOLDIERS.[1]

the Hittites were in sight. Their first onslaught was so violent that they threw down one side of the camp wall, and penetrated into the enclosure. Ramses charged them at the head of his household troops. Eight times he engaged the chariotry which threatened to surround him, and each time he broke their ranks. Once he found himself alone with Manna, his shield-bearer, in the midst of a knot of warriors who were bent on his destruction,

[1] Drawn by Faucher-Gudin, from the picture in the temple at Abu Simbel.

and he escaped solely by his coolness and bravery. The tame lion which accompanied him on his expeditions did terrible work by his side, and felled many an Asiatic with his teeth and claws.[1] The soldiers, fired by the king's

THE EGYPTIAN CAMP AND THE COUNCIL OF WAR ON THE MORNING OF THE BATTLE OF QODSHÛ.[2]

example, stood their ground resolutely during the long hours of the afternoon; at length, as night was drawing on, the legions of Phrâ and Sûtkhû, who had hastily

[1] The lion is represented and named in the battle-scenes at Abu Simbel, at Derr, and at Luxor, where we see it in camp on the eve of the battle, with its two front paws tied, and its keeper threatening it.

[2] Drawn by Boudier, from a photograph by Beato of the west front of the Ramesseum.

retraced their steps, arrived on the scene of action. A large body of Khâti, who were hemmed in in that part of the camp which they had taken in the morning, were at once killed or made prisoners, not a man of them

THE FUGITIVES WELCOMED BY THE GARRISON OF QODSHÛ.[1]

escaping. Khâtusaru, disconcerted by this sudden reinforcement of the enemy, beat a retreat, and nightfall suspended the struggle. It was recommenced at dawn the following morning with unabated fury, and terminated in the rout of the confederates. Garbatusa, the shield-bearer

[1] Drawn by Faucher-Gudin, from a photograph by Beato.

of the Hittite prince, the generals in command of his infantry and chariotry, and Khalupsaru, the "writer of books," fell during the action. The chariots, driven back to the Orontes, rushed into the river in the hope of fording it, but in so doing many lives were lost. Mazraîma, the Prince of Khâti's brother, reached the opposite bank in

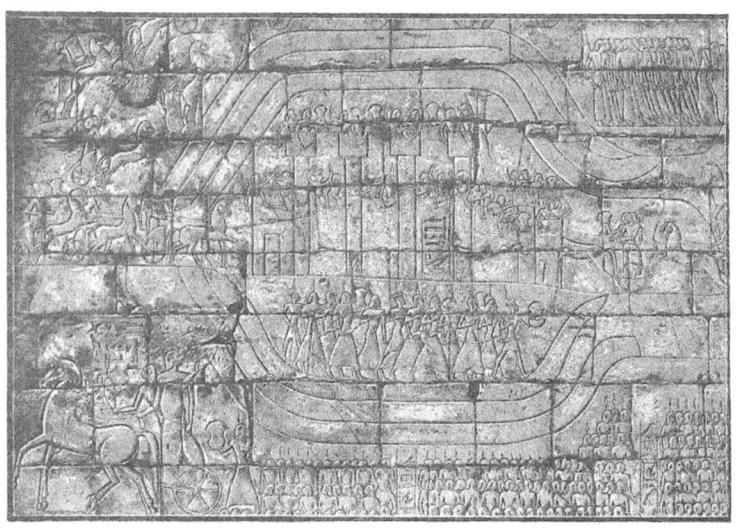

THE GARRISON OF QODSHÛ ISSUING FORTH TO HELP THE PRINCE OF KHÂTI.[1]

safety, but the Chief of Tonisa was drowned, and the lord of Khalupu was dragged out of the water more dead than alive, and had to be held head downwards to disgorge the water he had swallowed before he could be restored to consciousness. Khâtusaru himself was on the point of perishing, when the troops which had been shut up in Qodshû, together with the inhabitants, made a general

[1] Drawn by Faucher-Gudin, from a photograph by Bénédite.

sortie; the Egyptians were for a moment held in check, and the fugitives meanwhile were able to enter the town. Either there was insufficient provision for so many mouths, or the enemy had lost all heart from the disaster; at any rate, further resistance appeared useless. The next morning Khâtusaru sent to propose a truce or peace to the victorious Pharaoh. The Egyptians had probably suffered at least as much as their adversaries, and perhaps regarded the eventuality of a siege with no small distaste; Ramses, therefore, accepted the offers made to him and prepared to return to Egypt. The fame of his exploits had gone before him, and he himself was not a little proud of the energy he had displayed on the day of battle. His predecessors had always shown themselves to be skilful generals and brave soldiers, but none of them had ever before borne, or all but borne, single-handed the brunt of an attack. Ramses loaded his shield-bearer Manna with rewards for having stood by him in the hour of danger, and ordered abundant provender and sumptuous harness for the good horses—" Strength-in-Thebaid " and " Nûrit the satisfied "—who had drawn his chariot.[1] He determined that the most characteristic episodes of the campaign—the beating of the spies, the surprise of the camp, the king's repeated charges, the arrival of his veterans, the flight of the Syrians, and the surrender of Qodshû—should be represented on the walls and pylons of the temples. A poem in rhymed strophes in every case accompanies these records of his glory, whether at Luxor, at the

[1] A gold ring in the Louvre bears in relief on its bezel two little horses, which are probably "Strength-in-Thebaid " and " Nûrit satisfied."

Ramesseum, at the Memnonium of Abydos, or in the heart of Nubia at Abu Simbel. The author of the poem must have been present during the campaign, or must have had the account of it from the lips of his sovereign, for his work bears no traces of the coldness of official reports, and a warlike strain runs through it from one end to the other, so as still to invest it with life after a lapse of more than thirty centuries.[1]

But little pains are bestowed on the introduction, and the poet does not give free vent to his enthusiasm until the moment when he describes his hero, left almost alone, charging the enemy in the sight of his followers. The Pharaoh was surrounded by two thousand five hundred chariots, and his retreat was cut off by the warriors of the "perverse" Khâti and of the other nations who accompanied them—the peoples of Arvad, Mysia, and Pedasos; each of their chariots contained three men, and the ranks were so serried that they formed but one dense mass. "No other prince was with me, no general officers, no one in command of the archers or chariots. My foot-soldiers deserted me, my charioteers fled before the foe, and not one of them stood firm beside me to fight against them." Then said His Majesty: "Who art thou, then, my father Amon? A father who forgets his son? Or have I committed aught against thee? Have I not marched and halted according to thy command? When he does not violate thy orders, the lord of Egypt is indeed great, and he

---

[1] The author is unknown: Pentaûr, or rather Pentaûirît, to whom E. de Rougé attributed the poem, is merely the transcriber of the copy we possess on papyrus.

overthrows the barbarians in his path! What are these Asiatics to thy heart? Amon will humiliate those who know not the god. Have I not consecrated innumerable offerings to thee? Filling thy holy dwelling-place with my prisoners, I build thee a temple for millions of years, I lavish all my goods on thy storehouses, I offer thee the whole world to enrich thy domains. . . . A miserable fate indeed awaits him who sets himself against thy will, but happy is he who finds favour with thee by deeds done for thee with a loving heart. I invoke thee, O my father Amon! Here am I in the midst of people so numerous that it cannot be known who are the nations joined together against me, and I am alone among them, none other is with me. My many soldiers have forsaken me, none of my charioteers looked towards me when I called them, not one of them heard my voice when I cried to them. But I find that Amon is more to me than a million soldiers, than a hundred thousand charioteers, than a myriad of brothers or young sons, joined all together, for the number of men is as nothing, Amon is greater than all of them. Each time I have accomplished these things, Amon, by the counsel of thy mouth, as I do not transgress thy orders, I rendered thee glory even to the ends of the earth." So calm an invocation in the thick of the battle would appear misplaced in the mouth of an ordinary man, but Pharaoh was a god, and the son of a god, and his actions and speeches cannot be measured by the same standard as that of a common mortal. He was possessed by the religious spirit in the hour of danger, and while his body continued to fight, his soul took wing to the throne of Amon. He contemplates the lord of heaven face to face, reminds him of the benefits which he had received from him, and summons him to his aid with an imperiousness which betrays the sense of his own divine origin. The expected help was not delayed. " While the voice resounds in Hermonthis, Amon arises at my behest, he stretches out his hand to me, and I cry out with joy when he hails me from behind : ' Face to face with thee, face to face with thee, Ramses Miamun, I am with thee ! It is I, thy father ! My hand is with thee, and I am worth more to thee than hundreds of thousands. I am the strong one who loves valour; I have beheld in thee a courageous heart, and my heart is satisfied; my will is about to be accomplished ! ' I am like Montû; from the right I shoot with the dart, from the left I seize the enemy. I am like Baal in his hour, before them; I have encountered two thousand five hundred chariots, and as soon as I am in their midst, they are overthrown before my mares. Not one of all these people has found a hand wherewith to fight; their hearts sink within their breasts, fear paralyses their limbs ; they know not how to throw their darts, they have no strength to hold their lances. I precipitate them into the water like as the crocodile plunges therein ; they are prostrate face to the earth, one upon the other, and I slay in the midst of them, for I have willed that not one should look behind him, nor that one should return; he who falls rises not again." This sudden descent of the god has, even at the present day,·an effect upon the reader, prepared though he is by his education to consider it as a literary artifice ; but on the Egyptian, brought up to regard Amon with boundless reverence, its influence was irresistible. The Prince of the Khâti, repulsed at the very moment when he was certain of victory, "recoiled with terror. He sends against the enemy the various chiefs, followed by their chariots and skilled warriors,—the chiefs of Arvad, Lycia, and Ilion, the leaders of the Lycians and Dardanians, the lords of Carchemish, of the Girgashites, and of Khalupu; these allies of the Khâti, all together, comprised three thousand chariots." Their efforts, however, were in vain. "I fell upon them like Montû, my hand devoured them in the space of a moment, in the midst of them I hewed down and slew. They said one to another: This is no man who is amongst us; it is Sûtkhû the great warrior, it is Baal incarnate! These are not human actions which he accomplishes: alone, by himself, he repulses hundreds of thousands, without leaders or men. Up, let us flee before him, let us seek to save our lives, and let us breathe again!" When at last, towards evening, the army again rallies round the king, and finds the enemy completely defeated, the men hang their heads with mingled shame and admiration as the Pharaoh reproaches them: "What will the whole earth say when it is known that you left me alone, and without any to succour me? that not a prince, not a charioteer, not a captain of archers, was found to place his hand in mine? I fought, I repulsed millions of people by myself alone. 'Victory-in-Thebes' and 'Nûrit satisfied' were my glorious horses; it was they that I found under my hand when I was alone in the midst of the quaking foe. I myself will cause them to take their food before me, each day, when I shall be in my palace, for I was with them when I was in the midst of the enemy, along with the Prince Manna my shield-bearer, and with the officers of my house who accompanied me, and who are my witnesses for the combat; these are those whom I was with. I have returned after a victorious struggle, and I have smitten with my sword the assembled multitudes."

The ordeal was a terrible one for the Khâti; but when the first moment of defeat was over, they again took courage and resumed the campaign. This single effort had not exhausted their resources, and they rapidly filled up the gaps which had been made in their ranks. The plains of Naharaim and the mountains of Cilicia supplied them with fresh chariots and foot-soldiers in the place of those they had lost, and bands of mercenaries were furnished from the table-lands of Asia Minor, so that when Ramses II. reappeared in Syria, he found himself confronted by a completely fresh army. Khâtusaru, having profited by experience, did not again attempt a general engagement, but contented himself with disputing step by step the upper valleys of the Litâny and Orontes. Meantime his emissaries spread themselves over Phœnicia and Kharû, sowing the seeds of rebellion, often only too successfully. In the king's VIIIth year there was a general rising in Galilee, and its towns—Galaput in the hill-country of Bît-Aniti, Merom, Shalama, Dapur, and Anamaîm [1]—had to be

[1] Episodes from this war are represented at Karnak. The list of the towns taken, now much mutilated, comprised twenty-four names, which proves the importance of the revolt.

THE TAKING OF DAPUR IN GALILEE.

reduced one after another. Dapur was the hardest to carry. It crowned the top of a rocky eminence, and was protected by a double wall, which followed the irregularities of the hillside. It formed a rallying-point for a large force, which had to be overcome in the open country before the investment of the town could be attempted. The siege was at last brought to a conclusion, after a series of skirmishes, and the town taken by scaling, four Egyptian princes having been employed in conducting the attack. In the Pharaoh's IXth year a revolt broke out on the Egyptian frontier, in the Shephelah, and the king placed himself at the head of his troops to crush it. Ascalon, in which the peasantry and their families had found, as they hoped, a safe refuge, opened its gates to the Pharaoh, and its fall brought about the submission of several neighbouring places. This, it appears, was the first time since the beginning of the conquests in Syria that the inhabitants of these regions attempted to take up arms, and we may well ask what could have induced them thus to renounce their ancient loyalty. Their defection reduced Egypt for the moment almost to her natural frontiers. Peace had scarcely been resumed when war again broke out with fresh violence in Cœle-Syria, and one year it reached even to Naharaim, and raged around Tunipa as in the days of Thûtmosis III. "Pharaoh assembled his foot-soldiers and chariots, and he commanded his foot-soldiers and his chariots to attack the perverse Khâti who were in the neighbourhood of Tunipa, and he put on his armour and mounted his chariot, and he waged battle against the town of the perverse Khâti at the head of his foot-soldiers and his chariots, covered with his armour;" the fortress, however, did not yield till the second attack. Ramses carried his arms still further afield, and with such results, that, to judge merely from the triumphal lists engraved on the walls of the temple of Karnak, the inhabitants on the banks of the Euphrates, those in Carchemish, Mitanni, Singar, Assyria, and Mannus found themselves once more at the mercy of the Egyptian battalions. These victories, however brilliant, were not decisive; if after any one of them the princes of Assyria and Singar may have sent presents to the Pharaoh, the Hittites, on the other hand, did not consider themselves beaten, and it was only after fifteen campaigns that they were at length sufficiently subdued to propose a treaty. At last, in the Egyptian king's XXIst year, on the 21st of the month Tybi, when the Pharaoh, then residing in his good town of Ânakhîtû, was returning from the temple where he had been offering prayers to his father Amon-Râ, to Harmakhis of Heliopolis, to Phtah, and to Sûtkhû the valiant son of Nûît, Ramses, one of the "messengers" who filled the office of lieutenant for the king in Asia, arrived at the palace and presented to him Tartisubu, who was authorised to make peace with Egypt in the name of Khâtusaru.[1] Tartisubu carried in his hand a tablet of silver, on which his master had prescribed the conditions which appeared to him just and equitable. A short preamble recalling the alliances made between the ancestors of both parties, was followed by a declaration of friendship, and a reciprocal obligation to avoid in future

[1] The treaty of Ramses II. with the Prince of the Khâti was sculptured at Karnak.

all grounds of hostility. Not only was a perpetual truce declared between both peoples, but they agreed to help each other at the first demand. " Should some enemy march against the countries subject to the great King of Egypt, and should he send to the great Prince of the Khâti, saying: ' Come, bring me forces against them,' the great Prince of the Khâti shall do as he is asked by the great King of Egypt, and the great Prince of the Khâti shall destroy his enemies. And if the great Prince of the Khâti shall prefer not to come himself, he shall send his archers and his chariots to the great King of Egypt to destroy his enemies." A similar clause ensured aid in return from Ramses to Khâtusaru, " his brother," while two articles couched in identical terms made provision against the possibility of any town or tribe dependent on either of the two sovereigns withdrawing its allegiance and placing it in the hands of the other party. In this case the Egyptians as well as the Hittites engaged not to receive, or at least not to accept, such offers, but to refer them at once to the legitimate lord. The whole treaty was placed under the guarantee of the gods both of Egypt and of the Khâti, whose names were given at length: "Whoever shall fail to observe the stipulations, let the thousand gods of Khâti and the thousand gods of Egypt strike his house, his land, and his servants. But he who shall observe the stipulations engraved on the tablet of silver, whether he belong to the Hittite people or whether he belong to the people of Egypt, as he has not neglected them, may the thousand gods of Khâti and the thousand gods of Egypt give him health, and grant that he may prosper, himself, the people of his house, and also his land and his servants." The treaty itself ends by a description of the plaque of silver on which it was engraved. It was, in fact, a facsimile in metal of one of those clay tablets on which the Chaldæans inscribed their contracts. The preliminary articles occupied the upper part in closely written lines of cuneiform characters, while in the middle, in a space left free for the purpose, was the impress of two seals, that of the Prince of the Khâti and of his wife Pûûkhîpa. Khâtusaru was represented on them as standing upright in the arms of Sûtkhû, while around the two figures ran the inscription, "Seal of Sûtkhû, the sovereign of heaven." Pûûkhîpa leaned on the breast of a god, the patron of her native town of Aranna in Qazauadana, and the legend stated that this was the seal of the Sun of the town of Aranna, the regent of the earth. The text of the treaty was continued beneath, and probably extended to the other side of the tablet. The original draft had terminated after the description of the seals, but, to satisfy the Pharaoh, certain additional articles were appended for the protection of the commerce and industry of the two countries, for the prevention of the emigration of artisans, and for ensuring that steps taken against them should be more effectual and less cruel. Any criminal attempting to evade the laws of his country, and taking refuge in that of the other party to the agreement, was to be expelled without delay and consigned to the officers of his lord; any fugitive not a criminal, any subject carried off or detained by force, any able artisan quitting either territory to take up permanent residence in the other, was to be conducted to the frontier, but his act of folly was not to expose him to judicial condemnation. " He who shall thus act, his fault shall not be brought up against him; his house shall not be touched, nor his wife, nor his children; he shall not have his throat cut, nor shall his eyes be touched, nor his mouth, nor his feet; no criminal accusation shall be made against him."

This treaty is the most ancient of all those of which the text has come down to us; its principal conditions were—perfect equality and reciprocity between the contracting sovereigns, an offensive and defensive alliance, and the extradition of criminals and refugees. The original was drawn up in Chaldæan script by the scribes of Khâtusaru, probably on the model of former conventions between the Pharaohs and the Asiatic courts, and to this the Egyptian ministers had added a few clauses relative to the pardon of emigrants delivered up by one or other of the contracting parties. When, therefore, Tartisubu arrived in the city of Ramses, the acceptance of the treaty was merely a matter of form, and peace was virtually concluded. It did not confer on the conqueror the advantages which we might have expected from his successful campaigns : it enjoined, on the contrary, the definite renunciation of those countries, Mitanni, Naharaim, Alasia, and Amurru, over which Thûtmosis III. and his immediate successors had formerly exercised an effective sovereignty. Sixteen years of victories had left matters in the same state as they were after the expedition of Harmhabî, and, like his predecessor, Ramses was able to retain merely those Asiatic provinces which were within the immediate influence of Egypt, such as the Phœnician coast proper, Kharû, Peræa beyond Jordan, the oases of the Arabian desert, and the peninsula of Sinai.[1] This apparently unsatisfactory result, after such supreme efforts, was, however, upon closer examination, not so disappointing. For more than half a century at least, since the Hittite kingdom had been developed and established under the impulse given to it by Sapalulu, everything had been in its favour. The campaign of Seti had opposed merely a passing obstacle to its expansion, and had not succeeded in discouraging its ambitions, for its rulers still nursed the hope of being able one day to conquer Syria as far as the isthmus. The check received at Qodshû, the abortive attempts to foment rebellion in Galilee and the Shephelah, the obstinate persistence with which Ramses and his army returned year after year to the attack, the presence of the enemy at Tunipa, on the banks of the Euphrates, and in the provinces then forming the very centre of the Hittite kingdom—in short, all the incidents of this long struggle—at length convinced Khâtusaru that he was powerless to extend his rule in this direction at the expense of Egypt. Moreover, we have no knowledge of the events which occupied him on the other

---

[1] The *Anastasi Papyrus I.* mentions a place called *Zarû of Sesostris*, in the neighbourhood of Aleppo, in a part of Syria which was not in Egyptian territory: the frontier in this locality must have passed between Arvad and Byblos on the coast, and between Qodshû and Hazor from Merom inland. Egyptian rule on the other side of the Jordan seems to be proved by the monument discovered a few years ago in the Haurân, and known under the name of the "Stone of Job" by the Bedawin of the neighbourhood.

frontiers of his kingdom, where he may have been engaged at the same time in a conflict with Assyria, or in repelling an incursion of the tribes on the Black Sea. The treaty with Pharaoh, if made in good faith and likely to be lasting, would protect the southern extremities of his kingdom, and allow of his removing the main body of his forces to the north and east in case of attack from either of these quarters. The security which such an alliance would ensure made it, therefore, worth his while to sue for peace, even if the Egyptians should construe his overtures as an acknowledgment of exhausted supplies or of inferiority of strength. Ramses doubtless took it as such, and openly displayed on the walls at Karnak and in the Ramesseum a copy of the treaty so flattering to his pride, but the indomitable resistance which he had encountered had doubtless given rise to reflections resembling those of Khâtusaru, and he had come to realise that it was his own interest not to lightly forego the good will of the Khâti. Egypt had neighbours in Africa who were troublesome though not dangerous: the Timihû, the Tihonû, the Mashûasha, the negroes of Kûsh and of Pûanît, might be a continual source of annoyance and disturbance, even though they were incapable of disturbing her supremacy. The coast of the Delta, it is true, was exposed to the piracy of northern nations, but up to that time this had been merely a local trouble, easy to meet if not to obviate altogether. The only real danger was on the Asiatic side, arising from empires of ancient constitution like Chaldæa, or from hordes who, arriving at irregular intervals from the north, and carrying all before them, threatened, after the example of the Hyksôs, to enter the Delta. The Hittite kingdom acted as a kind of buffer between the Nile valley and these nations, both civilized and barbarous; it was a strongly armed force on the route of the invaders, and would henceforth serve as a protecting barrier, through which if the enemy were able to pass it would only be with his strength broken or weakened by a previous encounter. The sovereigns loyally observed the peace which they had sworn to each other, and in his XXXIVth year the marriage

KHÂTUSARU, PRINCE OF KHÂTI, AND HIS DAUGHTER.[1]

of Ramses with the eldest daughter of Khâtusaru strengthened their friendly relations. Pharaoh was not a little proud of this union, and he has left us a naïve record of the manner in which it came about. The inscription is engraved on the face of the rock at Abu Simbel in Nubia; and Ramses begins by boasting, in a heroic strain, of his own energy and exploits, of the fear with which his victories inspired the whole world, and of the anxiety of the Syrian kinglets to fulfil his least wishes. The Prince of the Khâti

[1] Drawn by Faucher-Gudin, from the plate in Lepsius; the triad worshipped by Khâtusaru and his daughter is composed of Ramses II., seated between Amon-Râ and Phtah-Totûnen.

had sent him sumptuous presents at every opportunity, and, not knowing how further to make himself agreeable to the Pharaoh, had finally addressed the great lords of his court, and reminded them how their country had formerly been ruined by war, how their master Sûtkhû had taken part against them, and how they had been delivered from their ills by the clemency of the Sun of Egypt. "Let us therefore take our goods, and placing my eldest daughter at the head of them, let us repair to the domains of the great god, so that the King Sesostris may recognise us." He accordingly did as he had proposed, and the embassy set out with gold and silver, valuable horses, and an escort of soldiers, together with cattle and provisions to supply them with food by the way. When they reached the borders of Khâru, the governor wrote immediately to the Pharaoh as follows: "Here is the Prince of the Khâti, who brings his eldest daughter with a number of presents of every kind; and now this princess and the chief of the country of the Khâti, after having crossed many mountains and undertaken a difficult journey from distant parts, have arrived at the frontiers of His Majesty. May we be instructed how we ought to act with regard to them." The king was then in residence at Ramses. When the news reached him, he officially expressed his great joy at the event, since it was a thing unheard of in the annals of the country that so powerful a prince should go to such personal inconvenience in order to marry his daughter to an ally. The Pharaoh, therefore, despatched his nobles and an army to receive them, but he was careful to conceal the anxiety which he felt all the while, and, according to custom, took counsel of his patron god Sûtkhû : " Who are these people who come with a message at this time to the country of Zahi ? " The oracle, however, reassured him as to their intentions, and he thereupon hastened to prepare for their proper reception. The embassy made a triumphal entry into the city, the princess at its head, escorted by the Egyptian troops told off for the purpose, together with the foot-soldiers and charioteers of the Khâti, comprising the flower of their army and militia. A solemn festival was held in their honour, in which food and drink were served without stint, and was concluded by the celebration of the marriage in the presence of the Egyptian lords and of the princes of the whole earth.[1] Ramses, unwilling to relegate a princess of such noble birth to the companionship of his ordinary concubines, granted her the title of queen, as if she were of solar blood, and with the cartouche gave her the new name of Ûirimaûnofîrurî—" She who sees the beauties of the Sun." She figures henceforth in the ceremonies and on the monuments in the place usually occupied by women of Egyptian race only, and these unusual honours may have compensated, in the eyes of the young princess, for the disproportion in age between herself and a veteran more

[1] The fact of the marriage is known to us by the decree of Phtah Totûnen at Abu Simbel in the XXXVth year of the king's reign. The account of it in the text is taken from the stele at Abu Simbel. The last lines are so mutilated that I have been obliged to paraphrase them. The stele of the Princess of Bakhtan has preserved the romantic version of this marriage, such as was current about the Saite period. The King of the Khâti must have taken advantage of the expedition which the Pharaoh made into Asia to send him presents by an embassy, at the head of which he placed his eldest daughter : the princess found favour with Ramses, who married her.

than sixty years old. The friendly relations between the two courts became so intimate that the Pharaoh invited his father-in-law to visit him in his own country. "The great Prince of Khâti informed the Prince of Qodi: 'Prepare thyself that we may go down into Egypt. The word of the king has gone forth, let us obey Sesostris. He gives the breath of life to those who love him; hence all the earth loves him, and Khâti forms but one with him.'" They were received with pomp at Ramses-Ânakhîtû, and perhaps at Thebes. It was with a mixture of joy and astonishment that Egypt beheld her bitterest foe become her most faithful ally, " and the men of Qimît having but one heart with the chiefs of the Khâti, a thing which had not happened since the ages of Rá."

The half-century following the conclusion of this alliance was a period of world-wide prosperity. Syria was once more able to breathe freely, her commerce being under the combined protection of the two powers who shared her territory. Not only caravans, but isolated travellers, were able to pass through the country from north to south without incurring any risks beyond those occasioned by an untrustworthy guide or a few highwaymen. It became in time a common task in the schools of Thebes to describe the typical Syrian tour of some soldier or functionary, and we still possess one of these imaginative stories in which the scribe takes his hero from Qodshû across the Lebanon to Byblos, Berytus, Tyre, and Sidon, "the fish" of which latter place " are more numerous than the grains of sand;" he then makes him cross Galilee and the forest of oaks to Jaffa, climb the mountains of the Dead

Sea, and following the maritime route by Raphia, reach Pelusium. The Egyptian galleys thronged the Phœnician ports, while those of Phœnicia visited Egypt. The latter drew so little water that they had no difficulty in coming up the Nile, and the paintings in one of the tombs represent them at the moment of their reaching Thebes. The hull of these vessels was similar to that of the Nile

PHŒNICIAN BOATS LANDING AT THEBES.[1]

boats, but the bow and stern were terminated by structures which rose at right angles, and respectively gave support to a sort of small platform. Upon this the pilot maintained his position by one of those wondrous feats of equilibrium of which the Orientals were masters. An open rail ran round the sides of the vessel, so as to prevent goods stowed upon the deck from falling into the sea when the vessel lurched. Voyages to Pûanît were undertaken more

[1] Drawn by Boudier, from the photograph published by Daressy.

frequently in quest of incense and precious metals. The working of the mines of Akiti had been the source of considerable outlay at the beginning of the reign. The measures taken by Seti to render the approaches to them practicable at all seasons had not produced the desired results; as far back as the IIIrd year of Ramses the overseers of the south had been forced to acknowledge that the managers of the convoys could no longer use any of the cisterns which had been hewn and built at such great expense. "Half of them die of thirst, together with their asses, for they have no means of carrying a sufficient number of skins of water to last during the journey there and back." The friends and officers whose advice had been called in, did not doubt for a moment that the king would be willing to complete the work which his father had merely initiated. "If thou sayest to the water, 'Come upon the mountain,' the heavenly waters will spring out at the word of thy mouth, for thou art Râ incarnate, Khopri visibly created, thou art the living image of thy father Tûmû, the Heliopolitan."—" If thou thyself sayest to thy father the Nile, father of the gods," added the Viceroy of Ethiopia, "'Raise the water up to the mountain,' he will do all that thou hast said, for so it has been with all thy projects which have been accomplished in our presence, of which the like has never been heard, even in the songs of the poets." The cisterns and wells were thereupon put into such a condition that the transport of gold was rendered easy for years to come. The war with the Khâti had not suspended building and other works of public utility; and now, owing to the establishment of peace, the sovereign was able to devote himself entirely to them. He deepened the canal at Zalû; he repaired the walls and the fortified places which protected the frontier on the side of the Sinaitic Peninsula, and he built or enlarged the strongholds along the Nile at those points most frequently threatened by the incursions of nomad tribes. Ramses was the royal builder *par excellence*, and we may say without fear of contradiction that, from the second cataract to the mouths of the Nile, there is scarcely an edifice on whose ruins we do not find his name. In Nubia, where the desert approaches close to the Nile, he confined himself to cutting in the solid rock the monuments which, for want of space, he could not build in the open. The idea of the cave-temple must have occurred very early to the Egyptians; they were accustomed to house their dead in the mountain-side, why then should they not house their gods in the same manner? The oldest forms of speos, those near to Beni-Hasan, at Deîr el-Baharî, at El-Kab, and at Gebel Silsileh, however, do not date further back than the time of the XVIIIth dynasty. All the forms of architectural plan observed in isolated temples were utilised by Ramses and applied to rock-cut buildings with more or less modification, according to the nature of the stratum in which he had to work. Where space permitted, a part only of the temple was cut in the rock, and the approaches to it were built in the open air with blocks brought to the spot, so that the completed speos became only in part a grotto—a hemi-speos of varied construction. It was in this manner that the architects of Ramses arranged the court and pylon at Beît-Wally, the hypostyle hall, rectangular court and pylon at Gerf-Hosseîn, and the avenue of sphinxes at Wady es-Sebuah, where the entrance to the avenue was guarded by two statues overlooking the river. The pylon at Gerf-Hosseîn has been demolished, and merely a few traces of the foundations appear here and there above the soil, but a

THE PROJECTING COLUMNS OF THE SPEOS OF GERF-HOSSEÎN.[1]

portion of the portico which surrounded the court is still standing, together with its massive architraves and statues, which stand with their backs against the pillars. The sanctuary itself comprised an antechamber, supported by two columns and flanked by two oblong recesses; this led into the Holy of Holies, which was a narrow niche with a

[1] Drawn by Faucher-Gudin, from a photograph by Insinger.

low ceiling, placed between two lateral chapels. A hall, nearly square in shape, connected these mysterious

THE CARYATIDES OF GERF-HOSSEÎN.[1]

chambers with the propylæa, which were open to the sky and faced with Osiride caryatides. These appear to keep

[1] Drawn by Faucher-Gudin, from a photograph by Insinger and Daniel Héron.

THE GREAT SPEOS OF ABU SIMBEL

rigid and solemn watch over the approaches to the tabernacle, and their faces, half hidden in the shadow, still present such a stern appearance that the semi-barbaric Nubians of the neighbouring villages believe them to be possessed by implacable genii. They are supposed to move from their places during the hours of night, and the fire which flashes from their eyes destroys or fascinates whoever is rash enough to watch them.

Other kings before Ramses had constructed buildings in these spots, and their memory would naturally become associated with his in the future; he wished, therefore, to find a site where he would be without a rival, and to this end he transformed the cliff at Abu Simbel into a monument of his greatness. The rocks here project into the Nile and form a gigantic conical promontory, the face of which was covered with triumphal stelæ, on which the sailors or troops going up or down the river could spell out as they passed the praises of the king and his exploits. A few feet of shore on the northern side, covered with dry and knotty bushes, affords in winter a landing-place for tourists. At the spot where the beach ends near the point of the promontory, sit four colossi, with their feet nearly touching the water, their backs leaning against a sloping wall of rock, which takes the likeness of a pylon. A band of hieroglyphs runs above their heads underneath the usual cornice, over which again is a row of crouching cynocephali looking straight before them, their hands resting upon their knees, and above this line of sacred images rises the steep and naked rock. One of the colossi is broken, and the bust of the statue, which must have been detached by some great shock, has fallen to the ground; the others rise to the height of 63 feet, and appear to look across the Nile as if watching the wadys leading to the gold-mines. The

THE TWO COLOSSI OF ABU SIMBEL TO THE SOUTH OF THE DOORWAY.[1]

pschent crown surmounts their foreheads, and the two ends of the head-dress fall behind their ears; their features are of a noble type, calm and serious; the nose slightly aquiline, the under lip projecting above a square, but

[1] Drawn by Faucher-Gudin, from a photograph by Insinger and Daniel Héron.

rather heavy, chin. Of such a type we may picture Ramses, after the conclusion of the peace with the Khâti, in the full vigour of his manhood and at the height of

THE INTERIOR OF THE SPEOS OF ABU SIMBEL.[1]

his power. The doorway of the temple is in the centre of the façade, and rises nearly to a level with the elbows

[1] Drawn by Boudier, from a photograph by Insinger and Daniel Héron.

of the colossi; above the lintel, and facing the river, stands a figure of the god Râ, represented with a human body and the head of a sparrow-hawk, while two images of the king in profile, one on each side of the god, offer him a figure of Truth. The first hall, 130 feet long by 58 feet broad, takes the place of the court surrounded by a colonnade which in other temples usually follows the pylon. Here eight Osiride figures, standing against as many square pillars, appear to support the weight of the superincumbent rock. Their profile catches the light as it enters through the open doorway, and in the early morning, when the rising sun casts a ruddy ray over their features, their faces become marvellously life-like. We are almost tempted to think that a smile plays over their lips as the first beams touch them. The remaining chambers consist of a hypostyle hall nearly square in shape, the sanctuary itself being between two smaller apartments, and of eight subterranean chambers excavated at a lower level than the rest of the temple. The whole measures 178 feet from the threshold to the far end of the Holy of Holies. The walls are covered with bas-reliefs in which the Pharaoh has vividly depicted the wars which he carried on in the four corners of his kingdom; here we see raids against the negroes, there the war with the Khâti, and further on an encounter with some Libyan tribe. Ramses, flushed by the heat of victory, is seen attacking two Timihu chiefs: one has already fallen to the ground and is being trodden underfoot; the other, after vainly letting fly his arrows, is about to perish from a blow of the conqueror. His knees give

THE FACE OF THE ROCK AT ABU SIMBEL.
Drawn by Faucher-Gudin, from a photograph by Beato.

way beneath him, his head falls heavily backwards, and the features are contracted in his death-agony. Pharaoh with his left hand has seized him by the arm, while with his right he points his lance against his enemy's breast, and is about to pierce him through the heart. As a rule, this type of bas-relief is executed with a conventional

RAMSES II. PIERCES A LIBYAN CHIEF WITH HIS LANCE.[1]

grace which leaves the spectator unmoved, and free to consider the scene merely from its historical point of view, forgetful of the artist. An examination of most of the other wall-decorations of the speos will furnish several examples of this type: we see Ramses with a suitable gesture brandishing his weapon above a group of prisoners, and the composition furnishes us with a fair example of official sculpture, correct, conventional, but devoid of

[1] Drawn by Boudier, from a photograph by Mons. de Bock.

230   THE REACTION AGAINST EGYPT

interest. Here, on the contrary, the drawing is so full of energy that it carries the imagination back to the time and scene of those far-off battles. The indistinct light in

RAMSES II. STRIKES A GROUP OF PRISONERS.[1]

which it is seen helps the illusion, and we almost forget that it is a picture we are beholding, and not the action itself as it took place some three thousand years ago. A small speos, situated at some hundred feet further north,

[1] Drawn by Boudier, from a photograph by Insinger.

is decorated with standing colossi of smaller size, four of which represent Ramses, and two of them his wife, Isit Nofrîtari. This speos possesses neither peristyle nor crypt, and the chapels are placed at the two extremities of the transverse passage, instead of being in a parallel line with

THE FAÇADE OF THE LITTLE SPEOS OF HATHOR AT ABU SIMBEL.[1]

the sanctuary; on the other hand, the hypostyle hall rests on six pillars with Hathor-headed capitals of fine proportions. A third excavated grotto of modest dimensions served as an accessory chamber to the two others. An inexhaustible stream of yellow sand poured over the great temple from the summit of the cliff, and partially covered it every year. No sooner were the efforts to remove it relaxed, than it spreads into the chambers,

[1] Drawn by Faucher-Gudin, from the plates in Champollion.

concealing the feet of the colossi, and slowly creeping upwards to their knees, breasts, and necks; at the beginning of this century they were entirely hidden. In spite of all that was done to divert it, it ceaselessly reappeared, and in a few summers regained all the ground which had been previously cleared. It would seem as if the desert, powerless to destroy the work of the conqueror, was seeking nevertheless to hide it from the admiration of posterity.*

Seti had worked indefatigably at Thebes, but the shortness of his reign prevented him from completing the buildings he had begun there. There existed everywhere, at Luxor, at Karnak, and on the left bank of the Nile, the remains of his unfinished works; sanctuaries partially roofed in, porticoes incomplete, columns raised to merely half their height, halls as yet imperfect with blank walls, here and there covered with only the outlines in red and black ink of their future bas-reliefs, and statues hardly blocked out, or awaiting the final touch of the polisher.[1] Ramses took up the work where his father had relinquished it. At Luxor there was not enough space to give to the hypostyle hall the extension which the original plans proposed, and the great colonnade has an unfinished appearance. The Nile, in one of its capricious floods, had

---

* The English engineers have succeeded in barring out the sand, and have prevented it from pouring over the cliff any more.—ED.

[1] This is the description which Ramses gave of the condition in which he found the Memnonium of Abydos. An examination of the inscriptions existing in the Theban temples which Seti I. had constructed, shows that it must have applied also to the appearance of certain portions of Qurneh, Luxor, and Karnak in the time of Ramses II.

carried away the land upon which the architects had intended to erect the side aisles; and if they wished to add to the existing structure a great court and a pylon, without which no temple was considered complete, it was necessary

THE CHAPEL OF THÛTMOSIS III. AND ONE OF THE PYLONS OF RAMSES II. AT LUXOR.[1]

to turn the axis of the building towards the east. In their operations the architects came upon a beautiful little edifice of rose granite, which had been either erected or restored by Thûtmosis III. at a time when the town was an independent municipality and was only beginning to extend

[1] Drawn by Faucher-Gudin, from a photograph by Beato.

its suburban dwellings to meet those of Karnak. They took care to make no change in this structure, but set to work to incorporate it into their final plans. It still stands at the north-west corner of the court, and the elegance of its somewhat slender little columns contrasts happily with the heaviness of the structure to which it is attached. A portion of its portico is hidden by the brickwork of the mosque of Abu'l Haggag : the part brought to light in the course of the excavations contains between each row of columns a colossal statue of Ramses II. We are accustomed to hear on all sides of the degeneracy of the sculptor's art at this time, and of its having fallen into irreparable neglect. Nothing can be further from the truth than this sweeping statement. There are doubtless many statues and bas-reliefs of this epoch which shock us by their crudity and ugliness, but these owed their origin for the most part to provincial workshops which had been at all times of mediocre repute, and where the artists did not receive orders enough to enable them to correct by practice the defects of their education. We find but few productions of the Theban school exhibiting bad technique, and if we had only this one monument of Luxor from which to form our opinion of its merits, it would be sufficient to prove that the sculptors of Ramses II. were not a whit behind those of Harmhabi or Seti I. Adroitness in cutting the granite or hard sandstone had in no wise been lost, and the same may be said of the skill in bringing out the contour and life-like action of the figure, and of the art of infusing into the features and demeanour of the Pharaoh something of the superhuman majesty with which the

Egyptian people were accustomed to invest their monarchs. If the statues of Ramses II. in the portico are not perfect models of sculpture, they have many good points, and their bold treatment makes them effectively decorative. Eight

THE COLONNADE OF SETI I. AND THE THREE COLOSSAL STATUES OF RAMSES II. AT LUXOR [1]

other statues of Ramses are arranged along the base of the façade, and two obelisks—one of which has been at Paris for half a century [2]—stood on either side of the entrance.

[1] Drawn by Faucher-Gudin, from a photograph by Beato.

[2] The colonnade and the little temple of Thûtmosis III. were concealed under the houses of the village; they were first brought to light in the excavations of 1884-86.

The whole structure lacks unity, and there is nothing corresponding to it in this respect anywhere else in Egypt. The northern half does not join on to the southern, but seems to belong to quite a distinct structure, or the two parts might be regarded as having once formed a single edifice which had become divided by an accident, which the architect had endeavoured to unite together again by a line of columns running between two walls. The masonry of the hypostyle hall at Karnak was squared and dressed, but the walls had been left undecorated, as was also the case with the majority of the shafts of the columns and the surface of the architraves. Ramses covered the whole with a series of sculptured and painted scenes which had a rich ornamental effect; he then decorated the pylon, and inscribed on the outer wall to the south the list of cities which he had captured. The temple of Amon then assumed the aspect which it preserved henceforward for centuries. The Ramessides and their successors occupied themselves in filling it with furniture, and in taking steps for the repair of any damage that might accrue to the hall or pillars; they had their cartouches or inscriptions placed in vacant spaces, but they did not dare to modify its arrangement. It was reserved for the Ethiopian and Greek Pharaohs, in presence of the hypostyle and pylon of the XIXth dynasty, to conceive of others on a still vaster scale. Ramses, having completed the funerary chapel of Seti at Qurneh upon the left bank of the river, then began to think of preparing the edifice destined for the cult of his " double "—that Ramesseum whose majestic ruins still stand at a short distance to the north of the giants of

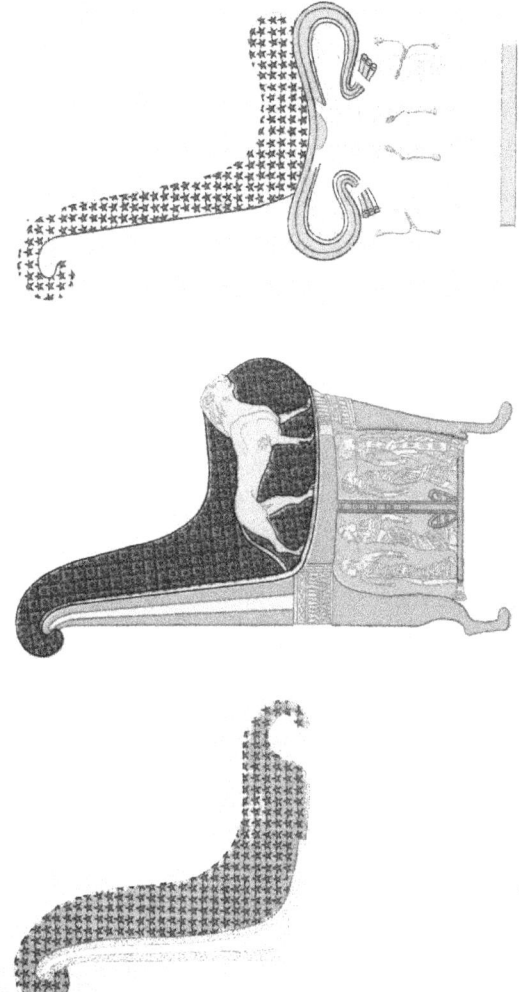

PAINTINGS OF CHAIRS IN THE FIFTH TOMB OF THE KINGS TO THE EAST. THEBES (BŶBAN EL MOLOUK).

Amenôthes. Did these colossal statues stimulate his spirit of emulation to do something yet more marvellous? He erected here, at any rate, a still more colossal figure. The earthquake which shattered Memnon brought it to the ground, and fragments of it still strew the soil where they fell some nineteen centuries ago. There are so many of them that the spectator would

THE REMAINS OF THE COLOSSAL STATUE OF RAMSES II. AT THE RAMESSEUM.[1]

think himself in the middle of a granite quarry.[2] The portions forming the breast, arms, and thighs are in detached pieces, but they are still recognisable where they lie close to each other. The head has lost nothing of its characteristic expression, and its proportions are

---

[1] Drawn by Faucher-Gudin, from a photograph by Beato.

[2] The ear measures 3 feet 4 inches in length; the statue is 58 feet high from the top of the head to the sole of the foot, and the weight of the whole has been estimated at over a thousand tons.

so enormous, that a man could sleep crouched up in the hollow of one of its ears as if on a sofa. Behind the court overlooked by this colossal statue lay a second court, surrounded by a row of square pillars, each having a figure of Osiris attached to it. The god is represented as a mummy, the swathings throwing the body

THE RAMESSEUM.[1]

and limbs into relief. His hands are freed from the bandages and are crossed on the breast, and hold respectively the flail and crook; the smiling face is surmounted by an enormous head-dress. The sanctuary with the buildings attached to it has perished, but enormous brick structures extend round the ruins, forming an enclosure of storehouses. Here the priests

[1] Drawn by Boudier, from a photograph by Beato; the great blocks in the foreground are the fragments of the colossal statue of Ramses II.

of the "double" were accustomed to dwell with their wives and slaves, and here they stored up the products of their domains—meat, vegetables, corn, fowls dried or preserved in fat, and wines procured from all the vineyards of Egypt.

These were merely the principal monuments put up by Ramses II. at Thebes during the sixty-seven years of his rule. There would be no end to the enumeration of his works if we were to mention all the other edifices which he constructed in the necropolis or among the dwellings of the living, all those which he restored, or those which he merely repaired or inscribed with his cartouches. These are often cut over the name of the original founder, and his usurpations of monuments are so numerous that he might be justly accused of having striven to blot out the memory of his predecessors, and of claiming for himself the entire work of the whole line of Pharaohs. It would seem as if, in his opinion, the glory of Egypt began with him, or at least with his father, and that no victorious campaigns had been ever heard of before those which he conducted against the Libyans and the Hittites.

The battle of Qodshû, with its attendant episodes—the flogging of the spies, the assault upon the camp, the charge of the chariots, the flight of the Syrians—is the favourite subject of his inscriptions; and the poem of Pentaûîrît adds to the bas-reliefs a description worthy of the acts represented. This epic reappears everywhere, in Nubia and in the Sâîd, at Abu Simbel, at Beît-Wally, at Derr, at Luxor, at Karnak, and on the Ramesseum, and the same battle-scenes, with the same accompanying texts, reappear in the

Memnonium, whose half-ruined walls still crown the necropolis of Abydos. He had decided upon the erection of this latter monument at the very beginning of his reign, and the artisans who had worked at the similar structure of Seti I. were employed to cover its walls with admirable

THE RUINS OF THE MEMNONIUM OF RAMSES II. AT ABYDOS.[1]

bas-reliefs. Ramses also laid claim to have his own resting-place at "the Cleft;" in this privilege he associated all the Pharaohs, from whom he imagined himself to be descended, and the same list of their names, which we find engraved in the chapel of his father, appears on his building also. Some ruins, lying beyond Abydos, are too formless to do more than indicate the site of some

[1] Drawn by Boudier, from a photograph by Émil Brugsch-Bey.

THE BUILDINGS OF RAMSES ON THE DELTA 241

of his structures. He enlarged the temple of Harshafîtû and that of Osiris at Heracleopolis, and, to accomplish these works the more promptly, his workmen had recourse for material to the royal towns of the IVth and XIIth dynasties; the pyramids of Ûsirtasen II. and Snofrûi at Medûm suffered accordingly the loss of the best part of their covering. He finished the mausoleum at Memphis, and dedicated the statue which Seti had merely blocked out; he then set to work to fill the city with buildings of his own device—granite and sandstone chambers to the east of the Sacred Lake,[1] monumental gateways to the south,[2] and before one of them a fine colossal figure in granite.[3] It lay not long ago at the bottom of a hole among the palm trees, and was covered by the inundation every year; it has now been so raised as to be safe from the waters. Ramses could hardly infuse new life into all the provinces which had been devastated years before by the Shepherd-kings; but Heliopolis,[4] Bubastes, Athribis, Patûmû, Mendis, Tell Moqdam, and all the cities of the eastern corner of the Delta, constitute a museum of his monuments, every object within them testifying to

[1] Partly excavated and published by Mariette, and partly by M. de Morgan. This is probably the temple mentioned in the *Great Inscription of Abu Simbel*.

[2] These are probably those mentioned by Herodotus, when he says that Sesostris constructed a propylon in the temple of Hephaistos.

[3] This is Abu-l-hôl of the Arabs.

[4] Ruins of the temple of Râ bear the cartouche of Ramses II. "Cleopatra's Needle," transported to Alexandria by one of the Ptolemies, had been set up by Ramses at Heliopolis; it is probably one of the four obelisks which the traditional Sesostris is said to have erected in that city, according to Pliny.

his activity. He colonised these towns with his prisoners, rebuilt them, and set to work to rouse them from the torpor into which they had fallen after their capture by Âhmosis. He made a third capital of Tanis, which rivalled both Memphis and Thebes. Before this it had been little more than a deserted ruin: he cleared out the *débris*, brought a population to the

THE COLOSSAL STATUE OF RAMSES II. AT MITRAHINEH.[1]

place; rebuilt the temple, enlarging it by aisles which extended its area threefold; and here he enthroned, along with the local divinities, a triad, in which Amonrâ and Sûtkhû sat side by side with his own deified "double." The ruined walls, the overturned stelæ, the obelisks recumbent in the dust, and the statues of his usurped

[1] Drawn by Faucher-Gudin, from a photograph brought back by Bénédite.

predecessors, all bear his name. His colossal figure of statuary sandstone, in a sitting attitude like that at the Ramesseum, projected from the chief court, and seemed to look down upon the confused ruin of his works.[1] We do not know how many wives he had in his harem, but one of the lists of his children which has come down to us enumerates, although mutilated at the end, one hundred and eleven sons, while of his daughters we know of fifty-five.[2] The majority of these were the offspring of mere concubines or foreign princesses, and possessed but a secondary rank in comparison with himself; but by his union with his sisters Nofrîtari Marîtmût and Isîtnofrît, he he had at least half a dozen sons and daughters who might aspire to the throne. Death robbed him of several of these before an opportunity was open to them to succeed him, and among them Amenhikhopshûf, Amenhiunamif, and Ramses, who had distinguished themselves in the campaign against the Khâti; and some of his daughters—Bitanîti, Marîtamon, Nibîttaûi—by becoming his wives lost their right to the throne. About the XXXth year of his reign, when he was close upon sixty, he began to think of an associate, and his choice rested on the eldest surviving son of his queen Isîtnofrît, who was called Khâmoîsît. This prince was born before the succession of his father, and had

---

[1] The fragments of the colossus were employed in the Græco-Roman period as building material, and used in the masonry of a boundary wall.

[2] The list of Abydos enumerates thirty-three of his sons and thirty-two of his daughters, that of Wady-Sebua one hundred and eleven of his sons and fifty-one of his daughters; both lists are mutilated. The remaining lists for the most part record only some of the children living at the time they were drawn up, at Derr, at the Ramesseum, and at Abu Simbel.

exhibited distinguished bravery under the walls of Qodshû and at Ascalon. When he was still very young he had been invested with the office of high priest of the Memphite Phtah, and thus had secured to him the revenues of the possessions of the god, which were the largest in all Egypt after those of the Theban Amon. He had a great reputation for his knowledge of abstruse theological questions and of the science of magic—a later age attributing to him the composition of several books on magic giving directions for the invocation of spirits belonging to this world and the world beyond. He became the hero also of fantastic romances, in which it was related of him how, in consequence of his having stolen from the mummy of an old wizard the books of Thot, he became the victim of possession by a sort of lascivious and sanguinary ghoul. Ramses relieved himself of the cares of state by handing over to Khâmoîsît the government of the country, without, however, conferring upon him the titles and insignia of royalty. The chief concern of Khâmoîsît was to secure the scrupulous observance of the divine laws. He celebrated at Silsilis the festivals of the inundation; he presided at the commemoration of his father's apotheosis, and at the funeral rites of the Apis who died in the XXXth year of the king's reign. Before his time each sacred bull had its separate tomb in a quarter of the Memphite Necropolis known to the Greeks as the Serapeion. The tomb was a small cone-roofed building erected on a square base, and containing only one chamber. Khâmoîsît substituted for this a rock-tomb similar to those used by ordinary individuals. He had a tunnel cut in the

THE LEGEND OF SESOSTRIS

solid rock to a depth of about a hundred yards, and on either side of this a chamber was prepared for each Apis on its death, the masons closing up the wall after the installation of the mummy. His regency had lasted for nearly a quarter of a century, when, the burden of government becoming too much for him, he was succeeded in the LVth year of Ramses by his younger brother Mînephtah, who was like himself a son of Isîtnofrît.[1] Mînephtah acted, during the first twelve years of his rule, for his father, who, having now almost attained the age of a hundred, passed peacefully away at Thebes in the LXVIIth year of his reign, full of days and sated with glory.[2] He became the subject of legend almost before he had closed his eyes upon the world.

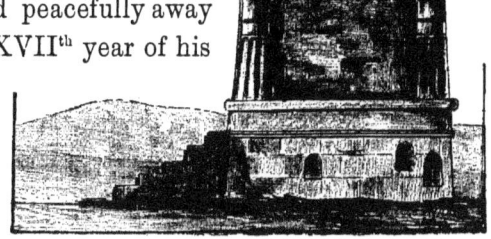

THE CHAPEL OF THE APIS OF AMENÔTHES III.[3]

He had obtained brilliant successes during his life, and the scenes describing them were depicted in scores of places. Popular fancy believed everything which he had related of himself, and added to this all that it knew of other kings, thus making him the Pharaoh of Pharaohs—the embodiment of all preceding monarchs. Legend preferred to recall him by the name

---

[1] Mînephtah was in the order of birth the thirteenth son of Ramses II.
[2] A passage on a stele of Ramses IV. formally attributes to him a reign of sixty-seven years. I procured at Koptos a stele of his year LXVI.
[3] Drawn by Faucher-Gudin, from a sketch by Mariette.

Sesûsû, Sesûstûrî—a designation which had been applied to him by his contemporaries, and he thus became better known to moderns as Sesostris than by his proper name Ramses Mîamûn.[1] According to tradition, he was at first sent to Ethiopia with a fleet of four hundred ships, by which he succeeded in conquering the coasts of the Red Sea as far as the Indus. In later times several stelæ in the cinnamon country were ascribed to him. He is credited after this with having led into the east a great army, with which he conquered Syria, Media, Persia, Bactriana, and India as far as the ocean; and with having on his return journey through the deserts of Scythia reached the Don [Tanais], where, on the shore of the Mæotic Sea, he left a number of his soldiers, whose descendants afterwards peopled Colchis. It was even alleged that he had ventured into Europe, but that the lack of provisions and the inclemency of the climate had prevented him from advancing further than Thrace. He returned

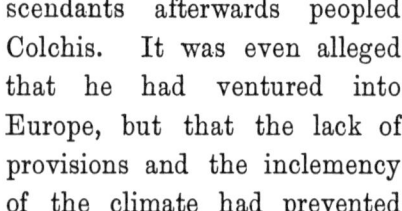

STATUE OF KHÂMOÎSÎT.[2]

[1] This designation, which is met with at Medinet-Habu and in the *Anastasi Papyrus I.*, was shown by E. de Rougé to refer to Ramses II.; the various readings Sesû, Sesûsû, Sesûstûrî, explain the different forms Sesosis, Sesoosis, Sesostris. Wiedemann saw in this name the mention of a king of the XVIIIth dynasty not yet classified.

[2] Drawn by Faucher-Gudin, from a statue in the British Museum.

to Egypt after an absence of nine years, and after having set up on his homeward journey statues and stelæ everywhere in commemoration of his victories. Herodotus asserts that he himself had seen several of these monuments in his travels in Syria and Ionia. Some of these are of genuine Egyptian manufacture, and are to be attributed to our Ramses; they are to be found near Tyre, and on the banks of the Nahr el-Kelb, where they mark the frontier to which his empire extended in this direction. Others have but little resemblance to Egyptian monuments, and were really the work of the Asiatic peoples among whom they were found. The two figures referred to long ago by Herodotus, which have been discovered near Ninfi between Sardis and Smyrna, are instances of the latter. The shoes of the figures are turned up at the toe, and the head-dress has more resemblance to the high hats of the people of Asia Minor than to the double crown of Egypt, while the lower garment is striped horizontally in place of vertically. The inscription, moreover, is in an Asiatic form of writing, and has nothing Egyptian about it.

Ramses II. in his youth was the handsomest man of

STELE OF THE NAHR EL-KELB.[1]

[1] Drawn by Faucher-Gudin, from a photograph.

his time. He was tall and straight; his figure was well moulded—the shoulders broad, the arms full and vigorous, the legs muscular; the face was oval, with a firm and

THE BAS-RELIEF OF NINFI.[1]

smiling mouth, a thin aquiline nose, and large open eyes. Old age and death did not succeed in marring the face sufficiently to disfigure it. The coffin containing his body is not the same as that in which his children placed

[1] Drawn by Faucher-Gudin, from a photograph.

him on the day of his obsequies; it is another substituted for it by one of the Ramessides, and the mask upon it has but a distant resemblance to the face of the victorious

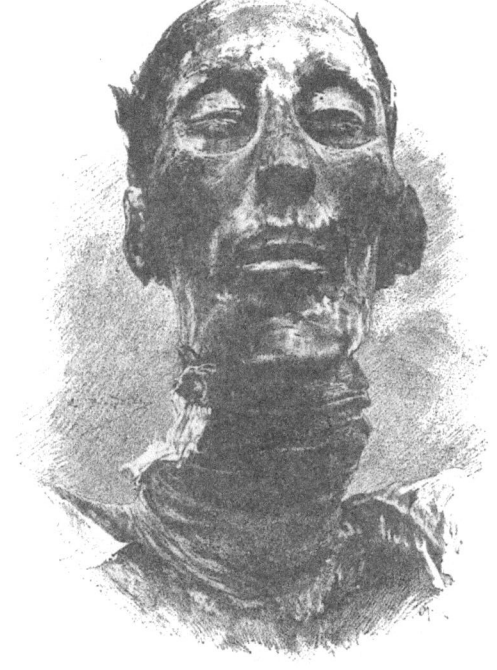

COFFIN OF RAMSES II.[1]   RAMSES II.[2]

Pharaoh. The mummy is thin, much shrunken, and light; the bones are brittle, and the muscles atrophied, as one would expect in the case of a man who had

[1] Drawn by Faucher-Gudin, from a photograph by Émil Brugsch-Bey. There may be seen below the cartouche the lines of the official report of inspection written during the XXIst dynasty.

[2] Drawn by Boudier, from a photograph taken from the mummy itself, by Émil Brugsch-Bey.

attained the age of a hundred; but the figure is still tall and of perfect proportions.[1] The head, which is bald on the top, is somewhat long, and small in relation to the bulk of the body; there is but little hair on the forehead, but at the back of the head it is thick, and in smooth stiff locks, still preserving its white colour beneath the yellow balsams of his last toilet. The forehead is low, the supra-orbital ridges accentuated, the eyebrows thick, the eyes small and set close to the nose, the temples hollow, the cheek-bones prominent; the ears, finely moulded, stand out from the head, and are pierced, like those of a woman, for the usual ornaments pendant from the lobe. A strong jaw and square chin, together with a large thick-lipped mouth, which reveals through the black paste within it a few much-worn but sound teeth, make up the features of the mummied king. His moustache and beard, which were closely shaven in his lifetime, had grown somewhat in his last sickness or after his death; the coarse and thick hairs in them, white like those of the head and eyebrows, attain a length of two or three millimetres. The skin shows an ochreous yellow colour under the black bituminous plaster. The mask of the mummy, in fact, gives a fair idea of that of the living king; the somewhat unintelligent expression, slightly brutish perhaps, but haughty and firm of purpose, displays itself with an air of royal majesty beneath the sombre materials used by the embalmer. The disappearance of

[1] Even after the coalescence of the vertebræ and the shrinkage produced by mummification, the body of Ramses II. still measures over 5 feet 8 inches.

THE LIBYAN KINGDOM 251

the old hero did not produce many changes in the position of affairs in Egypt: Mînephtah from this time forth possessed as Pharaoh the power which he had previously wielded as regent. He was now no longer young. Born somewhere about the beginning of the reign of Ramses II., he was now sixty, possibly seventy, years old; thus an old man succeeded another old man at a moment when Egypt must have needed more than ever an active and vigorous ruler. The danger to the country did not on this occasion rise from the side of Asia, for the relations of the Pharaoh with his Kharu[1] subjects continued friendly, and, during a famine which desolated Syria, he sent wheat to his Hittite allies. The nations, however, to the north and east, in Libya and in the Mediterranean islands, had for some time past been in a restless condition, which boded little good to the empires of the old world. The Timihû, some of them tributaries from the XIIth, and others from the first years of the XVIIIth dynasty, had always been troublesome, but never really dangerous neighbours. From time to time it was necessary to send light troops against them, who, sailing along the coast or following the caravan routes, would enter their territory, force them from their retreats, destroy their palm groves, carry off their cattle, and place garrisons in the principal oases—even in Sîwah itself. For more than a century, however, it would seem that more active and numerically

[1] A document preserved in the *Anastasi Papyrus III.* shows how regular the relations with Syria had become. It is the journal of a custom-house officer, or of a scribe placed at one of the frontier posts, who notes from day to day the letters, messengers, officers, and troops which passed from the 15th to the 25th of Pachons, in the IIIrd year of the reign.

stronger populations had entered upon the stage. A current of invasion, having its origin in the region of the Atlas, or possibly even in Europe, was setting towards the Nile, forcing before it the scattered tribes of the Sudan. Who were these invaders? Were they connected with the race which had planted its dolmens over the plains of the Maghreb? Whatever the answer to this question may be, we know that a certain number of Berber tribes[1]—the Labû and Mashaûasha—who had occupied a middle position between Egypt and the people behind them, and who had only irregular communications with the Nile valley, were now pushed to the front and forced to descend upon it.[2] They were men tall of stature and large of limb, with fair skins, light hair, and blue eyes; everything, in fact, indicating their northern origin. They took pleasure in tattooing the skin, just as the Tuaregs and Kabyles are now accustomed to do, and some, if not all, of them practised circumcision, like a portion of the Egyptians and Semites. In the arrangement of the hair, a curl fell upon the shoulder, while the remainder was arranged in small frizzled locks. Their chiefs and braves wore on their heads two flowering plumes. A loin-cloth, a wild-beast's skin thrown over the back, a mantle, or rather a covering of woollen or dyed cloth, fringed and

---

[1] The nationality of these tribes is evidenced by the names of their chiefs, which recall exactly those of the Numidians—Massyla, Massinissa, Massiva.

[2] The Labû, Laûbû, Lobû, are mentioned for the first time under Ramses II.; these are the Libyans of classical geographers. The Mashaûasha answer to the Maxyes of Herodotus; they furnished mercenaries to the armies of Ramses II.

ornamented with many-coloured needlework, falling from the left shoulder with no attachment in front, so as to leave the body unimpeded in walking,—these constituted the ordinary costume of the people. Their arms were

A LIBYAN.[1]

similar to those of the Egyptians, consisting of the lance, the mace, the iron or copper dagger, the boomerang, the bow and arrow, and the sling. They also employed horses and chariots. Their bravery made them a foe not to be despised, in spite of their ignorance of tactics and their want of discipline. When they were afterwards formed

[1] Drawn by Faucher-Gudin, from a photograph.

into regiments and conducted by experienced generals, they became the best auxiliary troops which Egypt could boast of. The Labû from this time forward were the most energetic of the tribes, and their chiefs prided themselves upon possessing the leadership over all the other clans in this region of the world.[1].

The Labû might very well have gained the mastery over the other inhabitants of the desert at this period, who had become enfeebled by the frequent defeats which they had sustained at the hands of the Egyptians. At the moment when Mînephtah ascended the throne, their king, Mâraîû, son of Didi, ruled over the immense territory lying between the Fayûm and the two Syrtes: the Timihu, the Kahaka, and the Mashaûasha rendered him the same obedience as his own people. A revolution had thus occurred in Africa similar to that which had taken place a century previously in Naharaim, when Sapalulu founded the Hittite empire. A great kingdom rose into being where no state capable of disturbing Egyptian control had existed before. The danger was serious. The Hittites, separated from the Nile by the whole breadth of Kharu, could not directly threaten any of the Egyptian cities; but the Libyans, lords of the desert, were in contact with the Delta, and could in a few days fall upon any point in the valley they chose. Mînephtah, therefore, hastened to resist the assault of the westerns, as his father had formerly done that of the easterns, and, strange as it may

[1] This was the case in the wars of Mînephtah and Ramses III., in which the Labû and their kings took the command of the confederate armies assembled against Egypt.

THE FIRST LIBYAN INVASION 255

seem, he found among the troops of his new enemies some of the adversaries with whom the Egyptians had fought under the walls of Qodshû sixty years before. The Shardana, Lycians, and others, having left the coasts of the Delta and the Phœnician seaports owing to the vigilant watch kept by the Egyptians over their waters, had betaken themselves to the Libyan littoral, where they met with a favourable reception. Whether they had settled in some places, and formed there those colonies of which a Greek tradition of a recent age speaks, we cannot say. They certainly followed the occupation of mercenary soldiers, and many of them hired out their services to the native princes, while others were enrolled among the troops of the King of the Khâti or of the Pharaoh himself. Mâraîû brought with him Achæans, Shardana, Tûrsha, Shagalasha,[1] and Lycians in considerable numbers when he resolved to begin the strife.[2] This was not one of those conventional little wars which aimed at nothing further than the imposition of the payment of a tribute upon the conquered, or the conquest of one of their provinces. Mâraiû had nothing less in view than the transport of his whole people into the Nile valley, to settle permanently there as the Hyksôs had done before him. He set out on his march towards the end of the IVth year of the Pharaoh's reign, or the beginning of his V[th], surrounded by the *élite* of his troops, " the first choice from among all the soldiers and

[1] The Shakalasha, Shagalasha, identified with the Sicilians by E. de Rougé, were a people of Asia Minor whose position there is approximately indicated by the site of the town Sagalassos, named after them.
[2] The *Inscription of Mînephtah* distinguishes the Libyans of Mâraîû from "the people of the Sea."

all the heroes in each land." The announcement of their approach spread terror among the Egyptians. The peace which they had enjoyed for fifty years had cooled their warlike ardour, and the machinery of their military organisation had become somewhat rusty. The standing army had almost melted away; the regiments of archers and charioteers were no longer effective, and the neglected fortresses were not strong enough to protect the frontier. As a consequence, the oases of Farafrah and of the Natron lakes fell into the hands of the enemy at the first attack, and the eastern provinces of the Delta became the possession of the invader before any steps could be taken for their defence. Memphis, which realised the imminent danger, broke out into open murmurs against the negligent rulers who had given no heed to the country's ramparts, and had allowed the garrisons of its fortresses to dwindle away. Fortunately Syria remained quiet. The Khâti, in return for the aid afforded them by Mînephtah during the famine, observed a friendly attitude, and the Pharaoh was thus enabled to withdraw the troops from his Asiatic provinces. He could with perfect security take the necessary measures for ensuring "Heliopolis, the city of Tûmû," against surprise, "for arming Memphis, the citadel of Phtah-Tonen, and for restoring all things which were in disorder: he fortified Pibalîsît, in the neighbourhood of the Shakana canal, on a branch of that of Heliopolis," and he rapidly concentrated his forces behind these quickly organised lines.[1] Mâraîû, however, continued to advance; in the

[1] Chabas would identify Pibalîsît with Bubastis; I agree with Brugsch in placing it at Belbeis.

early months of the summer he had crossed the Canopic branch of the Nile, and was now about to encamp not far from the town of Piriû. When the king heard of this "he became furious against them as a lion that fascinates its victim; he called his officers together and addressed them: 'I am about to make you hear the words of your master, and to teach you this: I am the sovereign shepherd who feeds you; I pass my days in seeking out that which is useful for you: I am your father; is there among you a father like me who makes his children live? You are trembling like geese, you do not know what is good to do: no one gives an answer to the enemy, and our desolated land is abandoned to the incursions of all nations. The barbarians harass the frontier, rebels violate it every day, every one robs it, enemies devastate our seaports, they penetrate into the fields of Egypt; if there is an arm of a river they halt there, they stay for days, for months; ... they come as numerous as reptiles, and no one is able to sweep them back, these wretches who love death and hate life, whose hearts meditate the consummation of our ruin. Behold, they arrive with their chief; they pass their time on the land which they attack in filling their stomachs every day; this is the reason why they come to the land of Egypt, to seek their sustenance, and their intention is to install themselves there; mine is to catch them like fish upon their bellies. Their chief is a dog, a poor devil, a madman; he shall never sit down again in his place.'" He then announced that on the 14th of Epiphi he would himself conduct the troops against the enemy.

These were brave words, but we may fancy the figure that this king of more than sixty years of age would have presented in a chariot in the middle of the fray, and his competence to lead an effective charge against the enemy. On the other hand, his absence in such a critical position of affairs would have endangered the *morale* of his soldiers and possibly compromised the issue of the battle. A dream settled the whole question.[1] While Mînephtah was asleep one night, he saw a gigantic figure of Phtah standing before him, and forbidding him to advance. "'Stay,' cried the god to him, while handing him the curved khopesh: 'put away discouragement from thee!' His Majesty said to him: 'But what am I to do then?' And Phtah answered him: 'Despatch thy infantry, and send before it numerous chariots to the confines of the territory of Piriû.'"[2] The Pharaoh obeyed the command, and did not stir from his position. Mâraiû had, in the mean time, arranged his attack for the 1st of Epiphi, at the rising of the sun: it did not take place, however, until the 3rd. "The archers of His Majesty made havoc of the barbarians for six hours; they were cut off by the edge of the sword." When Mâraîû saw the carnage, "he was afraid, his heart failed him; he betook himself to flight as fast as his feet

---

[1] Ed. Meyer sees in this nothing but a customary rhetorical expression, and thinks that the god spoke in order to encourage the king to defend himself vigorously.

[2] This name was read Pa-ari by E. de Rougé, Pa-ali by Lauth, and was transcribed Pa-ari-shop by Brugsch, who identified with Prosopitis. The orthography of the text at Athribis shows that we ought to read Piri, Pirû, Piriû; possibly the name is identical with that of Iarû which is mentioned in the Pyramid-texts.

could bear him to save his life, so successfully that his bow and arrows remained behind him in his precipitation, as well as everything else he had upon him." His treasure, his arms, his wife, together with the cattle which he had brought with him for his use, became the prey of the conqueror; " he tore out the feathers from his head-dress, and took flight with such of those wretched Libyans as escaped the massacre, but the officers who had the care of His Majesty's team of horses followed in their steps" and put most of them to the sword. Mâraîû succeeded, however, in escaping in the darkness, and regained his own country without water or provisions, and almost without escort. The conquering troops returned to the camp laden with booty, and driving before them asses carrying, as bloody tokens of victory, quantities of hands and *phalli* cut from the dead bodies of the slain. The bodies of six generals and of 6359 Libyan soldiers were found upon the field of battle, together with 222 Shagalasha, 724 Tursha, and some hundreds of Shardana and Achæans : several thousands of prisoners passed in procession before the Pharaoh, and were distributed among such of his soldiers as had distinguished themselves. These numbers show the gravity of the danger from which Egypt had escaped : the announcement of the victory filled the country with enthusiasm, all the more sincere because of the reality of the panic which had preceded it. The fellahîn, intoxicated with joy, addressed each other: "'Come, and let us go a long distance on the road, for there is now no fear in the hearts of men.' The fortified posts may at last be left; the citadels are now open; messengers stand at the foot of the walls and wait in the shade for the guard to awake after their siesta, to give them entrance. The military police sleep on their accustomed rounds, and the people of the marshes once more drive their herds to pasture without fear of raids, for there are no longer marauders near at hand to cross the river; the cry of the sentinels is heard no more in the night: ' Halt, thou that comest, thou that comest under a name which is not thine own—sheer off!' and men no longer exclaim on the following morning: ' Such or such a thing has been stolen;' but the towns fall once more into their usual daily routine, and he who works in the hope of the harvest, will nourish himself upon that which he shall have reaped." The return from Memphis to Thebes was a triumphal march.

STATUE OF MÎNEPHTAH.[1]

"He is very strong, Binrî Mînephtah," sang the court poets, "very wise are his projects—his words have as beneficial effect as those of Thot—everything which he does is completed to the end.—When he is like a guide at the head of his armies—his voice penetrates the fortress walls.—Very friendly to those who bow their backs—before Mîamun—his valiant soldiers spare him who humbles himself—before his courage and before his strength;—they

[1] Drawn by Faucher-Gudin, from a photograph by Dévéria.

fall upon the Libyans—they consume the Syrian;—the Shardana whom thou hast brought back by thy sword—make prisoners of their own tribes.—Very happy thy return to Thebes—victorious! Thy chariot is drawn by hand—the conquered chiefs march backwards before thee—whilst thou leadest them to thy venerable father—Amon, husband of his mother." And the poets amuse themselves with summoning Mâraîû to appear in Egypt, pursued as he was by his own people and obliged to hide himself from them. " He is nothing any longer but a beaten man, and has become a proverb among the Labû, and his chiefs repeat to themselves: 'Nothing of the kind has occurred since the time of Râ.' The old men say each one to his children : 'Misfortune to the Labû! it is all over with them! No one can any longer pass peacefully across the country ; but the power of going out of our land has been taken from us in a single day, and the Tihonû have been withered up in a single year ; Sûtkhû has ceased to be their chief, and he devastates their "duars; " there is nothing left but to conceal one's self, and one feels nowhere secure except in a fortress.'" The news of the victory was carried throughout Asia, and served to discourage the tendencies to revolt which were beginning to make themselves manifest there. " The chiefs gave there their salutations of peace, and none among the nomads raised his head after the crushing defeat of the Libyans; Khâti is at peace, Canaan is a prisoner as far as the disaffected are concerned, the inhabitant of Ascalon is led away, Gezer is carried into captivity, Ianuâmîm is brought to nothing, the Israîlû are destroyed and have no longer seed,

Kharu is like a widow of the land of Egypt."[1] Mînephtah ought to have followed up his opportunity to the end, but he had no such intention, and his inaction gave Maraîû time to breathe. Perhaps the effort which he had made had exhausted his resources, perhaps old age prevented him from prosecuting his success; he was content, in any case, to station bodies of pickets on the frontier, and to fortify a few new positions to the east of the Delta. The Libyan kingdom was now in the same position as that in which the Hittite had been after the campaign of Seti I.: its power had been checked for the moment, but it remained intact on the Egyptian frontier, awaiting its opportunity.

Mînephtah lived for some time after this memorable year V.,[2] and the number of monuments which belong to this period show that he reigned in peace. We can see that he carried out works in the same places as his father before him; at Tanis as well as Thebes, in Nubia as well as in the Delta. He worked the sandstone quarries for his building materials, and continued the custom of celebrating the feasts of the inundation at Silsileh. One at least of the stelæ which he set up on the occasion of these feasts is

[1] This passage is taken from a stele discovered by Petrie in 1896, on the site of the Amenophium at Thebes. The mention of the Israîlû immediately calls to mind the place-names Yushaph-ilu, Yakob-ilu, on lists of Thûtmosis III. which have been compared with the names Jacob and Joseph.

[2] The last known year of his reign is the year VIII. The lists of Manetho assign to him a reign of from twenty to forty years; Brugsch makes it out to have been thirty-four years, from 1300 to 1266 B.C., which is evidently too much, but we may attribute to him without risk of serious error a reign of about twenty years.

really a chapel, with its architraves and columns, and still excites the admiration of the traveller on account both of its form and of its picturesque appearance. The last years of his life were troubled by the intrigues of princes who

THE CHAPELS OF RAMSES II. AND MÎNEPHTAH AT SILSILEH.[1]

aspired to the throne, and by the ambition of the ministers to whom he was obliged to delegate his authority. One of the latter, a man of Semite origin, named Ben-Azana, of Zor-bisana, who had assumed the appellation of his first patron, Ramsesûpirniri, appears to have acted for him as regent. Mînephtah was succeeded, apparently, by one of

[1] Drawn by Faucher-Gudin, from a photograph by Beato.

his sons, called Seti, after his great-grandfather.¹ Seti II. had doubtless reached middle age at the time of his accession, but his portraits represent him, nevertheless, with the face and figure of a young man.² The expression in these is gentle, refined, haughty, and somewhat melancholic. It is the type of Seti I. and Ramses II., but enfeebled and, as it were, saddened. An inscription of his second year attributes to him victories in Asia,³ but others of the same period indicate the existence of disturbances similar to those which had troubled the last years of his father. These were occasioned by a certain Aiari, who was

STATUE OF SETI II.⁴

¹ E. de Rougé introduced Amenmeses and Siphtah between Mînephtah and Seti II., and I had up to the present followed his example; I have come back to the position of Chabas, making Seti II. the immediate successor of Mînephtah, which is also the view of Brugsch, Wiedemann, and Ed. Meyer. The succession as it is now given does not seem to me to be free from difficulties; the solution generally adopted has only the merit of being preferable to that of E. de Rougé, which I previously supported.

² The last date known of his reign is the year II. which is found at Silsilis; Chabas was, nevertheless, of the opinion that he reigned a considerable time.

³ The expressions employed in this document do not vary much from the usual protocol of all kings of this period. The triumphal chant of Seti II. preserved in the *Anastasi Papyrus IV.* is a copy of the triumphal chant of Mînephtah, which is in the same Papyrus.

⁴ Drawn by Faucher-Gudin, from a photograph.

high priest of Phtah, and who had usurped titles which belonged ordinarily to the Pharaoh or his eldest son, "heir in the house of Sibû, and hereditary prince of the two lands." Seti died, it would seem, without having had time to finish his tomb. We do not know whether he left any legitimate children, but two sovereigns succeeded him who were not directly connected with him, but were probably the grandsons of the Amenmesis and the Siphtah, whom we meet with among the children of Ramses. The first of these was also called Amenmesis, and he held sway for several years over the whole of Egypt, and over its foreign possessions.² The second, who was named

SETI II.¹

---

¹ Drawn by Boudier, from a photograph by Émil Brugsch-Bey.
² Graffiti of this sovereign have been found at the second cataract. Certain expressions have induced E. de Rougé to believe that he, as

Siphtah-Mînephtah, ascended "the throne of his father" thanks to the devotion of his minister Baî,[1] but in a greater degree to his marriage with a certain princess called Tausirît. He maintained himself in this position for at least six years, during which he made an expedition into Ethiopia, and received in audience at Thebes messengers from all foreign nations. He kept up so zealously the appearance of universal dominion, that to judge from his inscriptions he must have been the equal of the most powerful of his predecessors at Thebes.

Egypt, nevertheless, was proceeding at a quick pace towards its downfall. No sooner had this monarch disappeared than it began to break up.[2] There were no doubt many claimants for the crown, but none of them succeeded in disposing of the claims of his rivals, and anarchy reigned supreme from one end of the Nile valley to the other. "The land of Qîmît began to drift away, and the people within it had no longer a sovereign, and this, too, for many years, until other times came; for the land of Qîmît was in the hands of the princes ruling over the nomes, and they

---

well as Siphtah, came originally from Khibît in the Aphroditopolite nome. This was an allusion, as Chabas had seen, to the myth of Horus, similar to that relating to Thûtmosis III., and which we more usually meet with in the cases of those kings who were not marked out from their birth onwards for the throne.

[1] Bai has left two inscriptions behind him, one at Silsilis and the other at Sehêl, and the titles he assumes on both monuments show the position he occupied at the Theban court during the reign of Siphtah-Mînephtah. Chabas thought that Bai had succeeded in maintaining his rights to the crown against the claims of Amenmesis.

[2] The little that we know about this period of anarchy has been obtained from the *Harris Papyrus*.

put each other to death, both great and small. Other times came afterwards, during years of nothingness, in which Arisu, a Syrian,[1] was chief among them, and the whole country paid tribute before him; every one plotted with his neighbour to steal the goods of others, and it was the same with regard to the gods as with regard to men, offerings were no longer made in the temples." This was in truth the revenge of the feudal system upon Pharaoh. The barons, kept in check by Âhmosis and Amenôthes I., restricted by the successors of these sovereigns to the position of simple officers of the king, profited by the general laxity to recover as many as possible of their ancient privileges. For half a century and more, fortune had given them as masters only aged princes, not capable of maintaining continuous vigilance and firmness. The invasions of the peoples of the sea, the rivalry of the claimants to the throne, and the intrigues of ministers had, one after the other, served to break the bonds which fettered them, and in one generation they were able to regain that liberty of action of which they had been deprived for centuries. To this state of things Egypt had been drifting from the earliest times. Unity could be maintained only by a continuous effort, and once this became relaxed, the ties which bound the whole country together were soon broken. There was another danger threatening the country beside that arising from the

[1] The name of this individual was deciphered by Chabas; Lauth, and after him Krall, were inclined to read it as Ket, Ketesh, in order to identify it with the Ketes of Diodorus Siculus. A form of the name Arisai in the Bible may be its original, or that of Arish which is found in Phœnician, especially Punic, inscriptions.

weakening of the hands of the sovereign, and the turbulence of the barons. For some three centuries the Theban Pharaohs were accustomed to bring into the country after each victorious campaign many thousands of captives. The number of foreigners around them had, therefore, increased in a striking manner. The majority of these strangers either died without issue, or their posterity became assimilated to the indigenous inhabitants. In many places, however, they had accumulated in such proportions that they were able to retain among themselves the remembrance of their origin, their religion, and their customs, and with these the natural desire to leave the country of their exile for their former fatherland. As long as a strict watch was kept over them they remained peaceful subjects, but as soon as this vigilance was relaxed rebellion was likely to break out, especially amongst those who worked in the quarries. Traditions of the Greek period contain certain romantic episodes in the history of these captives. Some Babylonian prisoners brought back by Sesostris, these traditions tell us, unable to endure any longer the fatiguing work to which they were condemned, broke out into open revolt. They made themselves masters of a position almost opposite Memphis, and commanding

AMENMESIS.[1]

[1] Drawn by Faucher-Gudin, after a picture in Rosellini.

the river, and held their ground there with such obstinacy that it was found necessary to give up to them the province which they occupied : they built here a town, which they afterwards called Babylon. A similar legend attributes the building of the neighbouring village of Troîû to captives from Troy.[1] The scattered barbarian tribes of the Delta, whether Hebrews or the remnant of the Hyksôs, had endured there a miserable lot ever since the accession of the Ramessides. The rebuilding of the cities which had been destroyed there during the wars with the Hyksôs had restricted the extent of territory on which they could pasture their herds. Ramses II. treated them as slaves of the treasury,[2] and the Hebrews were not long under his rule before they began to look back with regret on the time of the monarchs " who knew Joseph." "The Egyptians set over them taskmasters to afflict them with their burdens. And they built for Pharaoh treasure cities, Pithom and Raamses. But the more they afflicted them, the more

[1] The name Babylon comes probably from *Banbonu, Barbonu, Babonu*—a term which, under the form *Hât-Banbonu*, served to designate a quarter of Heliopolis, or rather a suburban village of that city. Troja was, as we have seen, the ancient city of Troîû, now Tûrah, celebrated for its quarries of fine limestone. The narratives collected by the historians whom Diodorus consulted were products of the Saite period, and intended to explain to Greeks the existence on Egyptian territory of names recalling those of Babylon in Chaldæa and of Homeric Troy.

[2] A very ancient tradition identifies Ramses II. with the Pharaoh "who knew not Joseph" (*Exod.* i. 8). Recent excavations showing that the great works in the east of the Delta began under this king, or under Seti II. at the earliest, confirm in a general way the accuracy of the traditional view: I have, therefore, accepted it in part, and placed the Exodus after the death of Ramses II. Other authorities place it further back, and Lieblein in 1863 was inclined to put it under Amenôthes III.

they multiplied and grew. And they were grieved because of the children of Israel."[1] A secondary version of the same narrative gives a more detailed account of their condition: "They made their lives bitter with hard bondage, in mortar and in brick, and in all manner of service in the field."[2] The unfortunate slaves awaited only an opportunity to escape from the cruelty of their persecutors.

The national traditions of the Hebrews inform us that the king, in displeasure at seeing them increase so mightily notwithstanding his repression, commanded the midwives to strangle henceforward their male children at their birth. A woman of the house of Levi, after having concealed her infant for three months, put him in an ark of bulrushes and consigned him to the Nile, at a place where the daughter of Pharaoh was accustomed to bathe. The princess on perceiving the child had compassion on him, adopted him, called him Moses—saved from the waters— and had him instructed in all the knowledge of the Egyptians. Moses had already attained forty years of age, when he one day encountered an Egyptian smiting a Hebrew, and slew him in his anger, shortly afterwards fleeing into the land of Midian. Here he found an asylum,

---

[1] *Exod.* i. 11, 12. Excavations made by Naville have brought to light near Tel el-Maskhutah the ruins of one of the towns which the Hebrews of the Alexandrine period identified with the cities constructed by their ancestors in Egypt: the town excavated by Naville is Pitûmû, and consequently the Pithom of the Biblical account, and at the same time also the Succoth of *Exod.* xii. 37, xiii. 20, the first station of the Bnê-Israel after leaving Ramses.

[2] *Exod.* i. 13, 14.

and Jethro the priest gave him one of his daughters in marriage. After forty years of exile, God, appearing to him in a burning bush, sent him to deliver His people. The old Pharaoh was dead, but Moses and his brother Aaron betook themselves to the court of the new Pharaoh, and demanded from him permission for the Hebrews to sacrifice in the desert of Arabia. They obtained it, as we know, only after the infliction of the ten plagues, and after the firstborn of the Egyptians had been stricken.[1] The emigrants started from Ramses; as they were pursued by a body of troops, the Sea parted its waters to give them passage over the dry ground, and closing up afterwards on the Egyptian hosts, overwhelmed them to a man. Thereupon Moses and the children of Israel sang this song unto Jahveh, saying: "Jahveh is my strength and song—and He has become my salvation.—This is my God, and I will praise Him,—my father's God, and I will exalt Him.—The Lord is a man of war,—and Jahveh is His name.—Pharaoh's chariots and his hosts hath He cast into the sea,—and his chosen captains are sunk in the sea of weeds.—The deeps cover them—they went down into the depths like a stone. . . . The enemy said: 'I will pursue, I will overtake—I will divide the spoil—my lust shall be satiated upon them—I will draw my sword—my hand shall destroy them.'—Thou didst blow with Thy wind—the sea covered them—they sank as lead in the mighty waters."[2] From

---

[1] *Exod.* ii.–xiii. I have limited myself here to a summary of the Biblical narrative, without entering into a criticism of the text, which I leave to others.

[2] *Exod.* xv. 1-10 (R.V.)

this narrative we see that the Hebrews, or at least those of them who dwelt in the Delta, made their escape from their oppressors, and took refuge in the solitudes of Arabia. According to the opinion of accredited historians, this Exodus took place in the reign of Mînephtah, and the evidence of the triumphal inscription, lately discovered by Prof. Petrie, seems to confirm this view, in relating that the people of Israîlû were destroyed, and had no longer a seed. The context indicates pretty clearly that these ill-treated Israîlû were then somewhere south of Syria, possibly in the neighbourhood of Ascalon and Gezer. If it is the Biblical Israelites who are here mentioned for the first time on an Egyptian monument, one might suppose that they had just quitted the land of slavery to begin their wanderings through the desert. Although the peoples of the sea and the Libyans did not succeed in reaching their settlements in the land of Goshen, the Israelites must have profited both by the disorder into which the Egyptians were thrown by the invaders, and by the consequent withdrawal to Memphis of the troops previously stationed on the east of the Delta, to break away from their servitude and cross the frontier. If, on the other hand, the Israîlû of Mînephtah are regarded as a tribe still dwelling among the mountains of Canaan, while the greater part of the race had emigrated to the banks of the Nile, there is no need to seek long after Mînephtah for a date suiting the circumstances of the Exodus. The years following the reign of Seti II. offer favourable conditions for such a dangerous enterprise: the break-up of the monarchy, the discords of the barons, the revolts among the captives, and the supremacy of a Semite over the other chiefs, must have minimised the risk. We can readily understand how, in the midst of national disorders, a tribe of foreigners weary of its lot might escape from its settlements and betake itself towards Asia without meeting with strenuous opposition from the Pharaoh, who would naturally be too much preoccupied with his own pressing necessities to trouble himself much over the escape of a band of serfs.

Having crossed the Red Sea, the Israelites pursued their course to the north-east on the usual road leading into Syria, and then turning towards the south, at length arrived at Sinai. It was a moment when the nations of Asia were stirring. To proceed straight to Canaan by the beaten track would have been to run the risk of encountering their moving hordes, or of jostling against the Egyptian troops, who still garrisoned the strongholds of the Shephelah. The fugitives had, therefore, to shun the great military roads if they were to avoid coming into murderous conflict with the barbarians, or running into the teeth of Pharaoh's pursuing army. The desert offered an appropriate asylum to people of nomadic inclinations like themselves; they betook themselves to it as if by instinct, and spent there a wandering life for several generations.[1] The traditions collected in their sacred books described at length their marches and their halting-places, the great sufferings they endured, and the striking miracles which

[1] This explanation of the wanderings of the Israelites has been doubted by most historians: it has a cogency, once we admit the reality of the sojourn in Egypt and the Exodus.

God performed on their behalf.[1] Moses conducted them through all these experiences, continually troubled by their murmurings and seditions, but always ready to help them out of the difficulties into which they were led, on every occasion, by their want of faith. He taught them, under God's direction, how to correct the bitterness of brackish waters by applying to them the wood of a certain tree.[2] When they began to look back with regret to the "fleshpots of Egypt" and the abundance of food there, another signal miracle was performed for them. "At even the quails came up and covered the camp, and in the morning the dew lay round about the host; and when the dew that lay was gone up, behold, upon the face of the wilderness there lay a small round thing, as small as the hoar frost on the ground. And when the children of Israel saw it, they said one to another, 'What is it?' for they wist not what it was. And Moses said unto them, 'It is the bread which the Lord hath given you to eat.'"[3] "And the house of Israel called the name thereof 'manna:' and it was like coriander seed, white; and the taste of it was like wafers

---

[1] The itinerary of the Hebrew people through the desert contains a very small number of names which were not actually in use. They represent possibly either the stations at which the caravans of the merchants put up, or the localities where the Bedawin and their herds were accustomed to sojourn. The majority of them cannot be identified, but enough can still be made out to give us a general idea of the march of the emigrants.

[2] *Exod.* xv. 23-25. The station Marah, "the bitter waters," is identified by modern tradition with Ain Howarah. There is a similar way of rendering waters potable still in use among the Bedawin of these regions.

[3] *Exod.* xvi. 13-15.

THE MARCH OF THE HEBREWS TO SINAI 275

made with honey."[1] "And the children of Israel did eat the manna forty years, until they came to a land inhabited; they did eat the manna until they came unto the borders of the land of Canaan."[2] Further on, at Rephidim, the water failed: Moses struck the rocks at Horeb, and a spring gushed out.[3] The Amalekites, in the meantime, began to oppose their passage; and one might naturally doubt the power of a rabble of slaves, unaccustomed to war, to break through such an obstacle. Joshua was made their general, "and Moses, Aaron, and Hur went up to the top of the hill: and it came to pass, when Moses held up his hand, that Israel prevailed, and when he let down his hand, Amalek prevailed. But Moses' hands were heavy; and they took a stone, and put it under him, and he sat thereon; and Aaron and Hur stayed up his hands, the one on the one side, and the other on the other side, and his hands were steady until the going down of the sun. And Joshua discomfited Amalek and his people with the edge of the sword."[4] Three months after the departure of the Israelites from Egypt they encamped at the foot of Sinai, and "the Lord called unto Moses out of the mountain, saying, 'Thus shalt thou say to the house of Jacob, and

---

[1] *Exod.* xvi. 31. From early times the manna of the Hebrews had been identified with the *mann-es-sama*, "the gift of heaven," of the Arabs, which exudes in small quantities from the leaves of the tamarisk after being pricked by insects: the question, however, is still under discussion whether another species of vegetable manna may not be meant.

[2] *Exod.* xvi. 35.

[3] *Exod.* xvii. 1-7. There is a general agreement as to the identification of Rephidim with the Wady Feîrân, the village of Pharan of the Græco-Roman geographers.

[4] *Exod.* xvii. 8-13.

tell the children of Israel: Ye have seen what I did unto the Egyptians, and how I bare you on eagles' wings, and brought you unto Myself. Now therefore, if ye will obey My voice indeed, and keep My covenant, then ye shall be a peculiar treasure unto Me from among all peoples: for all the earth is Mine: and ye shall be unto Me a kingdom of priests, and an holy nation.' The people answered together and said, 'All that the Lord hath spoken we will do.' And the Lord said unto Moses, 'Lo, I come unto thee in a thick cloud, that the people may hear when I speak with thee, and may also believe thee for ever.'" "On the third day, when it was morning, there were thunders and lightnings, and a thick cloud upon the mount, and the voice of a trumpet exceeding loud; and all the people that were in the camp trembled. And Moses brought forth the people out of the camp to meet God; and they stood at the nether part of the mountain. And Mount Sinai was altogether on smoke, because the Lord descended upon it in fire: and the smoke thereof ascended as the smoke of a furnace, and the whole mount quaked greatly. And when the voice of the trumpet waxed louder and louder, Moses spake, and God answered him by a voice."[1] Then followed the giving of the supreme law, the conditions of the covenant which the Lord Himself deigned to promulgate directly to His people. It was engraved on two tables of stone, and contained, in ten concise statements, the commandments which the Creator of the Universe imposed upon the people of His choice.

[1] *Exod.* xix. 3-6, 9, 16-19.

THE TEN COMMANDMENTS

"I. I am Jahveh, which brought thee out of the land of Egypt. Thou shalt have none other gods before Me.

II. Thou shalt not make unto thee a graven image, etc.

III. Thou shalt not take the name of Jahveh thy God in vain.

IV. Remember the sabbath day to keep it holy.

V. Honour thy father and thy mother.

VI. Thou shalt do no murder.

VII. Thou shalt not commit adultery.

VIII. Thou shalt not steal.

IX. Thou shalt not bear false witness against thy neighbour.

X. Thou shalt not covet." [1]

"And all the people saw the thunderings, and the lightnings, and the voice of the trumpet, and the mountain smoking: and when the people saw it, they trembled, and stood afar off. And they said unto Moses, 'Speak thou with us, and we will hear: but let not God speak with us, lest we die.'" [2] God gave His commandments to Moses in instalments as the circumstances required them: on one occasion the rites of sacrifice, the details of the sacerdotal vestments, the mode of consecrating the priests, the composition of the oil and the incense for the altar; later on, the observance of the three annual festivals, and the orders as to absolute rest on the seventh day, as to the

---

[1] We have two forms of the Decalogue—one in *Exod.* xx. 2–17, and the other in *Deut.* v. 6–18.

[2] *Exod.* xx. 18, 19.

distinctions between clean and unclean animals, as to drink, as to the purification of women, and lawful and unlawful marriages.[1] The people waited from week to week until Jahveh had completed the revelation of His commands, and in their impatience broke the new law more than once. On one occasion, when "Moses delayed to come out of the mount," they believed themselves abandoned by heaven, and obliged Aaron, the high priest, to make for them a golden calf, before which they offered burnt offerings. The sojourn of the people at the foot of Sinai lasted eleven months. At the end of this period they set out once more on their slow marches to the Promised Land, guided during the day by a cloud, and during the night by a pillar of fire, which moved before them. This is a general summary of what we find in the sacred writings.

The Israelites, when they set out from Egypt, were not yet a nation. They were but a confused horde, flying with their herds from their pursuers; with no resources, badly armed, and unfit to sustain the attack of regular troops. After leaving Sinai, they wandered for some time among the solitudes of Arabia Petræa in search of some uninhabited country where they could fix their tents, and at length settled on the borders of Idumæa, in the

---

[1] This legislation and the history of the circumstances on which it was promulgated are contained in four of the books of the Pentateuch, viz. *Exodus*, *Leviticus*, *Numbers*, and *Deuteronomy*. Any one of the numerous text-books published in Germany will be found to contain an analysis of these books, and the prevalent opinions as to the date of the documents which it [the Hexateuch] contains. I confine myself here and afterwards only to such results as may fitly be used in a general history.

mountainous region surrounding Kadesh-Barnea.[1] Kadesh had from ancient times a reputation for sanctity among the Bedawin of the neighbourhood: it rejoiced in the possession of a wonderful well—the Well of Judgment—to which visits were made for the purpose of worship, and for obtaining the "judgment" of God. The country is a poor one, arid and burnt up, but it contains wells which never fail, and wadys suitable for the culture of wheat and for the rearing of cattle. The tribe which became possessed of a region in which there was a perennial supply of water was fortunate indeed, and a fragment of the psalmody of Israel at the time of their sojourn here still echoes in a measure the transports of joy which the people gave way to at the discovery of a new spring : " Spring up, O well; sing ye unto it: the well which the princes digged, which the nobles of the people delved with the sceptre and with their staves."[2] The wanderers took possession of this region after some successful brushes with the enemy, and settled there, without being further troubled by their neighbours or by their former masters. The Egyptians, indeed, absorbed in their civil discords, or in wars with foreign nations, soon forgot their escaped slaves, and never troubled themselves for centuries over what had become of the poor wretches, until in the reign of the Ptolemies, when they had learned from the Bible something of the

[1] The site of Kadesh-Barnea appears to have been fixed with certainty at Ain-Qadis by C. Trumbull.

[2] *Numb.* xxi. 17, 18. The context makes it certain that this song was sung at Beer, beyond the Arnon, in the land of Moab. It has long been recognised that it had a special reference, and that it refers to an incident in the wanderings of the people through the desert.

people of God, they began to seek in their own annals for traces of their sojourn in Egypt and of their departure from the country. A new version of the Exodus was the result, in which Hebrew tradition was clumsily blended with the materials of a semi-historical romance, of which Amenôthes III. was the hero. His minister and namesake, Amenôthes, son of Hâpû, left ineffaceable impressions on the minds of the inhabitants of Thebes: he not only erected the colossal figures in the Amenophium, but he constructed the chapel at Deîr el-Medineh, which was afterwards restored in Ptolemaic times, and where he continued to be worshipped as long as the Egyptian religion lasted. Profound knowledge of the mysteries of magic were attributed to him, as in later times to Prince Khâmoîsît, son of Ramses II. On this subject he wrote certain works which maintained their reputation for more than a thousand years after his death,[1] and all that was known about him marked him out for the important part he came to play in those romantic stories so popular among the Egyptians. The Pharaoh in whose good graces he lived had a desire, we are informed, to behold the gods, after the example of his ancestor Horus. The son of Hâpû, or Pa-Apis, informed him that he could not succeed in his design until he had expelled from the country all the lepers and unclean persons who contaminated it. Acting on this information, he brought together all those who suffered from physical defects, and confined them, to the number of eighty thousand, in the quarries of Tûrah. There were priests

---

[1] One of these books, which is mentioned in several religious texts, is preserved in the *Louvre Papyrus*.

among them, and the gods became wrathful at the treatment to which their servants were exposed; the soothsayer, therefore, fearing the divine anger, predicted that certain people would shortly arise who, forming an alliance with the Unclean, would, together with them, hold sway in Egypt for thirteen years. He then committed suicide, but the king nevertheless had compassion on the outcasts, and granted to them, for their exclusive use, the town of Avaris, which had been deserted since the time of Âhmosis. The outcasts formed themselves into a nation under the rule of a Heliopolitan priest called Osarsyph, or Moses, who gave them laws, mobilised them, and joined his forces with the descendants of the Shepherds at Jerusalem. The Pharaoh Amenôphis, taken by surprise at this revolt, and remembering the words of his minister Amenôthes, took flight into Ethiopia. The shepherds, in league with the Unclean, burned the towns, sacked the temples, and broke in pieces the statues of the gods: they forced the Egyptian priests to slaughter even their sacred animals, to cut them up and cook them for their foes, who ate them derisively in their accustomed feasts. Amenôphis returned from Ethiopia, together with his son Ramses, at the end of thirteen years, defeated the enemy, driving them back into Syria, where the remainder of them became later on the Jewish nation.[1]

---

[1] A list of the Pharaohs after Ai, as far as it is possible to make them out, is here given :

ZOSIRKHOPIRÛRÎ-SOTPÛNIRÎ HARMHABÎ MÎAMON.	ÛSIRKHOPÎRÛRÎ MÎAMON SÎTI II. MÎNEPHTAH.
MANPAHÎTIRÎ RAMSÎSÛ I.	MANMIRÎ-SOTPÛNIRÎ AMENDESÎSÛ HAQOÎSÎT.
MANMÂÎTRÎ SÎTI I. MÎAMON.	
ÛSIRMÂÎTRÎ RAMSÎSÛ II. MÎAMON.	KHÛNIRÎ-SOTPÛNIRÎ SIPHTAH MÎNEPHTAH.
BANIRÎ MÎAMON MÎNEPHTAH HOTPÛHIMÂÎT.	

This is but a romance, in which a very little history is mingled with a great deal of fable : the scribes as well as the people were acquainted with the fact that Egypt had been in danger of dissolution at the time when the Hebrews left the banks of the Nile, but they were ignorant of the details, of the precise date and of the name of the reigning Pharaoh. A certain similarity in sound suggested to them the idea of assimilating the prince whom the Chroniclers called Menepthes or Amenepthes with Amenôthes, *i.e.* Amenophis III. ; and they gave to the Pharaoh of the XIXth dynasty the minister who had served under a king of the XVIIIth : they metamorphosed at the same time the Hebrews into lepers allied with the Shepherds. From this strange combination there resulted a narrative which at once fell in with the tastes of the lovers of the marvellous, and was a sufficient substitute for the truth which had long since been forgotten. As in the case of the Egyptians of the Greek period, we can see only through a fog what took place after the deaths of Mînephtah and Seti II. We know only for certain that the chiefs of the nomes were in perpetual strife with each other, and that a foreign power was dominant in the country as in the time of Apôphis. The days of the empire would have

---

Harmhabî himself belonged to the XVIIIth dynasty, for he modelled the form of his cartouches on those of the Ahmesside Pharaohs : the XIXth dynasty began only, in all probability, with Ramses I., but the course of the history has compelled me to separate Harmhabî from his predecessors. Not knowing the length of the reigns, we cannot determine the total duration of the dynasty : we shall not, however, be far wrong in assigning to it a length of 130 years or thereabouts, *i.e.* from 1350 to somewhere near 1220 B.C.

been numbered if a deliverer had not promptly made his appearance. The direct line of Ramses II. was extinct, but his innumerable sons by innumerable concubines had left a posterity out of which some at least might have the requisite ability and zeal, if not to save the empire, at least to lengthen its duration, and once more give to Thebes days of glorious prosperity. Egypt had set out some five centuries before this for the conquest of the world, and fortune had at first smiled upon her enterprise. Thûtmosis I., Thûtmosis III., and the several Pharaohs bearing the name of Amenôthes had marched with their armies from the upper waters of the Nile to the banks of the Euphrates, and no power had been able to withstand them. New nations, however, soon rose up to oppose her, and the Hittites in Asia and the Libyans of the Sudan together curbed her ambition. Neither the triumphs of Ramses II. nor the victory of Mînephtah had been able to restore her prestige, or the lands of which her rivals had robbed her beyond her ancient frontier. Now her own territory itself was threatened, and her own well-being was in question; she was compelled to consider, not how to rule other tribes, great or small, but how to keep her own possessions intact and independent: in short, her very existence was at stake.

THE CLOSE OF THE THEBAN EMPIRE

RAMSES III.—THE THEBAN CITY UNDER THE RAMESSIDES—MANNERS AND CUSTOMS.

Nakhtûsît and Ramses III.: the decline of the military spirit in Egypt—The reorganisation of the army and fleet by Ramses—The second Libyan invasion—The Asiatic peoples, the Pulasati, the Zakkala, and the Tyrseni: their incursions into Syria and their defeat—The campaign of the year XI. and the fall of the Libyan kingdom—Cruising on the Red Sea—The buildings at Medinet-Habû—The conspiracy of Pentaûîrît—The mummy of Ramses III.

The sons and immediate successors of Ramses III.—Thebes and the Egyptian population: the transformation of the people and of the great lords: the feudal system from being military becomes religious—The wealth of precious metals, jewellery, furniture, costume—Literary education, and the influence of the Semitic language on the Egyptian: romantic stories, the historical novel, fables, caricatures and satires, collections of maxims and moral dialogues, love-poems.

THE BATTLE OF THE RATS AND CATS, A PARODY OF THE EGYPTIAN WARS.[1]

CHAPTER III

THE CLOSE OF THE THEBAN EMPIRE

Ramses III.—The Theban city under the Ramessides—Manners and customs.

AS in a former crisis, Egypt once more owed her salvation to a scion of the old Theban race. A descendant of Seti I. or Ramses II., named Nakhtûsît, rallied round him the forces of the southern nomes, and succeeded, though not without difficulty, in dispossessing the Syrian Arisû. "When he arose, he was like Sûtkhû, providing for all the

[1] Drawn by Faucher-Gudin, from a facsimile in Lepsius. The vignette, executed by Faucher-Gudin from a photograph by Lanzone, represents a functionary of the Theban necropolis.

necessities of the country which, for feebleness, could not stand, killing the rebels which were in the Delta, purifying the great throne of Egypt; he was regent of the two lands in the place of Tûmû, setting himself to reorganise that which had been overthrown, to such good purpose, that each one recognised as brethren those who had been separated from him as by a wall for so long a time, strengthening the temples by pious gifts, so that the traditional rites could be celebrated at the divine cycles."[1] Many were the difficulties that he had to encounter before he could restore to his country that peace and wealth which she had enjoyed under the long reign of Sesostris. It seems probable that his advancing years made him feel unequal to the task, or that he desired to guard against the possibility of disturbances in the event of his sudden death; at all events, he associated with himself on the throne his eldest son Ramses—not, however, as a Pharaoh who had full rights to the crown, like the coadjutors of the Amenemhâîts and Ûsirtasens, but as a prince invested with extraordinary powers, after the example of the sons of the Pharaohs Thûtmosis and Seti I. Ramses recalls with pride, towards the close of his life, how his father "had promoted him to the dignity of heir-presumptive to the throne of Sibû," and how he had been acclaimed as "the supreme head of Qimît for the administration of the whole earth united

[1] The exact relationship between Nakhtûsît and Ramses II. is not known; he was probably the grandson or great-grandson of that sovereign, though Ed. Meyer thinks he was perhaps the son of Seti II. The name should be read either Nakhîtsît, with the singular of the first word composing it, or Nakhîtûsît, Nakhtûsît, with the plural, as in the analogous name of the king of the XXXth dynasty, Nectanebo.

NAKHTÛSÎT AND RAMSES III.

together."[1] This constituted the rise of a new dynasty on the ruins of the old—the last, however, which was able to retain the supremacy of Egypt over the Oriental world.

We are unable to ascertain how long this double reign lasted. Nakhtûsît, fully occupied by enemies within the country, had no leisure either to build or to restore any monuments;[2] on his death, as no tomb had been prepared for him, his mummy was buried in that of the usurper Siphtah and the Queen Tausirît. He was soon forgotten, and but few traces of his services survived him; his name was subsequently removed from the official list of the kings, while others not so deserving as he —as, for instance, Siphtah-Mînephtah and Amenmesis —were honourably inscribed in it. The memory of his son overshadowed his own, and the series of the legitimate kings who formed the XXth dynasty did not include him. Ramses III. took for his hero his namesake, Ramses the Great, and endeavoured

NAKHTÛSÎT.

[1] The only certain monument that we as yet possess of this double reign is a large stele cut on the rock behind Medinet-Habû.

[2] Wiedemann attributes to him the construction of one of the doors of the temple of Mût at Karnak; it would appear that there is a confusion in his notes between the prenomen of this sovereign and that of Seti II., who actually did decorate one of the doorways of that temple. Nakhûsît must have also worked on the temple of Phtah at Memphis. His cartouche is met with on a statue originally dedicated by a Pharaoh of the XIIth dynasty, discovered at Tell-Nebêsheh.

to rival him in everything. This spirit of imitation was at times the means of leading him to commit somewhat puerile acts, as, for example, when he copied certain triumphal inscriptions word for word, merely changing the dates and the cartouches,[1] or when he assumed the prenomen of Usirmârî, and distributed among his male children the names and dignities of the sons of Sesostris. We see, moreover, at his court another high priest of Phtah at Memphis bearing the name of Khâmoîsît, and Marîtûmû, another supreme pontiff of Râ in Heliopolis. However, this ambition to resemble his ancestor at once instigated him to noble deeds, and gave him the necessary determination to accomplish them. He began by restoring order in the administration of affairs; " he established truth, crushed error, purified the temple from all crime," and made his authority felt not only in the length and breadth of the Nile valley, but in what was still left of the Asiatic provinces. The disturbances of the preceding years had weakened the prestige of Amon-Râ, and the king's supremacy would have been seriously endangered, had any one arisen in Syria of sufficient energy to take advantage of the existing state of affairs. But since the death of Khâtusaru, the power of the Khâti had considerably declined, and they retained their position merely through their former prestige; they were in as much need of peace, or even more so, than the Egyptians, for the same discords which had harassed the reigns of Seti II. and his successors had doubtless brought

[1] Thus the great decree of Phtah-Totûnen, carved by Ramses II. in the year XXXV. on the rocks of Abu Simbel, was copied by Ramses III. at Medinet-Habû in the year XII.

trouble to their own sovereigns. They had made no serious efforts to extend their dominion over any of those countries which had been the objects of the cupidity of their forefathers, while the peoples of Kharû and Phœnicia, thrown back on their own resources, had not ventured to take up arms against the Pharaoh. The yoke lay lightly upon them, and in no way hampered their internal liberty; they governed as they liked, they exchanged one prince or chief for another, they waged petty wars as of old, without, as a rule, exposing themselves to interference from the Egyptian troops occupying the country, or from the "royal messengers." These vassal provinces had probably ceased to pay tribute, or had done so irregularly, during the years of anarchy following the death of Siphtah, but they had taken no concerted action, nor attempted any revolt, so that when Ramses III. ascended the throne he was spared the trouble of reconquering them. He had merely to claim allegiance to have it at once rendered him—an allegiance which included the populations in the neighbourhood of Qodshû and on the banks of the Nahr el-Kelb. The empire, which had threatened to fall to pieces amid the civil wars, and which would indeed have succumbed had they continued a few years longer, again revived now that an energetic prince had been found to resume the direction of affairs, and to weld together those elements which had been on the point of disintegration.

One state alone appeared to regret the revival of the Imperial power; this was the kingdom of Libya. It had continued to increase in size since the days of Mînephtah, and its population had been swelled by the annexation of several strange tribes inhabiting the vast area of the Sahara. One of these, the Mashaûasha, acquired the ascendency among these desert races owing to their numbers and valour, and together with the other tribes— the Sabati, the Kaiakasha, the Shaîû, the Hasa, the Bikana, and the Qahaka[1]—formed a confederacy, which now threatened Egypt on the west. This federation was conducted by Didi, Mashaknû, and Mâraiû, all children of that Mâraîû who had led the first Libyan invasion, and also by Zamarû and Zaûtmarû, two princes of less important tribes.[2] Their combined forces had attacked Egypt for the second time during the years of anarchy, and had gained possession one after another of all the towns in the west of the Delta, from the neighbourhood of Memphis to the town of Qarbîna: the Canopic branch of the Nile now formed the limit of their dominion, and they often crossed it to devastate the central provinces.[3] Nakhtûsîti had been unable to drive them out, and Ramses had not ventured on the task immediately after his accession. The military institutions of the country had

---

[1] This enumeration is furnished by the summary of the campaigns of Ramses III. in *The Great Harris Papyrus*. The Sabati of this text are probably identical with the people of the Sapudiu or Spudi (Asbytæ), mentioned on one of the pylons of Medinet-Habû.

[2] The relationship is nowhere stated, but it is thought to be probable from the names of Didi and Mâraiû, repeated in both series of inscriptions.

[3] The town of Qarbîna has been identified with the Canopus of the Greeks, and also with the modern Korbani; and the district of Gautu, which adjoined it, with the territory of the modern town of Edkô. Spiegelberg throws doubt on the identification of Qarbu or Qarbîna, with Canopus. Révillout prefers to connect Qarbîna with Heracleopolis Parva in Lower Egypt.

become totally disorganised after the death of Mînephtah, and that part of the community responsible for furnishing the army with recruits had been so weakened by the late troubles, that they were in a worse condition than before the first Libyan invasion. The losses they had suffered since Egypt began its foreign conquests had not been repaired by the introduction of fresh elements, and the hope of spoil was now insufficient to induce members of the upper classes to enter the army. There was no difficulty in filling the ranks from the fellahin, but the middle class and the aristocracy, accustomed to ease and wealth, no longer came forward in large numbers, and disdained the military profession. It was the fashion in the schools to contrast the calling of a scribe with that of a foot-soldier or a charioteer, and to make as merry over the discomforts of a military occupation as it had formerly been the fashion to extol its glory and profitableness. These scholastic exercises represented the future officer dragged as a child to the barracks, "the side-lock over his ear.—He is beaten and his sides are covered with scars,—he is beaten and his two eyebrows are marked with wounds,—he is beaten and his head is broken by a badly aimed blow; he is stretched on the ground" for the slightest fault, "and blows fall on him as on a papyrus,—and he is broken by the stick." His education finished, he is sent away to a distance, to Syria or Ethiopia, and fresh troubles overtake him. "His victuals and his supply of water are about his neck like the burden of an ass,—and his neck and throat suffer like those of an ass,—so that the joints of his spine are broken.—He drinks putrid water, keeping perpetual guard the while." His fatigues soon tell upon his health and vigour: "Should he reach the enemy,—he is like a bird which trembles.—Should he return to Egypt,—he is like a piece of old worm-eaten wood.—He is sick and must lie down, he is carried on an ass,—while thieves steal his linen,—and his slaves escape." The charioteer is not spared either. He, doubtless, has a moment of vain-glory and of flattered vanity when he receives, according to regulations, a new chariot and two horses, with which he drives at a gallop before his parents and his fellow-villagers; but once having joined his regiment, he is perhaps worse off than the foot-soldier. "He is thrown to the ground among thorns:—a scorpion wounds him in the foot, and his heel is pierced by its sting.—When his kit is examined,—his misery is at its height." No sooner has the fact been notified that his arms are in a bad condition, or that some article has disappeared, than "he is stretched on the ground—and overpowered with blows from a stick." This decline of the warlike spirit in all classes of society had entailed serious modifications in the organisation of both army and navy. The native element no longer predominated in most battalions and on the majority of vessels, as it had done under the XVIIIth dynasty; it still furnished those formidable companies of archers—the terror of both Africans and Asiatics—and also the most important part, if not the whole, of the chariotry, but the main body of the infantry was composed almost exclusively of mercenaries, particularly of the Shardana and the Qahaka. Ramses began his reforms by rebuilding the fleet, which, in a country like Egypt, was always an artificial creation, liable to fall into decay, unless a strong and persistent effort were made to keep it in an efficient condition. Shipbuilding had made considerable progress in the last few centuries, perhaps from the impulse received through Phœnicia, and the vessels turned out of the dockyards were far superior to those constructed under Hâtshopsîtû. The general outlines of the hull remained the same, but the stem and stern were finer, and not so high out of the water; the bow ended, moreover, in a lion's head of metal, which rose above the cut-water. A wooden structure running between the forecastle and quarter-deck protected the rowers during the fight, their heads alone being exposed. The mast had only one curved yard, to which the sail was fastened; this was run up from the deck by halyards when the sailors wanted to make sail, and thus differed from the Egyptian arrangement, where the sail was fastened to a fixed upper yard. At least half of the crews consisted of Libyan prisoners, who were branded with a hot iron like cattle, to prevent desertion; the remaining half was drawn from the Syrian or Asiatic coast, or else were natives of Egypt. In order to bring the army into better condition, Ramses revived the system of classes, which empowered him to compel all Egyptians of unmixed race to take personal service, while he hired mercenaries from Libya, Phœnicia, Asia Minor, and wherever he could get them, and divided them into regular regiments, according to their extraction and the arms that they bore. In the field, the archers always headed the column, to meet the advance of the foe with their arrows; they were followed by the Egyptian lancers—the Shardana and the

Tyrseni with their short spears and heavy bronze swords—while a corps of veterans, armed with heavy maces, brought up the rear.[1] In an engagement, these various troops formed three lines of infantry disposed one behind the other—the light brigade in front to engage the adversary, the swordsmen and lancers who were to come into close quarters with the foe, and the mace-bearers in reserve, ready to advance on any threatened point, or to await the critical moment when their intervention would decide the victory: as in the times of Thûtmosis and Ramses II. the chariotry covered the two wings.

It was well for Ramses that on ascending the throne he had devoted himself to the task of recruiting the Egyptian army, and of personally and carefully superintending the instruction and equipment of his men; for it was thanks to these precautions that, when the confederated Libyans attacked the country about the Vth year of his reign, he was enabled to repulse them with complete success. "Didi, Mashaknû, Maraîû, together with Zamarû and Zaûtmarû, had strongly urged them to attack Egypt and to carry fire before them from one end of it to the other."—"Their warriors confided to each other in their counsels, and their hearts were full: 'We will be drunk!' and their princes said within their breasts: 'We will fill our hearts with violence!' But their plans were overthrown, thwarted, broken against the heart of the god, and the prayer of their chief, which their lips repeated, was

[1] This is the order of march represented during the Syrian campaign, as gathered from the arrangement observed in the pictures at Medinet-Habu.

not granted by the god." They met the Egyptians at a place called "Ramsisû-Khasfi-Timihû" ("Ramses repulses the Timihû"), but their attack was broken by the latter, who were ably led and displayed considerable valour. "They bleated like goats surprised by a bull who stamps its foot, who pushes forward its horn and shakes the mountains, charging whoever seeks to annoy it." They fled afar, howling with fear, and many of them, in endeavouring to escape their pursuers, perished in the canals. "It is, said they, the breaking of our spines which threatens us in the land of Egypt, and its lord destroys our souls for ever and ever. Woe be upon them! for they have seen their dances changed into carnage, Sokhît is behind them, fear weighs upon them. 'We march no longer upon roads where we can walk, but we run across fields, all the fields! And their soldiers did not even need to measure arms with us in the struggle! Pharaoh alone was our destruction, a fire against us every time that he willed it, and no sooner did we approach than the flame curled round us, and no water could quench it on us.'" The victory was a brilliant one; the victors counted 12,535 of the enemy killed,[1] and many more who surrendered at discretion. The latter were formed into a brigade, and were distributed throughout the valley of the Nile in military settlements. They submitted to their fate with that resignation which we know to have been a characteristic of the vanquished at that date. They

---

[1] The number of the dead is calculated from that of the hands and phalli brought in by the soldiers after the victory, the heaps of which are represented at Medinet-Habu.

regarded their defeat as a judgment from God against which there was no appeal; when their fate had been once pronounced, nothing remained to the condemned except to submit to it humbly, and to accommodate themselves to the master to whom they were now bound by a decree from on high. The prisoners of one day became on the next the devoted soldiers of the prince against whom they had formerly fought resolutely, and they were employed against their own tribes, their employers having no fear of their deserting to the other side during the engagement. They were lodged in the barracks at Thebes, or in the provinces under the feudal lords and governors of the Pharaoh, and were encouraged to retain their savage customs and warlike spirit. They intermarried either with the fellahîn or with women of their own tribes, and were reinforced at intervals by fresh prisoners or volunteers. Drafted principally into the Delta and the cities of Middle Egypt, they thus ended by constituting a semi-foreign population, destined by nature and training to the calling of arms, and forming a sort of warrior caste, differing widely from the militia of former times, and known for many generations by their national name of Mashaûasha. As early as the XIIth dynasty, the Pharaohs had, in a similar way, imported the Mazaîû from Nubia, and had used them as a military police; Ramses III. now resolved to naturalise the Libyans for much the same purpose. His victory did not bear the immediate fruits that we might have expected from his own account of it; the memory of the exploits of Ramses II. haunted him, and, stimulated by the example of his ancestor at Qodshû, he doubtless desired to have the sole credit of the victory over the Libyans. He certainly did overcome their kings, and arrested their invasion; we may go so far as to allow that he wrested from them the provinces which they had occupied on the left bank of the Canopic branch, from Marea to the Natron Lakes, but he did not conquer them, and their power still remained as formidable as ever. He had gained a respite at the point of the sword, but he had not delivered Egypt from their future attacks.

He might perhaps have been tempted to follow up his success and assume the offensive, had not affairs in Asia at this juncture demanded the whole of his atten-

ONE OF THE LIBYAN CHIEFS VANQUISHED BY RAMSES III.[1]

tion. The movement of great masses of European tribes in a southerly and easterly direction was beginning to be felt by the inhabitants of the Balkans, who were forced to set out in a double stream of emigration—one crossing the Bosphorus and the Propontis towards the centre of Asia Minor, while the other made for what was later known as Greece Proper, by way of the passes over Olympus and Pindus. The nations who had hitherto inhabited these regions, now found themselves thrust forward by the pressure of invading hordes, and were constrained to move towards the south and east by every avenue which presented itself. It was probably the irruption of the Phrygians into the high table-land which

[1] Drawn by Faucher-Gudin, from Champollion.

gave rise to the general exodus of these various nations—
the Pulasati, the Zakkala, the Shagalasha, the Danauna,
and the Ûashasha—some of whom had already made their
way into Syria and taken part in campaigns there, while
others had as yet never measured strength with the
Egyptians. The main body of these migrating tribes
chose the overland route, keeping within easy distance
of the coast, from Pamphylia as far as the confines of
Naharaim. They were accompanied by their families, who

THE WAGGONS OF THE PULASATI AND THEIR CONFEDERATES.[1]

must have been mercilessly jolted in the ox-drawn square
waggons with solid wheels in which they travelled. The
body of the vehicle was built either of roughly squared
planks, or else of something resembling wicker-work.
The round axletree was kept in its place by means of
a rude pin, and four oxen were harnessed abreast to the
whole structure. The children wore no clothes, and had,
for the most part, their hair tied into a tuft on the top
of their heads; the women affected a closely fitting cap,
and were wrapped in large blue or red garments drawn

[1] Drawn by Faucher-Gudin, from Champollion.

ASIATIC TRIBES

close to the body.[1] The men's attire varied according to the tribe to which they belonged. The Pulasati undoubtedly held the chief place; they were both soldiers and sailors, and we must recognise in them the foremost of those tribes known to the Greeks of classical times as the Carians, who infested the coasts of Asia Minor as well as those of Greece and the Ægean islands.[2] Crete was at this time the seat of a maritime empire, whose chiefs were perpetually cruising the seas and harassing the civilized states of the Eastern Mediterranean. These sea-rovers had grown wealthy through piracy, and contact with the merchants of Syria and Egypt had awakened in them a taste for a certain luxury and refinement, of which we find no traces in the remains of their civilization anterior to this period. Some of the symbols in the inscriptions found on their monuments recall certain of the Egyptian characters, while others present an original

PULASATI.[3]

---

[1] These details are taken from the battle-scenes at Medinet-Habu.

[2] The Pulasati have been connected with the Philistines by Champollion, and subsequently by the early English Egyptologists, who thought they recognised in them the inhabitants of the Shephelah. Chabas was the first to identify them with the Pelasgi; Unger and Brugsch prefer to attribute to them a Libyan origin, but the latter finally returns to the Pelasgic and Philistine hypothesis. They were without doubt the Philistines, but in their migratory state, before they settled on the coast of Palestine.

[3] Drawn by Faucher-Gudin, from a photograph by Beato.

aspect and seem to be of Ægean origin. We find in them, arranged in juxtaposition, signs representing flowers, birds, fish, quadrupeds of various kinds, members of the human body, and boats and household implements. From the little which is known of this script we are inclined to derive it from a similar source to that which has furnished those we meet with in several parts of Asia Minor and Northern Syria. It would appear that in ancient times, somewhere in the centre of the Peninsula—but under what influence or during what period we know not—a syllabary was developed, of which varieties were handed on from tribe to tribe, spreading on the one side to the Hittites, Cilicians, and the peoples on the borders of Syria and Egypt, and on the other to the Trojans, to the people of the Cyclades, and into Crete and Greece. It is easy to distinguish the Pulasati by the felt helmet which they wore fastened under the chin by two straps and surmounted by a crest of feathers. The upper part of their bodies was covered by bands of leather or some thick material, below which hung a simple loin-cloth, while their feet were bare or shod with short sandals. They carried each a round buckler with two handles, and the stout bronze sword common to the northern races, suspended by a cross belt passing over the left shoulder, and were further armed with two daggers and two javelins. They hurled the latter from a short distance while attacking, and then drawing their sword or daggers, fell upon the enemy; we find among them a few chariots of the Hittite type, each manned by a driver and two fighting men. The Tyrseni appear to have been the most numerous after the Pulasati, next to whom came the Zakkala. The latter are thought to have been a branch of the Siculo-Pelasgi whom Greek tradition represents as scattered at this period among the Cyclades and along the coast of the Hellespont;[1] they wore a casque surmounted with plumes like that of the Pulasati. The Tyrseni may be distinguished by their feathered head-dress, but the Shagalasha affected a long ample woollen cap falling on the neck behind, an article of apparel which is still worn by the sailors of the Archipelago; otherwise they were equipped in much the same manner as their allies. The other members of the confederation, the Shardana, the Dananna, and the Uashasha, each furnished an inconsiderable contingent, and, taken all together, formed but a small item of the united force.[2] Their fleet sailed along the coast and kept within sight of the force on land. The squadrons depicted on the monuments are without doubt those of the two peoples, the Pulasati and Zakkala. Their ships resembled in many respects those of Egypt, except in the fact that they had no cut-water. The bow and stern rose up straight like the neck of a goose or swan; two structures for fighting purposes were erected above the deck, while a rail running round the sides of

[1] The Zakkara, or Zakkala, have been identified with the Teucrians by Lauth, Chabas, and Fr. Lenormant, with the Zygritæ of Libya by Unger and Brugsch, who subsequently returned to the Teucrian hypothesis; W. Max Müller regards them as an Asiatic nation probably of the Lydian family. The identification with the Siculo-Pelasgi of the Ægean Sea was proposed by Maspero.

[2] The form of the word shows that it is of Asiatic origin, Uasasos, Uassos, which refers us to Caria or Lycia.

the vessel protected the bodies of the rowers. An upper yard curved in shape hung from the single mast, which terminated in a top for the look-out during a battle. The upper yard was not made to lower, and the top-men managed the sail in the same manner as the Egyptian sailors. The resemblance between this fleet and that of Ramses is easily explained. The dwellers on the Ægean,

A SHAGALASHA CHIEF.[1]

owing to the knowledge they had acquired of the Phœnician galleys, which were accustomed to cruise annually in their waters, became experts in shipbuilding. They copied the lines of the Phœnician craft, imitated the rigging, and learned to manœuvre their vessels so well, both on ordinary occasions and in a battle, that they could now oppose to the skilled eastern navigators ships as well fitted out and commanded by captains as experienced as those of Egypt or Asia.

[1] Drawn by Faucher-Gudin, from a photograph by Petrie.

ASIATIC INCURSIONS

There had been a general movement among all these peoples at the very time when Ramses was repelling the attack of the Libyans; "the isles had quivered, and had vomited forth their people at once."[1] They were subjected to one of those irresistible impulses such as had driven the Shepherds into Egypt; or again, in later times, had carried away the Cimmerians and the Scyths to the pillage of Asia Minor: "no country could hold out against their arms, neither Khâti, nor Qodi, nor Carchemish, nor Arvad, nor Alasia, without being brought to nothing." The ancient kingdoms of Sapalulu and Khâtusaru, already tottering, crumbled to pieces under the shock, and were broken up into their primitive elements. The barbarians, unable to carry the towns by assault, and too impatient to resort to a lengthened siege, spread over the valley of the Orontes, burning and devastating the country everywhere. Having reached the frontiers of the empire, in the country of the Amorites, they came to a halt, and constructing an entrenched camp, installed within it their women and the booty they had acquired. Some of their predatory bands, having ravaged the Bekâa, ended by attacking the subjects of the Pharaoh himself, and their chiefs dreamed of an invasion of Egypt. Ramses, informed of their design by the despatches of his officers and vassals, resolved to prevent its accomplishment. He summoned his troops together, both indigenous and mercenary, in

[1] This campaign is mentioned in the inscription of Medinet-Habu. We find some information about the war in the *Great Harris Papyrus*, also in the inscription of Medinet-Habu which describes the campaign of the year V., and in other shorter texts of the same temple.

his own person looked after their armament and commissariat, and in the VIIIth year of his reign crossed the frontier near Zalu. He advanced by forced marches to meet the enemy, whom he encountered somewhere in Southern Syria, on the borders of the Shephelah,[1] and after a stubbornly contested campaign obtained the victory. He carried off from the field, in addition to the treasures of the confederate tribes, some of the chariots which had been used for the transport of their families. The survivors made their way hastily to the north-west, in the direction of the sea, in order to receive the support of their navy, but the king followed them step by step. It is recorded that he occupied himself with lion-hunting *en route* after the example of the victors of the XVIIIth dynasty, and that he killed three of these animals in the long grass on one occasion on the banks of some river. He rejoined his ships, probably at Jaffa, and made straight for the enemy. The latter were encamped on the level shore, at the head of a bay wide enough to offer to their ships a commodious space for naval evolutions—possibly the mouth of the Belos, in the neighbourhood of Magadil. The king drove their foot-soldiers into the water at the

[1] No site is given for these battles. E. de Rougé placed the theatre of war in Syria, and his opinion was accepted by Brugsch. Chabas referred it to the mouth of the Nile near Pelusium, and his authority has prevailed up to the present. The remarks of W. Max Muller have brought me back to the opinion of the earlier Egyptologists; but I differ from him in looking for the locality further south, and not to the mouth of Nahr el-Kelb as the site of the naval battle. It seems to me that the fact that the Zakkala were prisoners at Dor, and the Pulasati in the Shephelah, is enough to assign the campaign to the regions I have mentioned in the text.

same moment that his admirals attacked the combined fleet of the Pulasati and Zakkala. Some of the Ægean galleys were capsized and sank when the Egyptian vessels rammed them with their sharp stems, and the crews, in endeavouring to escape to land by swimming, were picked

THE ARMY OF RAMSES III. ON THE MARCH, AND THE LION-HUNT.[1]

off by the arrows of the archers of the guard who were commanded by Ramses and his sons; they perished in the waves, or only escaped through the compassion of the victors. "I had fortified," said the Pharaoh, "my frontier at Zahi; I had drawn up before these people my generals, my provincial governors, the vassal princes, and the best of my soldiers. The mouths of the river seemed to be a

[1] Drawn by Faucher-Gudin, from a photograph by Beato.

mighty rampart of galleys, barques, and vessels of all kinds, equipped from the bow to the stern with valiant armed men. The infantry, the flower of Egypt, were as lions roaring on the mountains; the charioteers, selected from among the most rapid warriors, had for their captains only officers confident in themselves; the horses quivered in all their limbs, and were burning to trample the nations underfoot. As for me, I was like the warlike Montû: I stood up before them and they saw the vigour of my arms. I, King Ramses, I was as a hero who is conscious of his valour, and who stretches his hands over the people in the day of battle. Those who have violated my frontier will never more garner harvests from this earth: the period of their soul has been fixed for ever. My forces were drawn up before them on the 'Very Green,' a devouring flame approached them at the river mouth, annihilation embraced them on every side. Those who were on the strand I laid low on the seashore, slaughtered like victims of the butcher. I made their vessels to capsize, and their riches fell into the sea.'" Those who had not fallen in the fight were caught, as it were, in the cast of a net. A rapid cruiser of the fleet carried the Egyptian standard along the coast as far as the regions of the Orontes and Saros. The land troops, on the other hand, following on the heels of the defeated enemy, pushed through Cœle-Syria, and in their first burst of zeal succeeded in reaching the plains of the Euphrates. A century had elapsed since a Pharaoh had planted his standard in this region, and the country must have seemed as novel to the soldiers of Ramses III. as to those of his predecessor Thûtmosis.

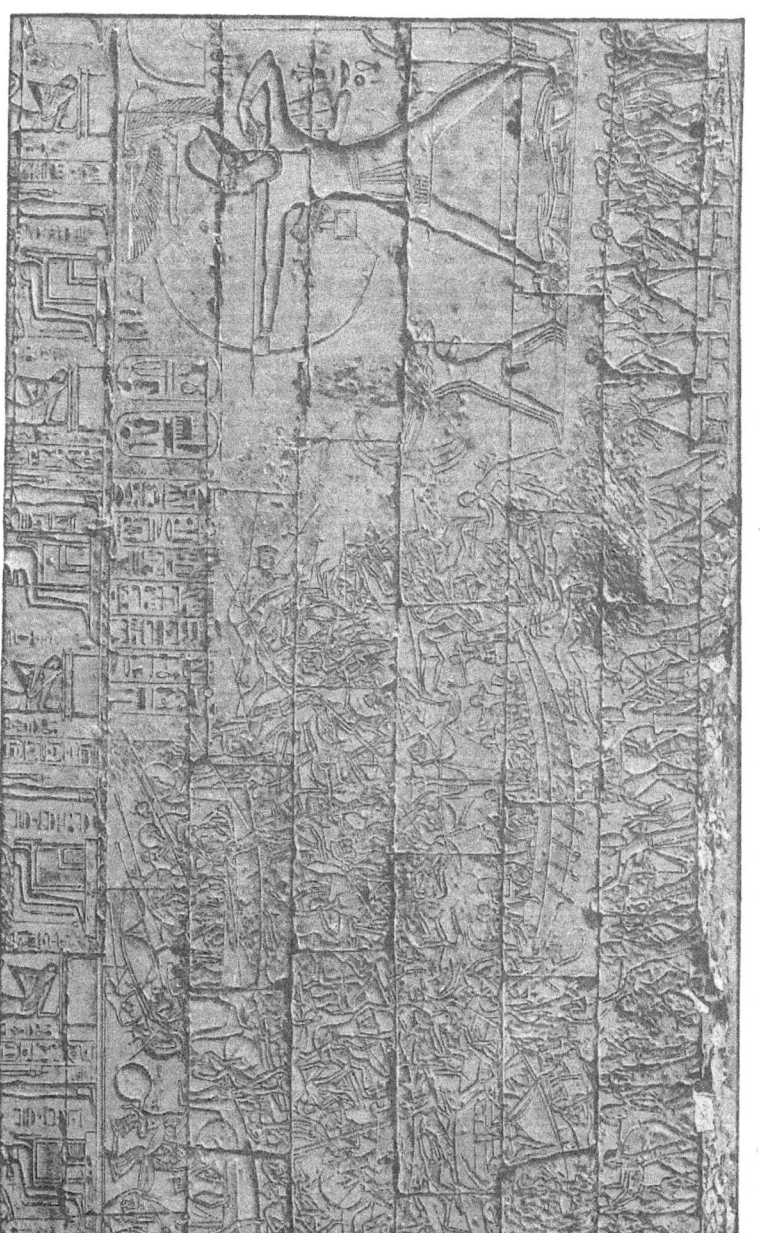

THE DEFEAT OF THE PEOPLES OF THE SEA AT MAGADÎL.

DEFEAT OF THE PEOPLES OF THE SEA   311

The Khâti were still its masters; and all enfeebled as they were by the ravages of the invading barbarians, were nevertheless not slow in preparing to resist their ancient enemies. The majority of the citadels shut their gates in the face of Ramses, who, wishing to lose no time, did not attempt to besiege them: he treated their territory with the usual severity, devastating their open towns, destroying their harvests, breaking down their fruit trees, and cutting away their forests. He was able, moreover, without arresting his march, to carry by assault several of their fortified towns, Alaza among the number, the destruction of which is represented in the scenes of his victories. The spoils were considerable, and came very opportunely to reward the soldiers or to provide funds for the erection of monuments. The last battalion of troops, however, had hardly recrossed the isthmus when Lotanû became again its own master, and Egyptian rule was once more limited to its traditional provinces of Kharû and Phœnicia. The King of the Khâti appears among the prisoners whom the Pharaoh is represented as bringing to his father Amon; Carchemish, Tunipa, Khalabu, Katna, Pabukhu, Arvad, Mitanni, Mannus, Asi, and a score of other famous towns of this period appear in the list of the subjugated nations, recalling the triumphs of Thûtmosis III. and Amenôthes II. Ramses did not allow himself to be deceived into thinking that his success was final. He accepted the protestations of obedience which were spontaneously offered him, but he undertook no further expedition of importance either to restrain or to provoke his enemies: the restricted rule which satisfied his exemplar Ramses II. ought, he thought, to be sufficient for his own ambition.

Egypt breathed freely once more on the announcement of the victory; henceforward she was "as a bed without anguish." "Let each woman now go to and fro according to her will," cried the sovereign, in describing the campaign, "her ornaments upon her, and directing her steps to any place she likes!" And in order to provide still further guarantees of public security, he converted his Asiatic captives, as he previously had his African prisoners, into a bulwark against the barbarians, and a safeguard of the frontier. The war must, doubtless, have decimated Southern Syria; and he planted along its coast what remained of the defeated tribes—the Philistines in the Shephelah, and the Zakkala on the borders of the great oak forest stretching from Carmel to Dor.[1] Watch-towers were erected for the supervision of this region, and for rallying-points in case of internal revolts or attacks from without. One of these, the Migdol of Ramses III., was erected, not far from the scene of the decisive battle, on the spot where the spoils had been divided. This living barrier, so to speak, stood between the Nile valley and the dangers which threatened it from Asia, and it was not long before its value was put to the proof. The Libyans, who had been saved from destruction by the diversion created in their favour on the eastern side of the empire, having now recovered their courage, set about collecting

---

[1] It is in this region that we find henceforward the Hebrews in contact with the Philistines: at the end of the XXIst Egyptian dynasty a scribe makes Dor a town of the Zakkala.

their hordes together for a fresh invasion. They returned to the attack in the XIth year of Ramses, under the leadership of Kapur, a prince of the Mashauasha.[1] "Their soul had said to them for the second time that they would end

THE CAPTIVE CHIEFS OF RAMSES III. AT MEDINET-HABU.[2]

their lives in the nomes of Egypt, that they would till its valleys and its plains as their own land." The issue did

[1] The second campaign against the Libyans is known to us from the inscriptions of the year XI. at Medinet-Habu.
[2] Drawn by Boudier, from a photograph by Beato. The first prisoner on the left is the Prince of the Khâti (cf. the cut on p. 318 of the present work), the second is the Prince of the Amâuru [Amorites], the third the Prince of the Zakkala, the fourth that of the Shardana, the fifth that of the Shakalasha (see the cut on p. 304 of this work), and the sixth that of the Tursha [Tyrseni].

not correspond with their intentions. "Death fell upon them within Egypt, for they had hastened with their feet to the furnace which consumes corruption, under the fire of the valour of the king who rages like Baal from the heights of heaven. All his limbs are invested with victorious strength; with his right hand he lays hold of the multitudes, his left extends to those who are against him, like a cloud of arrows directed upon them to destroy them, and his sword cuts like that of Montû. Kapur, who had come to demand homage, blind with fear, threw down his arms, and his troops did the same. He sent up to heaven a suppliant cry, and his son [Mashashalu] arrested his foot and his hand; for, behold, there rises beside him the god who knows what he has in his heart: His Majesty falls upon their heads as a mountain of granite and crushes them, the earth drinks up their blood as if it had been water . . .; their army was slaughtered, slaughtered their soldiers," near a fortress situated on the borders of the desert called the "Castle of Ûsirmarî-Miamou." They were seized, "they were stricken, their arms bound, like geese piled up in the bottom of a boat, under the feet of His Majesty."[1] The fugitives were pursued at the sword's point from the *Castle of Ûsirmarî-Miamon* to the *Castle of the Sands*, a distance of over thirty miles.[2] Two thousand

---

[1] The name of the son of Kapur, Mashashalu, Masesyla, which is wanting in this inscription, is supplied from a parallel inscription.

[2] The *Castle of Ûsirmarî-Miamon* was "on the mountain of the horn of the world," which induces me to believe that we must seek its site on the borders of the Libyan desert. The royal title entering into its name being liable to change with every reign, it is possible that we have an earlier reference to this stronghold in a mutilated passage of the Athribis

RAMSES III. BINDS THE CHIEFS OF THE LIBYANS.
From a photograph by Beato.

and seventy-five Libyans were left upon the ground that day, two thousand and fifty-two perished in other engagements, while two thousand and thirty-two, both male and female, were made prisoners. These were almost irreparable losses for a people of necessarily small numbers, and if we add the number of those who had succumbed in the disaster of six years before, we can readily realise how discouraged the invaders must have been, and how little likely they were to try the fortune of war once more. Their power dwindled and vanished almost as quickly as it had arisen; the provisional cohesion given to their forces by a few ambitious chiefs broke up after their repeated defeats, and the rudiments of an empire which had struck terror into the Pharaohs, resolved itself into its primitive elements, a number of tribes scattered over the desert. They were driven back beyond the Libyan mountains; fortresses guarded the routes they had previously followed, and they were obliged henceforward to renounce any hope of an invasion *en masse*, and to content themselves with a few raiding expeditions into the fertile plain of the Delta, where they had formerly found a transitory halting-place. Counter-raids organised by the local troops or by the mercenaries who garrisoned the principal towns in the neighbourhood of Memphis—Hermopolis and Thinis[1]—

Stele, which relates to the campaigns of Mînephtah; it must have commanded one of the most frequented routes leading to the oasis of Amon.

[1] *The Great Harris Papyrus* speaks of fortifications erected in the towns of Anhûri-Shû, possibly Thinis, and of Thot, possibly Hermopolis, in order to repel the tribes of the Tihonu who were ceaselessly harassing the frontier.

inflicted punishment upon them when they became too audacious. Their tribes, henceforward, as far as Egypt was concerned, formed a kind of reserve from which the Pharaoh could raise soldiers every year, and draw sufficient materials to bring his army up to fighting strength when internal revolt or an invasion from without called for military activity.

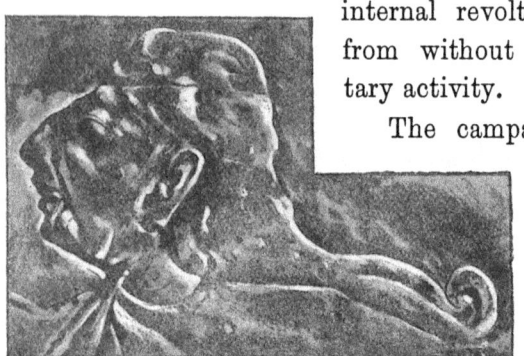

THE PRINCE OF THE KHÂTI.[1]

The campaign of the XIth year brought to an end the great military expeditions of Ramses III. Henceforward he never took the lead in any more serious military enterprise than that of repressing the Bedawin of Seîr for acts of brigandage,[2] or the Ethiopians for some similar reason. He confined his attention to the maintenance of commercial and industrial relations with manufacturing countries, and with the markets of Asia and Africa. He strengthened the garrisons of Sinai, and encouraged the working of the ancient mines in that region. He sent a colony of quarrymen and of smelters to the land of Atika, in order to work the veins of silver which were alleged to exist there.[3] He

[1] Drawn by Faucher-Gudin, from a photograph taken at Medinet-Habu.
[2] The Sâîrû of the Egyptian texts have been identified with the Bedawin of Seir.
[3] This is the Gebel-Ataka of our day. All this district is imperfectly

launched a fleet on the Red Sea, and sent it to the countries of fragrant spices. "The captains of the sailors were there, together with the chiefs of the *corvée* and accountants, to provide provision" for the people of the Divine Lands "from the innumerable products of Egypt; and these products were counted by myriads. Sailing through the great sea of Qodi, they arrived at Pûânît without mishap, and there collected cargoes for their galleys and ships, consisting of all the unknown marvels of Tonûtir, as well as considerable quantities of the perfumes of Pûâtîn, which they stowed on board by tens of thousands without number. The sons of the princes of Tonûtir came themselves into Qîmit with their tributes. They reached the region of Coptos safe and sound, and disembarked there in peace with their riches." It was somewhere about Sau and Tuau that the merchants and royal officers landed, following the example of the expeditions of the XIIth and XVIIIth dynasties. Here they organised caravans of asses and slaves, which taking the shortest route across the mountain—that of the valley of Rahanû—carried the precious commodities to Coptos, whence they were transferred to boats and distributed along the river. The erection of public buildings, which had been interrupted since the time of Mînephtah, began again with renewed activity. The captives in the recent victories furnished the requisite labour, while the mines, the voyages to the Somali coast, and the tributes of vassals provided the necessary money. Syria was not lost sight

explored, but we know that it contains mines and quarries some of which were worked as late as in the time of the Mameluk Sultans.

of in this resumption of peaceful occupations. The overthrow of the Khâti secured Egyptian rule in this region, and promised a long tranquillity within its borders. One temple at least was erected in the country—that of Pakanâna—where the princes of Kharû were to assemble to offer worship to the Pharaoh, and to pay each one his quota of the general tribute. The Pulasati were employed to protect the caravan routes, and a vast reservoir was erected near Aîna to provide a store of water for the irrigation of the neighbouring country. The Delta absorbed the greater part of the royal subsidies; it had suffered so much from the Libyan incursions, that the majority of the towns within it had fallen into a condition as miserable as that in which they were at the time of the expulsion of the Shepherds. Heliopolis, Bubastis, Thmuis, Amû, and Tanis still preserved some remains of the buildings which had already been erected in them by Ramses; he constructed also, at the place at present called Tel el-Yahûdîyeh, a royal palace of limestone, granite, and alabaster, of which the type is unique amongst all the structures hitherto discovered. Its walls and columns were not ornamented with the usual sculptures incised in stone, but the whole of the decorations—scenes as well as inscriptions—consisted of plaques of enamelled terra-cotta set in cement. The forms of men and animals and the lines of hieroglyphs, standing out in slight relief from a glazed and warm-coloured background, constitute an immense mosaic-work of many hues. The few remains of the work show great purity of design and an extraordinary delicacy of tone. All the knowledge of the

BEAUTY OF EGYPTIAN CERAMIC ART

Egyptian painters, and all the technical skill of their artificers in ceramic, must have been employed to compose such harmoniously balanced decorations, with their free handling of line and colour, and their thousands of rosettes, squares, stars, and buttons of varicoloured pastes.[1] The

THE COLOSSAL OSIRIAN FIGURES IN THE FIRST COURT AT MEDINET-HABU.[1]

difficulties to overcome were so appalling, that when the marvellous work was once accomplished, no subsequent

---

[1] This temple has been known since the beginning of the nineteenth century, and the Louvre is in possession of some fragments from it which came from Salt's collection; it was rediscovered in 1870, and some portions of it were transferred by Mariette to the Boulaq Museum. The remainder was destroyed by the fellahin, at the instigation of the enlightened amateurs of Cairo, and fragments of it have passed into various private collections. The decoration has been attributed to Chaldæan influence, but it is a work purely Egyptian, both in style and in technique.

[2] Drawn by Faucher-Gudin, from a photograph by Beato.

attempt was made to construct a second like it: all the remaining structures of Ramses III., whether at Memphis, in the neighbourhood of Abydos, or at Karnak, were in the conventional style of the Pharaohs. He determined, nevertheless, to give to the exterior of the Memnonium, which he built near Medinet-Habu for the worship of himself, the proportions and appearance of an Asiatic "Migdol," influenced probably by his remembrance of similar structures which he had seen during his Syrian campaign. The chapel itself is of the ordinary type, with its gigantic pylons, its courts surrounded by columns—each supporting a colossal Osirian statue—its hypostyle hall, and its mysterious cells for the deposit of spoils taken from the peoples of the sea and the cities of Asia. His tomb was concealed at a distant spot in the Biban-el-Moluk, and we see depicted on its walls the same scenes that we find in the last resting-place of Seti I. or Ramses II., and in addition to them, in a series of supplementary chambers, the arms of the sovereign, his standards, his treasure, his kitchen, and the preparation of offerings which were to be made to him. His sarcophagus, cut out of an enormous block of granite, was brought for sale to Europe at the beginning of this century, and Cambridge obtained possession of its cover, while the Louvre secured the receptacle itself.

These were years of profound tranquillity. The Pharaoh intended that absolute order should reign throughout his realm, and that justice should be dispensed impartially within it. There were to be no more exactions, no more crying iniquities: whoever was discovered oppressing

THE FIRST PYLON OF THE TEMPLE OF MEDINET-HABU, THE FAÇADE LOOKING INTO THE FIRST COURT.
Drawn by Faucher-Gudin, from a photograph by Beato.

the people, no matter whether he were court official or feudal lord—was instantly deprived of his functions, and replaced by an administrator of tried integrity. Ramses boasts, moreover, in an idyllic manner, of having planted trees everywhere, and of having built arbours wherein the people might sit in the shade in the open air; while women might go to and fro where they would in security, no one daring to insult them on the way. The Shardanian and Libyan mercenaries were restricted to the castles which they garrisoned, and were subjected to such a severe discipline that no one had any cause of complaint against these armed barbarians settled in the heart of Egypt. "I have," continues the king, "lifted up every miserable one out of his misfortune, I have granted life to him, I have saved him from the mighty who were oppressing him, and have secured rest for every one in his own town." The details of the description are exaggerated, but the general import of it is true. Egypt had recovered the peace and prosperity of which it had been deprived for at least half a century, that is, since the death of Mînephtah. The king, however, was not in such a happy condition as his people, and court intrigues embittered the later years of his life. One of his sons, whose name is unknown to us, but who is designated in the official records by the nickname of Pentaûîrît, formed a conspiracy against him. His mother, Tîi, who was a woman of secondary rank, took it into her head to secure the crown for him, to the detriment of the children of Queen Isît. An extensive plot was hatched in which scribes, officers of the guard, priests, and officials in high place, both natives and foreigners, were involved. A resort to the supernatural was at first attempted, and the superintendent of the Herds, a certain Panhûibaûnû, who was deeply versed in magic, undertook to cast a spell upon the Pharaoh, if he could only procure certain conjuring books of which he was not possessed. These were found to be in the royal library. He managed to introduce himself under cover of the night into the harem, where he manufactured certain waxen figures, of which some were to excite the hate of his wives against their husband, while others would cause him to waste away and finally perish. A traitor betrayed several of the conspirators, who, being subjected to the torture, informed upon others, and these at length brought the matter home to Pentaûirît and his immediate accomplices. All were brought before a commission of twelve members, summoned expressly to try the case, and the result was the condemnation and execution of six women and some forty men. The extreme penalty of the Egyptian code was reserved for Pentaûirît, and for the most culpable,—"they died of themselves," and the meaning of this phrase is indicated, I believe, by the appearance of one of the mummies disinterred at Deir el-Baharî.[1] The coffin in which it was placed was very

---

[1] The translations by Déveria, Lepage-Renouf, and Erman agree in making it a case of judicial suicide: there was left to the condemned a choice of his mode of death, in order to avoid the scandal of a public execution. It is also possible to make it a condemnation to death in person, which did not allow of the substitution of a proxy willing, for a payment to his family, to undergo death in place of the condemned; but, unfortunately, no other text is to be found supporting the existence of such a practice in Egypt.

plain, painted white and without inscription; the customary removal of entrails had not been effected, but the body was covered with a thick layer of natron, which was applied even to the skin itself and secured by wrappings. It makes one's flesh creep to look at it: the hands and feet are tied by strong bands, and are curled up as if under an intolerable pain; the abdomen is drawn up, the stomach projects like a ball, the chest is contracted, the head is thrown back, the face is contorted in a hideous grimace, the retracted lips expose the teeth, and the mouth is open as if to give utterance to a last despairing cry. The conviction is borne in upon us that the man was invested while still alive with the wrappings of the dead. Is this the mummy of Pentaûîrît, or of some other prince as culpable as he was, and condemned to this frightful punishment? In order to prevent the recurrence of such wicked plots, Pharaoh resolved to share his throne with that one of his sons who had most right to it. In the XXXIInd year of his reign he called together his military

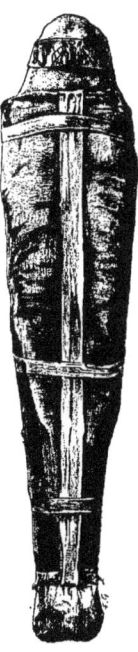

THE MUMMY OF RAMSES III.[1]

and civil chiefs, the generals of the foreign mercenaries, the Shardana, the priests, and the nobles of the court, and presented to them, according to custom, his heir-designate, who was also called Ramses. He placed the double crown upon his brow, and seated him beside himself upon the

[1] Drawn by Faucher-Gudin, from a photograph by Émil Brugsch-Bey.

throne of Horus. This was an occasion for the Pharaoh to bring to remembrance all the great exploits he had performed during his reign—his triumphs over the Libyans and over the peoples of the sea, and the riches he had lavished upon the gods: at the end of the enumeration he exhorted those who were present to observe the same fidelity towards the son which they had observed towards the father, and to serve the new sovereign as valiantly as they had served himself.

The joint reign lasted for only four years. Ramses III. was not much over sixty years of age when he died. He was still vigorous and muscular, but he had become stout and heavy. The fatty matter of the body having been dissolved by the natron in the process of embalming, the skin distended during life has gathered up into enormous loose folds, especially about the nape of the neck, under the chin, on the hips, and at the articulations of the limbs. The closely shaven head and cheeks present no trace of hair or beard. The forehead, although neither broad nor high, is better proportioned than that of Ramses II.; the supra-orbital ridges are less accentuated than his, the cheek-bones not so prominent, the nose not so arched, and the chin and jaw less massive. The eyes were perhaps larger, but no opinion can be offered on this point, for the eyelids have been cut away, and the cleared-out cavities have been filled with rags. The ears do not stand out so far from the head as those of Ramses II., but they have been pierced for ear-rings. The mouth, large by nature, has been still further widened in the process of embalming, owing to the awkwardness of the operator, who has cut into the cheeks at the side. The thin lips allow the white and regular teeth to be seen; the first molar on the right has been either broken in half, or has worn away more rapidly than the rest. Ramses III. seems, on the whole, to have been a sort of reduced copy, a little more delicate in make, of Ramses II.; his face shows more subtlety of expression and intelligence, though less nobility than that of the latter, while his figure is not so upright, his shoulders not so broad, and his general muscular vigour less. What has been said of his personality may be extended to his reign; it was evidently and designedly an imitation of the reign of Ramses II., but fell short of its model owing to the insufficiency of his resources in men and money. If Ramses III. did not succeed in becoming one of the most powerful of the Theban Pharaohs, it was not for lack of energy or ability; the depressed condition of Egypt at the time limited the success of his endeavours and caused them to fall short of his intentions. The work accomplished by him was not on this account less glorious. At his accession Egypt was in a wretched state, invaded on the west, threatened by a flood of barbarians on the east, without an army or a fleet, and with no resources in the treasury. In fifteen years he had disposed of his inconvenient neighbours, organised an army, constructed a fleet, re-established his authority abroad, and settled the administration at home on so firm a basis, that the country owed the peace which it enjoyed for several centuries to the institutions and prestige which he had given it. His associate in the government, Ramses IV., barely survived him. Then followed a series of *rois fainéants* bearing the name of Ramses, but in an order not yet clearly determined. It is generally assumed that Ramses V., brother of Ramses III., succeeded Ramses IV. by supplanting his nephews—who, however, appear to have soon re-established their claim to the throne, and to have followed each other in rapid succession as Ramses VI., Ramses VII., Ramses VIII., and Maritûmû.[1] Others endeavour to make out that Ramses V. was the son of Ramses IV., and that the prince called Ramses VI. never succeeded to the throne at all. At any rate, his son, who is styled Ramses VII., but who is asserted by some to have been a son of Ramses III., is considered to have succeeded Ramses V., and to have become the ancestor from whom the later Ramessides traced their descent.[2] The short reigns of these Pharaohs were marked by no events which would cast lustre on their names; one might say that they had nothing else to do than to enjoy peacefully the riches accumulated by their forefather. Ramses IV. was anxious to profit by the commercial relations which had been again established between Egypt and Puanît, and, in order to facilitate the transit between

[1] The order of the Ramessides was first made out by Champollion the younger and by Rosellini. Bunsen and Lepsius reckon in it thirteen kings; E. de Rougé puts the number at fifteen or sixteen; Maspero makes the number to be twelve, which was reduced still further by Sethe. Erman thinks that Ramses IX. and Ramses X. were also possibly sons of Ramses III.; he consequently declines to recognise King Maritûmû as a son of that sovereign, as Brugsch would make out.

[2] The monuments of these later Ramessides are so rare and so doubtful that I cannot yet see my way to a solution of the questions which they raise.

Coptos and Kosseir, founded a station, and a temple dedicated to Isis, in the mountain of Bakhni; by this route, we learn, more than eight thousand men had passed under the auspices of the high priest of Amon, Nakhtû-ramses. This is the only undertaking of public utility which we can attribute to any of these kings. As we see them in their statues and portraits, they are heavy and squat and without refinement, with protruding eyes, thick lips, flattened and commonplace noses, round and expressionless faces. Their work was confined to the engraving of their cartouches on the blank spaces of the temples at Karnak and Medinet-Habu, and the addition of a few stones to the buildings at Memphis, Abydos, and Heliopolis.

A RAMSES OF THE XXth DYNASTY.[1]

Whatever energy and means they possessed were expended on the construction of their magnificent tombs. These may still be seen in the Biban el-Moluk, and no visitor can refrain from admiring them for their

[1] Drawn by Faucher-Gudin, from a photograph by Émil Brugsch-Bey. This is the Ramses VI. of the series now generally adopted.

magnitude and decoration. As to funerary chapels, owing to the shortness of the reigns of these kings, there was not time to construct them, and they therefore made up for this want by appropriating the chapel of their father, which was at Medinet-Habu, and it was here consequently that their worship was maintained. The last of the sons of Ramses III. was succeeded by another and equally ephemeral Ramses; after whom came Ramses X. and Ramses XI., who re-established the tradition of more lasting reigns. There was now no need of expeditions against Kharu or Libya, for these enfeebled countries no longer disputed, from the force of custom, the authority of Egypt. From time to time an embassy from these countries would arrive at Thebes, bringing presents, which were pompously recorded as representing so much tribute.[1] If it is true that a people which has no history is happy, then Egypt ought to be reckoned as more fortunate under the feebler descendants of Ramses III. than it had ever been under the most famous Pharaohs.

Thebes continued to be the favourite royal residence. Here in its temple the kings were crowned, and in its palaces they passed the greater part of their lives, and here in its valley of sepulchres they were laid to rest when their reigns and lives were ended. The small city of the beginning of the XVIIIth dynasty had long encroached upon the plain, and was now transformed into an immense town, with magnificent monuments, and a motley population,

---

[1] The mention of a tribute, for instance, in the time of Ramses IV. from the Lotanu.

THEBES: ITS WALLS AND RAMPARTS   333

having absorbed in its extension the villages of Ashirû,[1] and
Madit, and even the southern Apît, which we now call
Luxor. But their walls could still be seen, rising up in the
middle of modern constructions, a memorial of the heroic
ages, when the power of the Theban princes was trembling
in the balance, and when conflicts with the neighbouring
barons or with the legitimate king were on the point of
breaking out at every moment.[2] The inhabitants of Apit
retained their walls, which coincided almost exactly with
the boundary of Nsîttauî, the great sanctuary of Amon;
Ashirû sheltered behind its ramparts the temple of Mût,
while Apit-rîsît clustered around a building consecrated by
Amenôthes III. to his divine father, the lord of Thebes.
Within the boundary walls of Thebes extended whole
suburbs, more or less densely populated and prosperous,
through which ran avenues of sphinxes connecting together
the three chief boroughs of which the sovereign city was
composed. On every side might have been seen the same
collections of low grey huts, separated from each other by
some muddy pool where the cattle were wont to drink and
the women to draw water; long streets lined with high
houses, irregularly shaped open spaces, bazaars, gardens,

[1] The village of Ashirû was situated to the south of the temple of
Karnak, close to the temple of Mût. Its ruins, containing the statues
of Sokhît collected by Amenôthes III., extend around the remains marked
X in Mariette's plan.

[2] These are the walls which are generally regarded as marking the
sacred enclosure of the temples: an examination of the ruins of Thebes
shows us that, during the XXth and XXIst dynasties, brick-built houses
lay against these walls both on the inner and outer sides, so that they
must have been half hidden by buildings, as are the ancient walls of Paris
at the present day.

courtyards, and shabby-looking palaces which, while presenting a plain and unadorned exterior, contained within them the refinements of luxury and the comforts of wealth. The population did not exceed a hundred thousand souls,[1] reckoning a large proportion of foreigners attracted

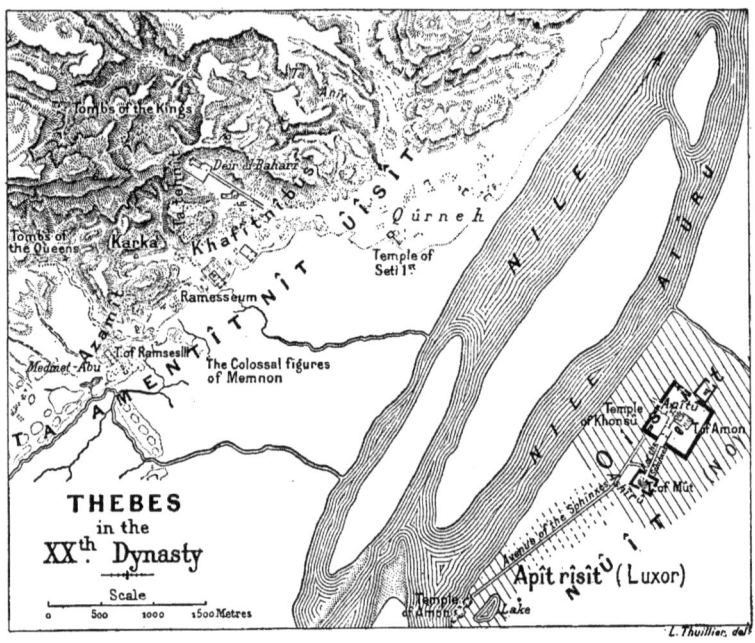

hither by commerce or held as slaves. The court of the Pharaoh drew to the city numerous provincials, who,

---

[1] Letronne, after having shown that we have no authentic ancient document giving us the population, fixes it at 200,000 souls. My estimate, which is, if anything, exaggerated, is based on the comparison of the area of ancient Thebes and that of such modern towns as Siût, Girgeh and Qina, whose populations are known for the last fifty years from the census.

coming thither to seek their fortune, took up their abode there, planting in the capital of Southern Egypt types from the north and the centre of the country, as well as from Nubia and the Oases; such a continuous infusion of foreign material into the ancient Theban stock gave rise to families of a highly mixed character, in which all the various races of Egypt were blended in the most capricious fashion. In every twenty officers, and in the same number of ordinary officials, about half would be either Syrians, or recently naturalised Nubians, or the descendants of both, and among the citizens such names as Pakhari the Syrian, Palamnani the native of the Lebanon, Pinahsî the negro, Palasiai the Alasian, preserved the indications of foreign origin.[1] A similar mixture of races was found in other cities, and Memphis, Bubastis, Tanis, and Siût must have presented as striking an aspect in this respect as Thebes.[2] At Memphis there were regular colonies of Phœnician, Canaanite, and Amorite merchants sufficiently prosperous to have temples there to their national gods, and influential enough to gain adherents to their religion from the indigenous inhabitants. They worshipped Baal, Anîti. Baal-Zaphuna, and Ashtoreth, side by side with Phtah, Nofirtûmû, and Sokhit,[3] and this condition of things at

[1] Among the forty-three individuals compromised in the conspiracy against Ramses III. whose names have been examined by Déveria, nine are foreigners, chiefly Semites, and were so recognised by the Egyptians themselves—Adiram, Balmahara, Garapusa, Iunîni the Libyan, Paiarisalama, possibly the Jerusalemite, Nanaîu, possibly the Ninevite, Paluka the Lycian, Qadendena, and Uarana or Uarámu.

[2] An examination of the stelæ of Abydos shows the extent of foreign influence in this city in the middle of the XVIIIth dynasty.

[3] These gods are mentioned in the preamble of a letter written on the

Memphis was possibly paralleled elsewhere—as at Tanis and Bubastis. This blending of races was probably not so extensive in the country districts, except in places where mercenaries were employed as garrisons; but Sudanese or Hittite slaves, brought back by the soldiers of the ranks, had introduced Ethiopian and Asiatic elements into many a family of the fellahîn.[1] We have only to examine in any of our museums the statues of the Memphite and Theban periods respectively, to see the contrast between the individuals represented in them as far as regards stature and appearance. Some members of the courts of the Ramessides stand out as genuine Semites notwithstanding the disguise of their Egyptian names; and in the times of Kheops and Ûsirtasen they would have been regarded as barbarians. Many of them exhibit on their faces a blending of the distinctive features of one or other of the predominant Oriental races of the time. Additional evidence of a mixture of races is forthcoming when we examine with an unbiased mind the mummies of the period, and the complexity of the new elements introduced among the people by the political movements of the later centuries is thus strongly confirmed. The new-comers had all been absorbed and assimilated by the country, but the

verso of the *Sallier Papyrus*. From the mode in which they are introduced we may rightly infer that they had, like the Egyptian gods who are mentioned with them, their chapels at Memphis. A place in Memphis is called " the district called the district of the Khâtiû " is an inscription of the IIIrd year of Ai, and shows that Hittites were there by the side of Canaanites.

[1] One of the letters in the *Great Bologna Papyrus* treats of a Syrian slave, employed as a cultivator at Hermopolis, who had run away from his master.

generations which arose from this continual cross-breeding, while representing externally the Egyptians of older epochs, in manners, language, and religion, were at bottom something different, and the difference became the more accentuated as the foreign elements increased. The people were thus gradually divested of the character which had distinguished them before the conquest of Syria; the dispositions and defects imported from without counteracted to such an extent their own native dispositions and defects that all marks of individuality were effaced and nullified. The race tended to become more and more what it long continued to be afterwards,—a lifeless and inert mass, without individual energy—endowed, it is true, with patience, endurance, cheerfulness of temperament, and good nature, but with little power of self-government, and thus forced to submit to foreign masters who made use of it and oppressed it without pity.

The upper classes had degenerated as much as the masses. The feudal nobles who had expelled the Shepherds, and carried the frontiers of the empire to the banks of the Euphrates, seemed to have expended their energies in the effort, and to have almost ceased to exist. As long as Egypt was restricted to the Nile valley, there was no such disproportion between the power of the Pharaoh and that of his feudatories as to prevent the latter from maintaining their privileges beside, and, when occasion arose, even against the monarch. The conquest of Asia, while it compelled them either to take up arms themselves or to send their troops to a distance, accustomed them and their soldiers to a passive obedience. The maintenance of a strict discipline in the army was the first condition of successful campaigning at great distances from the mother country and in the midst of hostile people, and the unquestioning respect which they had to pay to the orders of their general prepared them for abject submission to the will of their sovereign. To their bravery, moveover, they owed not only money and slaves, but also necklaces and bracelets of honour, and distinctions and offices in the Pharaonic administration. The king, in addition, neglected no opportunity for securing their devotion to himself. He gave to them in marriage his sisters, his daughters, his cousins, and any of the princesses whom he was not compelled by law to make his own wives. He selected from their harems nursing-mothers for his own sons, and this choice established between him and them a foster relationship, which was as binding among the Egyptians and other Oriental peoples as one of blood. It was not even necessary for the establishment of this relation that the foster-mother's connexion with the Pharaoh's son should be durable or even effective: the woman had only to offer her breast to the child for a moment, and this symbol was quite enough to make her his nurse—his true *monâît*. This fictitious fosterage was carried so far, that it was even made use of in the case of youths and persons of mature age. When an Egyptian woman wished to adopt an adult, the law prescribed that she should offer him the breast, and from that moment he became her son. A similar ceremony was prescribed in the case of men who wished to assume the quality of male nurse—*monâî*—or even, indeed, of female nurse—*monâît*—like that of their wives; according to which they were to place, it would seem, the end of one of their fingers in the mouth of the child.¹ Once this affinity was established, the fidelity of these feudal lords was established beyond question; and their official duties to the sovereign were not considered as accomplished when they had fulfilled their military obligations, for they continued to serve him in the palace as they had served him on the field. Wherever the necessities of the government called them—at Memphis, at Ramses, or elsewhere—they assembled around the Pharaoh; like him they had their palaces at Thebes, and when they died they were anxious to be buried there beside him.² Many of the old houses had become extinct, while others, owing to marriages, were absorbed into the royal family; the fiefs conceded to the relations or favourites of the Pharaoh continued to exist, indeed, as of old, but the ancient distrustful and turbulent feudality had given place to an aristocracy of courtiers, who lived oftener in attendance on the monarch than on their own estates, and whose authority continued to diminish to the profit of the absolute rule of the king. There would be nothing astonishing in the "count" becoming nothing more than

[1] These symbolical modes of adoption were first pointed out by Maspero. Legend has given examples of them: as, for instance, where Isis fosters the child of Malkander, King of Byblos, by inserting the tip of her finger in its mouth.

[2] The tomb of a prince of Tobûî, the lesser Aphroditopolis, was discovered at Thebes by Maspero. The rock-cut tombs of two Thinite princes were noted in the same necropolis. These two were of the time of Thûtmosis III. I have remarked in tombs not yet made public the mention of princes of El-Kab, who played an important part about the person of the Pharaohs down to the beginning of the XXth dynasty.

a governor, hereditary or otherwise, in Thebes itself; he could hardly be anything higher in the capital of the empire.[1] But the same restriction of authority was evidenced in all the provinces: the recruiting of soldiers, the receipt of taxes, most of the offices associated with the civil or military administration, became more and more affairs of the State, and passed from the hands of the feudal lord into those of the functionaries of the Crown. The few barons who still lived on their estates, while they were thus dispossessed of the greater part of their prerogatives, obtained some compensation, on the other hand, on the side of religion. From early times they had been by birth the heads of the local cults, and their protocol had contained, together with those titles which justified their possession of the temporalities of the nome, others which attributed to them spiritual supremacy. The sacred character with which they were invested became more and more prominent in proportion as their political influence became curtailed, and we find scions of the old warlike families or representatives of a new lineage at Thinis, at Akhmîm,[2] in the nome of Baalû, at Hierâconpolis,[3] at

[1] Rakhmirî and his son Manakhpirsonbû were both "counts" of Thebes under Thûtmosis III., and there is nothing to show that there was any other person among them invested with the same functions and belonging to a different family.

[2] For example, the tomb of Anhûrimôsû, high priest of Anhuri-Shû and prince of Thinis, under Mînephtah, where the sacerdotal character is almost exclusively prominent. The same is the case with the tombs of the princes of Akhmim in the time of Khûniatonû and his successors: the few still existing in 1884-5 have not been published. The stelæ belonging to them are at Paris and Berlin.

[3] Horimôsû, Prince of Hierâconpolis under Thûtmosis III., is, above everything else, a prophet of the local Horus.

El-Kab,[1] and in every place where we have information from the monuments as to their position, bestowing more concern upon their sacerdotal than on their other duties. This transfiguration of the functions of the barons, which had been completed under the XIXth and XXth dynasties, corresponded with a more general movement by which the Pharaohs themselves were driven to accentuate their official position as high priests, and to assign to their sons sacerdotal functions in relation to the principal deities. This rekindling of religious fervour would not, doubtless, have restrained military zeal in case of war;[2] but if it did not tend to suppress entirely individual bravery, it discouraged the taste for arms and for the bold adventures which had characterised the old feudality. The duties of sacrificing, of offering prayer, of celebrating the sacred rites according to the prescribed forms, and rendering due homage to the gods in the manner they demanded, were of such an exactingly scrupulous and complex character that the Pharaohs and the lords of earlier times had to assign them to men specially fitted for, and appointed to, the task; now that they had assumed these absorbing functions themselves, they were obliged to delegate to others an increasingly greater proportion of their civil and military duties. Thus, while the king and his great

[1] The princes of El-Kab during the XIXth and XXth dynasties were, before everything, priests of Nekhabît, as appears from an examination of their tombs, which, lying in a side valley, far away from the tomb of Pihirî, are rarely visited.

[2] The sons of Ramses II., Khâmoîsît and Marîtûmû, were brave warriors in spite of their being high priests of Phtah at Memphis, and of Râ at Heliopolis.

vassals were devoutly occupying themselves in matters of worship and theology, generals by profession were relieving them of the care of commanding their armies; and as these individuals were frequently the chiefs of Ethiopian, Asiatic, and especially of Libyan bands, military authority, and, with it, predominant influence in the State were quickly passing into the hands of the barbarians. A sort of aristocracy of veterans, notably of Shardana or Mashauasha, entirely devoted to arms, grew up and increased gradually side by side with the ancient noble families, now by preference devoted to the priesthood.[1]

The barons, whether of ancient or modern lineage, were possessed of immense wealth, especially those of priestly families. The tribute and spoil of Asia and Africa, when once it had reached Egypt, hardly ever left it: they were distributed among the population in proportion to the position occupied by the recipients in the social scale. The commanders of the troops, the attendants on the king, the administrators of the palace and temples, absorbed the greater part, but the distribution was carried down to the private soldier and his relations in town or country, who received some of the crumbs. When we remember for a moment the four centuries and more during which Egypt had been reaping the fruits of her foreign conquest, we cannot think without amazement of the quantities of gold and other precious metals which must have been brought

---

[1] This military aristocracy was fully developed in the XXIst and XXIInd dynasties, but it began to take shape after Ramses III. had planted the Shardana and Qahaka in certain towns as garrisons.

in divers forms into the valley of the Nile.[1] Every fresh expedition made additions to these riches, and one is at a loss to know whence in the intervals between two defeats the conquered could procure so much wealth, and why the sources were never exhausted nor became impoverished. This flow of metals had an influence upon commercial transactions, for although trade was still mainly carried on by barter, the mode of operation was becoming changed appreciably. In exchanging commodities, frequent use was now made of rings and ingots of a certain prescribed weight in *tabonû;* and it became more and more the custom to pay for goods by a certain number of *tabonû* of gold, silver, or copper, rather than by other commodities : it was the practice even to note down in invoices or in the official receipts, alongside the products or manufactured articles with which payments were made, the value of the same in weighed metal.[2] This custom, although not yet widely

---

[1] The quantity of gold in ingots or rings, mentioned in the *Annals of Thûtmosis III.*, represents altogether a weight of nearly a ton and a quarter, or in value some £140,000 of our money. And this is far from being the whole of the metal obtained from the enemy, for a large portion of the inscription has disappeared, and the unrecorded amount might be taken, without much risk of error, at as much as that of which we have evidence —say, some two and a half tons, which Thûtmosis had received or brought back between the years XXIII. and XLII. of his reign—an estimation rather under than over the reality. These figures, moreover, take no account of the vessels and statues, or of the furniture and arms plated with gold. Silver was not received in such large quantities, but it was of great value, and the like may be said of copper and lead.

[2] The facts justifying this position were observed and put together for the first time by Chabas : a translation is given in his memoir of a register of the XXth or XXIst dynasty, which gives the price of butcher's meat, both in gold and silver, at this date. Fresh examples have been

extended, placed at the disposal of trade enormous masses of metal, which were preserved in the form of ingots or bricks, except the portion which went to the manufacture of rings, jewellery, or valuable vessels.[1] The general prosperity encouraged a passion for goldsmith's work, and the use of bracelets, necklaces, and chains became common among classes of the people who were not previously accustomed to wear them. There was henceforward no scribe or merchant, however poor he might be, who had not his seal made of gold or silver, or at any rate of copper gilt. The stone was sometimes fixed, but frequently arranged so as to turn round on a pivot; while among people of superior rank it had some emblem or device upon it, such as a scorpion, a sparrow-hawk, a lion, or a cynocephalous monkey. Chains occupied the same position among the ornaments of Egyptian women as rings among men; they were indispensable decorations. Examples of silver chains are known of some five feet in length, while others do not exceed two to three inches. There are specimens in gold of all sizes, single, double, and triple, with large or small links, some thick and heavy, while others are as slight and flexible as the finest Venetian lace. The poorest peasant woman, alike with the lady of the court, could boast of the possession of a chain, and she must have been in dire poverty who had not some other ornament in her jewel-case. The jewellery of Queen

since collected by Spiegelberg, who has succeeded in drawing up a kind of tariff for the period between the XVIIIth and XXth dynasties.

[1] There are depicted on the monuments bags or heaps of gold dust, ingots in the shape of bricks, rings, and vases, arranged alongside each other.

Âhhotpû shows to what degree of excellence the work of the Egyptian goldsmiths had attained at the time of the expulsion of the Hyksôs: they had not only preserved the good traditions of the best workmen of the XIIth dynasty, but they had perfected the technical details, and had learned to combine form and colour with a greater skill. The pectorals of Prince Khâmoîsît and the Lord Psaru, now in the Louvre, but which were originally placed in the tomb of the Apis in the time of Ramses II., are splendid examples. The most common form of these represents in miniature the front of a temple with a moulded or flat border, surmounted by a curved cornice.

PECTORAL OF RAMSES II.[1]

In one of them, which was doubtless a present from the king himself, the cartouche, containing the first name of the Pharaoh-Usirmari, appears just below the frieze, and serves as a centre for the design within the frame. The wings of the ram-headed sparrow-hawk, the emblem of Amonrâ, are so displayed as to support it, while a large uræus and a vulture beneath embracing both the sparrow-hawk and the cartouche with outspread wings give the idea of divine protection. Two *didû*, each of them filling one of the lower corners, symbolise duration. The framework

[1] Drawn by Faucher-Gudin, from the jewel in the Louvre.

of the design is made up of divisions marked out in gold, and filled either with coloured enamels or pieces of polished stone. The general effect is one of elegance, refinement, and harmony, the three principal elements of the design becoming enlarged from the top downwards in a deftly adjusted gradation. The dead-gold of the cartouche in the upper centre is set off below by the brightly variegated and slightly undulating band of colours of the sparrow-hawk, while the uræus and vulture, associated together with one pair of wings, envelope the upper portions in a half-circle of enamels, of which the shades pass from red through green to a dull blue, with a freedom of handling and a skill in the manipulation of colour which do honour to the artist. It was not his fault if there is still an element of stiffness in the appearance of the pectoral as a whole, for the form which religious tradition had imposed upon the jewel was so rigid that no artifice could completely get over this defect. It is a type which arose out of the same mental concepts as had given birth to Egyptian architecture and sculpture—monumental in character, and appearing often as if designed for colossal rather than ordinary beings. The dimensions, too overpowering for the decoration of normal men or women, would find an appropriate place only on the breasts of gigantic statues: the enormous size of the stone figures to which alone they are adapted would relieve them, and show them in their proper proportions. The artists of the second Theban empire tried all they could, however, to get rid of the square framework in which the sacred bird is enclosed, and we find examples among the pectorals in the Louvre of the sparrow-hawk only with curved wings, or of the ram-headed hawk with the wings extended; but in both of them there is displayed the same brilliancy, the same purity of line, as in the square-shaped jewels, while the design, freed from the trammels of the hampering enamelled frame, takes on a more graceful form, and becomes more suitable for personal decoration. The ram's head in the second case excels in the beauty of its workmanship anything to be found elsewhere in the museums of Europe or Egypt. It is of the finest gold, but its value does not depend upon the precious material: the ancient engraver knew how to model it with a bold and free hand, and he has managed to invest it with as much dignity as if he had been carving his subject in heroic size out of a block of granite or limestone. It is not an example of pure industrial art, but of an art for which a designation is lacking. Other examples, although more carefully executed and of more costly materials, do not approach it in value: such, for instance, are the earrings of Ramses XII. at Gîzeh, which are made up of an ostentatious combination of disks, filigree-work, chains, beads, and hanging figures of the uræus.

THE RAM-HEADED SPARROW-HAWK IN THE LOUVRE.[1]

To get an idea of the character of the plate on the royal sideboards, we must have recourse to the sculptures in the temples, or to the paintings on the tombs: the

[1] Drawn by Faucher-Gudin, from a jewel in the Louvre.

engraved gold or silver centrepieces, dishes, bowls, cups, and amphoræ, if valued by weight only, were too precious to escape the avarice of the impoverished generations which followed the era of Theban prosperity. In the fabrication of these we can trace foreign influences, but not to the extent of a predominance over native art: even if the subject to be dealt with by the artist happened to be a Phœnician god or an Asiatic prisoner, he was not content with slavishly copying his model; he translated it and interpreted it, so as to give it an Egyptian character.

The household furniture was in keeping with these precious objects. Beds and armchairs in valuable woods, inlaid with ivory, carved, gilt, painted in subdued and bright colours, upholstered with mattresses and cushions of many-hued Asiatic stuffs, or of home-made materials, fashioned after Chaldæan patterns, were in use among the well-to-do, while people of moderate means had to be content with old-fashioned furniture of the ancient regime. The Theban dwelling-house was indeed more sumptuously furnished than the earliest Memphite, but we find the same general arrangements in both, which provided, in addition to quarters for the masters, a similar number of rooms intended for the slaves, for granaries, storehouses, and stables. While the outward decoration of life was subject to change, the inward element remained

DECORATED ARMCHAIR.[1]

[1] Drawn by Faucher-Gudin, from one of these objects in the tomb of Ramses III.

unaltered. Costume was a more complex matter than in former times: the dresses and lower garments were more gauffered, had more embroidery and stripes; the wigs were larger and longer, and rose up in capricious arrangements of curls and plaits. The use of the chariot had now become a matter of daily custom, and the number of domestics, already formidable, was increased by fresh additions in the shape of coachmen, grooms, and *saises*, who ran before their master to clear a way for the horses through the crowded streets of the city.[1] As material existence became more complex, intellectual life partook of the same movement, and, without deviating much from the lines prescribed for it by the learned and the scribes of the Memphite age, literature had become in the mean time larger, more complicated, more exacting, and more difficult to grapple with and to master. It had its classical authors, whose writings were committed to memory and taught in the schools. These were truly masterpieces, for if some felt that they understood and enjoyed them, others found them almost beyond their comprehension, and complained bitterly of their obscurity. The later writers followed them pretty closely, in taking pains, on

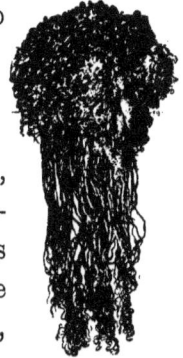

EGYPTIAN WIG.[2]

---

[1] The pictures at Tel el-Amarna exhibit the king, queen, and princesses driving in their chariots with escorts of soldiers and runners. We often find in the tomb-paintings the chariot and coachman of some dignitary, waiting while their master inspects a field or a workshop, or while he is making a visit to the palace for some reward.

[2] Drawn by Faucher-Gudin, from a photograph by M. de Mertens.

the one hand, to express fresh ideas in the forms consecrated by approved and ancient usage, or when they failed to find adequate vehicles to convey new thoughts, resorting in their lack of imagination to the foreigner for the requisite expressions. The necessity of knowing, at least superficially, something of the dialect and writings of Asia, compelled the Egyptian scribes to study to some degree the literature of Phœnicia and of Chaldæa. From these sources they had borrowed certain formulæ of incan-

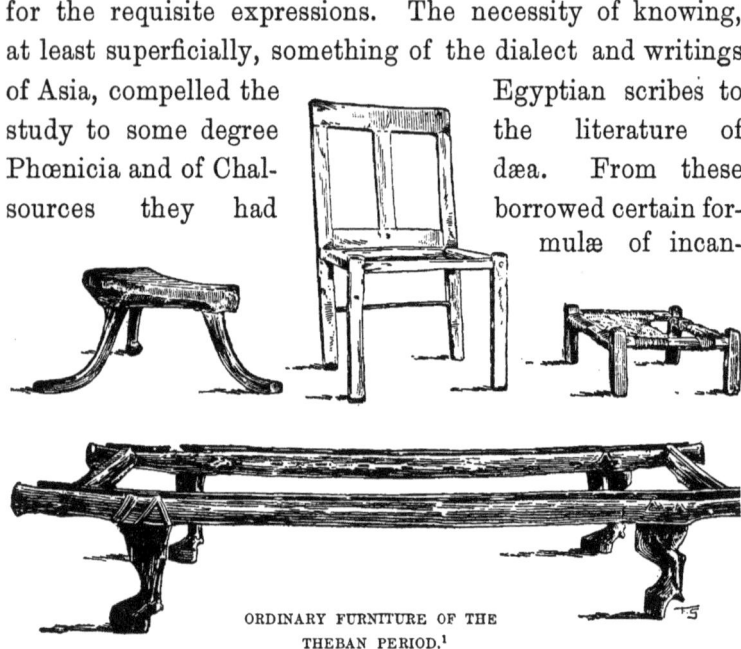

ORDINARY FURNITURE OF THE THEBAN PERIOD.[1]

tation, medical recipes, and devout legends, in which the deities of Assyria and especially Astartê played the chief part. They appropriated in this manner a certain number of words and phrases with which they were accustomed to interlard their discourses and writings. They thought it polite to call a door no longer by the

[1] Drawn by Faucher-Gudin, from photographs of the objects in the Museums of Berlin and Gizeh.

word *ro*, but the term *tirâ*, and to accompany themselves no longer with the harp *bonît*, but with the same instrument under its new name *kinnôr*, and to make the *salâm* in saluting the sovereign in place of crying before him, *aaû*. They were thorough-going Semiticisers; but one is less offended by their affectation when one considers that the number of captives in the country, and the intermarriages with Canaanite women, had familiarised a portion of the community from childhood with the sounds and ideas of the languages from which the scribes were accustomed to borrow unblushingly. This artifice, if it served to infuse an appearance of originality into their writings, had no influence upon their method of composition. Their poetical ideal remained what it had been in the time of their ancestors, but seeing that we are now unable to determine the characteristic cadence of sentences or the mental attitude which marked each generation of literary men, it is often difficult for us to find out the qualities in their writings which gave them popularity. A complete library of one of the learned in the Ramesside period must have contained a strange mixture of works, embracing, in addition to books of devotion, which were indispensable to those who were solicitous about their souls,[1] collections of hymns, romances, war and love songs, moral and philosophical treatises, letters, and legal documents. It

---

[1] There are found in the rubrics of many religious books, for example that dealing with the unseen world, promises of health and prosperity to the soul which, "while still on earth," had read and learned them. A similar formula appears at the end of several important chapters of the *Book of the Dead*.

would have been similar in character to the literary possessions of an Egyptian of the Memphite period,[1] but the language in which it was written would not have been so stiff and dry, but would have flowed more easily, and been more sustained and better balanced. The great odes to the deities which we find in the Theban *papyri* are better fitted, perhaps, than the profane compositions of the period, to give us an idea of the advance which Egyptian genius had made in the width and richness of its modes of expression, while still maintaining almost the same dead-level of idea which had characterised it from the outset. Among these, one dedicated to Harmakhis, the sovereign sun, is no longer restricted to a bare enumeration of the acts and virtues of the "Disk," but ventures to treat of his daily course and his final triumphs in terms which might have been used in describing the victorious campaigns or the apotheosis of a Pharaoh. It begins with his awakening, at the moment when he has torn himself away from the embraces of night. Standing upright in the cabin of the divine bark, "the fair boat of millions of years," with the coils of the serpent Mihni around him, he glides in silence on the eternal current of the celestial waters, guided and protected by those battalions of secondary deities with whose odd forms the

---

[1] The composition of these libraries may be gathered from the collections of papyri which have turned up from time to time, and have been sold by the Arabs to Europeans buyers; *e.g.* the Sallier Collection, the Anastasi Collections, and that of Harris. They have found their way eventually into the British Museum or the Museum at Leyden, and have been published in the *Select Papyri* of the former, or in the *Monuments Égyptiens* of the latter.

monuments have made us familiar. "Heaven is in delight, the earth is in joy, gods and men are making festival, to render glory to Phrâ-Harmakhis, when they see him arise in his bark, having overturned his enemies in his own time!" They accompany him from hour to hour, they fight the good fight with him against Apopi, they shout aloud as he inflicts each fresh wound upon the monster: they do not even abandon him when the west has swallowed him up in its darkness.[1] Some parts of the hymn remind us, in the definiteness of the imagery and in the abundance of detail, of a portion of the poem of Pentaûîrît, or one of those inscriptions of Ramses III. wherein he celebrates the defeat of hordes of Asiatics or Libyans.

The Egyptians took a delight in listening to stories. They preferred tales which dealt with the marvellous and excited their imagination, introducing speaking animals, gods in disguise, ghosts and magic.[1] One of them tells of a king who was distressed because he had no heir, and had no sooner obtained the favour he desired from the gods, than the Seven Hathors, the mistresses of Fate, destroyed his happiness by predicting that the child would meet with his death by a serpent, a dog, or a crocodile. Efforts were made to provide against such a fatality by shutting him up in a tower; but no sooner had he grown to man's estate, than he procured himself a dog, went off to wander through the world, and married the daughter of the Prince of Naharaim. His fate meets him first under the form of a

[1] The remains of Egyptian romantic literature have been collected and translated into French by Maspero, and subsequently into English by Flinders Petrie.

serpent, which is killed by his wife; he is next assailed by a crocodile, and the dog kills the crocodile, but as the oracles must be fulfilled, the brute turns and despatches his master without further consideration. Another story describes two brothers, Anûpû and Bitiû, who live happily together on their farm till the wife of the elder falls in love with the younger, and on his repulsing her advances, she accuses him to her husband of having offered her violence. The virtue of the younger brother would not have availed him much, had not his animals warned him of danger, and had not Phrâ-Harmakhis surrounded him at the critical moment with a stream teeming with crocodiles. He mutilates himself to prove his innocence, and announces that henceforth he will lead a mysterious existence far from mankind; he will retire to the Valley of the Acacia, place his heart on the topmost flower of the tree, and no one will be able with impunity to steal it from him. The gods, however, who frequent this earth take pity on his loneliness, and create for him a wife of such beauty that the Nile falls in love with her, and steals a lock of her hair, which is carried by its waters down into Egypt. Pharaoh finds the lock, and, intoxicated by its scent, commands his people to go in quest of the owner. Having discovered the lady, Pharaoh marries her, and ascertaining from her who she is, he sends men to cut down the Acacia, but no sooner has the flower touched the earth, than Bitiû droops and dies. The elder brother is made immediately acquainted with the fact by means of various prodigies. The wine poured out to him becomes troubled, his beer leaves a deposit. He seizes his shoes and staff and sets out to find the heart.

After a search of seven years he discovers it, and reviving it in a vase of water, he puts it into the mouth of the corpse, which at once returns to life. Bitiû, from this moment, seeks only to be revenged. He changes himself into the bull Apis, and, on being led to court, he reproaches the queen with the crime she has committed against him. The queen causes his throat to be cut; two drops of his blood fall in front of the gate of the palace, and produce in the night two splendid "Persea" trees, which renew the accusation in a loud voice. The queen has them cut down, but a chip from one of them flies into her mouth, and ere long she gives birth to a child who is none other than a reincarnation of Bitiû. When the child succeeds to the Pharaoh, he assembles his council, reveals himself to them, and punishes with death her who was first his wife and subsequently his mother. The hero moves throughout the tale without exhibiting any surprise at the strange incidents in which he takes part, and, as a matter of fact, they did not seriously outrage the probabilities of contemporary life. In every town sorcerers could be found who knew how to transform themselves into animals or raise the dead to life : we have seen how the accomplices of Pentaûîrît had recourse to spells in order to gain admission to the royal palace when they desired to rid themselves of Ramses III. The most extravagant romances differed from real life merely in collecting within a dozen pages more miracles than were customarily supposed to take place in the same number of years; it was merely the multiplicity of events, and not the events themselves, that gave to the narrative its romantic and improbable character. The rank of the heroes alone raised the tale out of the region of ordinary life; they are always the sons of kings, Syrian princes, or Pharaohs; sometimes we come across a vague and undefined Pharaoh, who figures under the title of Pîrûîaûi or Prûîti, but more often it is a well-known and illustrious Pharaoh who is mentioned by name. It is related how, one day, Kheops, suffering from *ennui* within his palace, assembled his sons in the hope of learning from them something which he did not already know. They described to him one after another the prodigies performed by celebrated magicians under Kanibri and Snofrûi; and at length Mykerinos assured him that there was a certain Didi, living then not far from Meîdum, who was capable of repeating all the marvels done by former wizards. Most of the Egyptian sovereigns were, in the same way, subjects of more or less wonderful legends—Sesostris, Amenôthes III., Thûtmosis III., Amenemhâît I., Khîti, Sahûri, Ûsirkaf, and Kakiû. These stories were put into literary shape by the learned, recited by public story-tellers, and received by the people as authentic history; they finally filtered into the writings of the chroniclers, who, in introducing them into the annals, filled up with their extraordinary details the *lacunæ* of authentic tradition. Sometimes the narrative assumed a briefer form, and became an apologue. In one of them the members of the body were supposed to have combined against the head, and disputed its supremacy before a jury; the parties all pleaded their cause in turn, and judgment was given in due form.[1] Animals also had their place in

[1] This version of the *Fable of the Members and the Stomach* was discovered upon a schoolboy's tablet at Turin.

this universal comedy. The passions or the weaknesses of humanity were attributed to them, and the narrator makes the lion, rat, or jackal to utter sentiments from which he draws some short practical moral. La Fontaine had predecessors on the banks of the Nile of whose existence he little dreamed.

As La Fontaine found an illustrator in Granville, so, too, in Egypt the draughtsman brought his reed to the aid

THE CAT AND THE JACKAL GO OFF TO THE FIELDS WITH THEIR FLOCKS.[1]

of the fabulist, and by his cleverly executed sketches gave greater point to the sarcasm of story than mere words could have conveyed. Where the author had briefly mentioned that the jackal and the cat had cunningly forced their services on the animals whom they wished to devour at their leisure, the artist would depict the jackal and the cat equipped as peasants, with wallets on their backs, and sticks over their shoulders, marching behind a troup of gazelles or a flock of fat geese: it was easy to foretell the fate of their unfortunate charges. Elsewhere it is an ox who brings up before his master a cat who has cheated him,

[1] Drawn by Faucher-Gudin, from Lepsius.

and his proverbial stupidity would incline us to think that he will end by being punished himself for the misdeeds of which he had accused the other. Puss's sly and artful expression, the ass-headed and important-looking judge, with the wand and costume of a high and mighty dignitary, give pungency to the story, and recall the daily scenes at the judgment-seat of the lord of Thebes. In another place we see a donkey, a lion, a crocodile, and a monkey giving

THE CAT BEFORE ITS JUDGE.[1]

an instrumental and vocal concert. A lion and a gazelle play a game of chess. A cat of fashion, with a flower in her hair, has a disagreement with a goose: they have come to blows, and the excitable puss, who fears she will come off worst in the struggle, falls backwards in a fright. The draughtsmen having once found vent for their satire, stopped at nothing, and even royalty itself did not escape their attacks. While the writers of the day made fun of the military calling, both in prose and verse, the

[1] Drawn by Faucher-Gudin, from Lepsius.

caricaturists parodied the combats and triumphal scenes of the Ramses or Thûtmosis of the day depicted on the walls of the pylons. The Pharaoh of all the rats, perched upon a chariot drawn by dogs, bravely charges an army of cats; standing in the heroic attitude of a conqueror, he pierces them with his darts, while his horses tread the fallen underfoot; his legions meanwhile in advance of him attack a fort defended by tomcats, with the same ardour that the

A CONCERT OF ANIMALS DEVOTED TO MUSIC.[1]

Egyptian battalions would display in assaulting a Syrian stronghold. This treatment of ethics did not prevent the Egyptian writers from giving way to their natural inclinations, and composing large volumes on this subject after the manner of Kaqîmni or Phtahhotpû. One of their books, in which the aged Ani inscribes his Instructions to his son, Khonshotpû, is compiled in the form of a dialogue, and contains the usual commonplaces upon virtue, temper-

[1] Drawn by Faucher-Gudin, from Lepsius.

ance, piety, the respect due to parents from children, or to the great ones of this world from their inferiors. The language in which it is written is ingenious, picturesque, and at times eloquent; the work explains much that is obscure in Egyptian life, and upon which the monuments have thrown no light. " Beware of the woman who goes out surreptitiously in her town, do not follow her or any like her, do not expose thyself to the experience of what it costs a man to face an Ocean of which the bounds are unknown.[1] The wife whose husband is far from home sends thee letters, and invites thee to come to her daily when she has no witnesses; if she succeeds in entangling thee in her net, it is a crime which is punishable by death as soon as it is known, even if no wicked act has taken place, for men will commit every sort of crime when under this temptation alone." " Be not quarrelsome in breweries, for fear that thou mayest be denounced forthwith for words which have proceeded from thy mouth, and of having spoken that of which thou art no longer conscious. Thou fallest, thy members helpless, and no one holds out a hand to thee, but thy boon-companions around thee say : ' Away with the drunkard!' Thou art wanted for some business, and thou art found rolling on the ground like an infant." In speaking of what a man owes to his mother, Ani waxes eloquent: "When she bore thee as all have to bear, she had in thee a heavy burden without being able to call on

[1] I have been obliged to paraphrase the sentence considerably to render it intelligible to the modern reader. The Egyptian text says briefly : " Do not know the man who braves the water of the Ocean whose bounds are unknown." *To know the man* means here *know the state of the man* who does an action.

thee to share it. When thou wert born, after thy months were fulfilled, she placed herself under a yoke in earnest, her breast was in thy mouth for three years; in spite of the increasing dirtiness of thy habits, her heart felt no disgust, and she never said: 'What is that I do here?' When thou didst go to school to be instructed in writing, she followed thee every day with bread and beer from thy house. Now thou art a full-grown man, thou hast taken a wife, thou hast provided thyself with a house; bear always in mind the pains of thy birth and the care for thy education that thy mother lavished on thee, that her anger may not rise up against thee, and that she lift not her hands to God, for he will hear her complaint!" The whole of the book does not rise to this level, but we find in it several maxims which appear to be popular proverbs, as for instance: "He who hates idleness will come without being called;" "A good walker comes to his journey's end without needing to hasten;" or, "The ox which goes at the head of the flock and leads the others to pasture is but an animal like his fellows." Towards the end, the son Khonshotpû, weary of such a lengthy exhortation to wisdom, interrupts his father roughly: "Do not everlastingly speak of thy merits, I have heard enough of thy deeds;" whereupon Ani resignedly restrains himself from further speech, and a final parable gives us the motive of his resignation: "This is the likeness of the man who knows the strength of his arm. The nursling who is in the arms of his mother cares only for being suckled; but no sooner has he found his mouth than he cries: "Give me bread!'"

It is, perhaps, difficult for us to imagine an Egyptian in love repeating madrigals to his mistress,[1] for we cannot easily realise that the hard and blackened bodies we see in our museums have once been men and women loving and beloved in their own day. The feeling which they entertained one for another had none of the reticence or delicacy of our love: they went straight to the point, and the language in which they expressed themselves is sometimes too coarse for our taste. The manners and customs of daily life among the Egyptians tended to blunt in them the feelings of modesty and refinement to which our civilization has accustomed us. Their children went about without clothes, or, at any rate, wore none until the age of puberty. Owing to the climate, both men and women left the upper part of the body more or less uncovered, or wore fabrics of a transparent nature. In the towns, the servants who moved about their masters or his guests had merely a narrow loin-cloth tied round their hips; while in the country, the peasants dispensed with even this covering, and the women tucked up their garments when at work so as to move more freely. The religious teaching and the ceremonies connected with their worship drew the attention of the faithful to the unveiled human form of their gods, and the hieroglyphs themselves contained pictures which shock our sense of

[1] The remains of Egyptian amatory literature have been collected, translated, and commentated on by Maspero. They have been preserved in two papyri, one of which is at Turin, the other in the British Museum. The first of these appears to be a sort of dialogue in which the trees of a garden boast one after another of the beauty of a woman, and discourse of the love-scenes which took place under their shadow.

propriety. Hence it came about that the young girl who was demanded in marriage had no idea, like the maiden of to-day, of the vague delights of an ideal union. The physical side was impressed upon her mind, and she was well aware of the full meaning of her consent. Her lover, separated from her by her disapproving parents, thus expresses the grief which overwhelms him: "I desire to lie down in my chamber,—for I am sick on thy account, —and the neighbours come to visit me.—Ah! if my sister but came with them,—she would show the physicians what ailed me,—for she knows my sickness!" Even while he thus complains, he sees her in his imagination, and his spirit visits the places she frequents: "The villa of my sister,—(a pool is before the house),—the door opens suddenly,—and my sister passes out in wrath.—Ah! why am I not the porter,—that she might give me her orders! —I should at least hear her voice, even were she angry,— and I, like a little boy, full of fear before her!" Meantime the young girl sighs in vain for "her brother, the beloved of her heart," and all that charmed her before has now ceased to please her. "I went to prepare my snare, my cage and the covert for my trap—for all the birds of Puânît alight upon Egypt, redolent with perfume;—he who flies foremost of the flock is attracted by my worm, bringing odours from Puânît,—its claws full of incense.— But my heart is with thee, and desires that we should trap them together,—I with thee, alone, and that thou shouldest be able to hear the sad cry of my perfumed bird,—there near to me, close to me, I will make ready my trap,—O my beautiful friend, thou who goest to the field of the well-beloved!" The latter, however, is slow to appear, the day passes away, the evening comes on: "The cry of the goose resounds—which is caught by the worm-bait,—but thy love removes me far from the bird, and I am unable to deliver myself from it; I will carry off my net, and what shall I say to my mother,—when I shall have returned to her?—Every day I come back laden with spoil,—but to-day I have not been able to set my trap,—for thy love makes me its prisoner!" "The goose flies away, alights,—it has greeted the barns with its cry;—the flock of birds increases on the river, but I leave them alone and think only of thy love,—for my heart is bound to thy heart—and I cannot tear myself away from thy beauty." Her mother probably gave her a scolding, but she hardly minds it, and in the retirement of her chamber never wearies of thinking of her brother, and of passionately crying for him: "O my beautiful friend! I yearn to be with thee as thy wife—and that thou shouldest go whither thou wishest with thine arm upon my arm,—for then I will repeat to my heart, which is in thy breast, my supplications.—If my great brother does not come to-night, —I am as those who lie in the tomb—for thou, art thou not health and life,—he who transfers the joys of thy health to my heart which seeks thee?" The hours pass away and he does not come, and already "the voice of the turtle-dove speaks,—it says: 'Behold, the dawn is here, alas! what is to become of me?' Thou, thou art the bird, thou callest me,—and I find my brother in his chamber,—and my heart is rejoiced to see him!—I will never go away again, my hand will remain in thy hand,—and when I wander forth, I will go with thee into the most beautiful places,—happy in that he makes me the foremost of women—and that he does not break my heart." We should like to quote the whole of it, but the text is mutilated, and we are unable to fill in the blanks. It is, nevertheless, one of those products of the Egyptian mind which it would have been easy for us to appreciate from beginning to end, without effort and almost without explanation. The passion in it finds expression in such sincere and simple language as to render rhetorical ornament needless, and one can trace in it, therefore, nothing of the artificial colouring which would limit it to a particular place or time. It translates a universal sentiment into the common language of humanity, and the hieroglyphic groups need only to be put into the corresponding words of any modern tongue to bring home to the reader their full force and intensity. We might compare it with those popular songs which are now being collected in our provinces before the peasantry have forgotten them altogether: the artlessness of some of the expressions, the boldness of the imagery, the awkwardness and somewhat abrupt character of some of the passages, communicate to both that wild charm which we miss in the most perfect specimens of our modern love-poets.

END OF VOL. V.

INDEX

A

Abd-el-Qûrnah, Cemetary of, 309
Abu Simbel (Ipsambul), 187, 239-242
Abu Simbel, Colossi of, 224
Abydos, 180
Abydos, Temple at, 176-179
Acre (Aku), 35
Ahhotpû (Aahotep) I., Queen, 345
Aî, 110, 119
Alasia, Kingdom of, 24, 32-36, 52, 132, 143
Amenhotep. *See* Amenôthes
Amenmesis, 265, 268, 289
Amenôthes II., 43-46
Amenôthes III., 26, 52, 55, 59, 76, 280
  Tomb of, 70
Amenôthes IV. (Khûniatonû *or* Amenhotep), 27, 28, 80, 81, 89, 95-101, 105, 126, 133
Amon (god of Thebes) and his priests, 73, 92, 93, 123
Amon's promise to Thûtmosis III., 9
Amorites (Amurru), The, 24, 34, 101, 143, 164, 313
Arisû (the Syrian), 267, 287
Arvad (Arados), 4, 14, 132, 191, 311
Asia Minor, 147-151
Aten. *See* Atonû
Atonû (solar disk), Worship of, 78, 80, 83, 86, 89
Augarit (Ugarît), 157
Azîru, 101

B

Babylon, 269
Baûki, 86
Beit-Wally, 187
Beni-Israel. *See* Israelites
Berber tribes, The, 252
Brick-making, 58
Bûrnabûriash (King of Babylon), 14, 27, 35, 100.
Byblos (Gublu), 3

C

Carchemish (Jerabis ?), 191, 208, 311
Caricatures and satires, 357-360
Chariots,
  Egyptian, 33, 349
  Hittite, 140
Commandments, The ten, 277

D

Damascus, 24
Dananna, The, 145
Dapûr (Tabor), 204, 205
Dardanos, 151
Deir-el-Baharî, 40
Deir-el-Baharî, Temple of, 40
Dushratta (King of Mitanni), 26-30, 54, 99, 137, 139
Dynasty XVIII. (table of kings) 112
Dynasty XIX., 117

E

Egyptian chariot, 33, 349
Egyptian costume, 349
Egyptian education, 349
Egyptian empire, Organization of, 11
Egyptian fables, 355
Egyptian fairy stories, 353
Egyptian furniture, 349
Egyptian goldsmiths' work, 345
Egyptian love-songs, 363-365
Egyptian ships, 295
Elephantinê, 62-65
Etbaî, Gold-mines of, 167-170
Ethiopia, 99, 132
  Tributes of, 5
Exodus, The, 271, 273
  Egyptian romance of the, 281

F

Fairy stories and fables, 353, 355

INDEX

G

Gebel-Barkal, 61, 62
Gebel Silsileh, 129, 131
Gerf-hossein, Temple at, 220, 221
Gilukhipa, 54, 55
Gold-mines, 169, 170
Goldsmiths' work, 31, 345
Gublu. *See* Byblos
Gurneh, Temple of. *See* Qurneh

H

Hamath (Hamatu), 24
Harmhabî (Hôremheb) 117, 119, 128, 158–161, 181
Harmhabî, Statue of, 117
Harmhabî (Wars in Ethiopia), 128, 131
Hâtshopsitû (Hatasu), Queen, 69
Hâtshopsitû II., 42
Haûi-nibû, 132, 144
Hebrews, The (Ibrim), 369
Hittite religion, 137
Hittite type and costume, 135
Hittites, The. *See* Khâti
Hittites, Campaign of Ramses II. against, 193

I

Ibrim. *See* Hebrews
Israelites, The, *or* Beni-Israel, 270, 271, 278

J

Jerabis. *See* Carchemish
Job, Stone of, 212

K

Kadesh. *See* Qodshu
Katiti, 9
Kallimasin (King of Babylon), 26, 29, 54
Karnak, 117, 118, 173, 175, 236
   Temple of Amon at, 67
Kefâtiû, 3
Khalupsaru, the "writer of books," 198
Khâmoisit, 243, 244, 280
Kharû, 24, 25, 34, 163–165, 320
Khâti *or* Khiti (Hittites), 12, 28, 29, 45, 52, 130, 133, 150, 153, 163, 190, 195, 311, 313, 318
Khâtusaru (Khatusharu), Hittite prince, 190, 197, 204, 208, 290
Khûitatonû. *See* Tel-el-Amarna
Khûniaton, *or* Khûniatonû (Khuenaten). *See* Amenothes IV.
Kings, Tombs of, 183, 331

Kûrigalzû I., 14
Kûsh, 165

L

Lapis-lazuli of Babylon, 33
Libya, 251, 291
Libyan defeat at Piriû, 257
Libyan invasions, 255, 297, 313
Libyan sailors, 295
Libyans *or* Labû (Timihû), 251–254, 295, 317
Lion, Tame, in battle, 196
Lions of Gebel-Barkal, 61, 62
Lotanû (*or* Rotanû), 3, 4, 31
Love-songs, 363–365
Luku, The, 145
Luxor, Temple at, 66, 185, 233, 235

M

Magadil, 306, 309
Manna, 274, 275
Marah, 274
Mâraiû (Libyan prince), 253, 254, 257, 291
Marriages, Royal, 27–30
Mashaûasha (Maxyes), 252, 254, 292, 313, 342
Maurusaru (Hittite King), 164, 190
Maxyes. *See* Mashaûasha
Mazaiû, 298
Medinet-Habu, 313, 321, 325, 331
Memnon, Colossi of, 73, 76
Memnonium (at Abydos), 240
Memnonium at Medinet-Habu, 323
Messengers, The royal, 21, 165
Minephtah, 245, 255, 256, 261, 263
Mitânni, 9, 25, 45, 54, 208, 311
Moses, 270
Musical instruments from Syria, 33
Mûtemûaû, 51, 52
Mûtnozmit, 114, 118, 121
   Head of, 114

N

Naharaim, 3, 24, 34, 43, 133, 142, 155, 191, 207
Nakhtûsit, 287–289
Nofritari, 81
Nubia, 57, 171
Nubia, Temples and religions of, 57

P

Pakanâna, 162
Pentaûr (Pentaûirit), 200
   Poem of, 201, 239
Pentaûirit, Conspiracy of, 326

INDEX

"People of the Sea," 255, 305, 309, 311
Philistines. *See* Pulasati
Phœnicia, 24, 25
Phœnician vessels, 218
Piriû, 259
Pithom (*or* Succoth), 269
Pûanit, 5, 218, 319
Pulasati (Philistines), 300, 301, 312, 319

Q

Qodi (Galilee?), 153
Qodshu (*or* Kadesh on the Orontes), 24, 164, 192, 193, 197
Qodshu, Battle of, 4, 195
Qodshu, Prince of, 4
Qurneh (*or* Gurneh), Temple of, 180, 181

R

Radesieh, 168, 169
Ramesseum, The, 238, 239
Rams of Amenôthes III., 59, 67
Ramses I., 160, 161, 180
Ramses II. (Miamûn, Sesostris), 160, 182-187, 208, 243-245, 249
  Head of, 116
  In the Delta, 189
  Marriage, 215
  Mummy of, 249
  Ring of, 283
Ramses III., 289, 299, 307, 327, 332
Ramses IV. and his successors, 329-332
Ramses (town), 189, 209

S

Sâakerî, 107
Sacred lake, 70
Sangar, 52
Sapalalu (Hittite king), 142, 158
Semitic influence in Egypt, 350, 351
Sesebi, Temple of, 171
Seti I., 11, 160-166, 177, 183
  Head of, 115
Seti II., 265
  Statue of, 265
Shabtuna, 192

Shagalasha (*or* Shakalasha), 255, 303
Shardanes, The, 145, 165, 193, 313, 342
Shaûsû, 4, 35, 161
Sidon (Ziduna), 13
Sinai, Mount, 276
Singar, 32, 208
Sıphtah-Minephtah, 265, 289
Soleb, Temple of, 59
Sparrow-hawk, Ram-headed, 347
Sphinx, The, 47
Stele of the Sphinx, 50
Sutarna (King of Mitanni), 54
Syria, Egyptian commerce with, 32, 217

T

Tabor. *See* Dapûr
Tanis, 242
Tel-el-Amarna (Khûitatonû), 83, 85, 103
Tel-el-Amarna tablets, 13, 16, 19, 21, 96
Tel-el-Yahûdiyeh, 320
Theban scribe, 285
Thebes and its people, 333
Thebes and its temples, 65-68
Thebes necropolis, Officer of, 287
Thûtii, a royal messenger, 21
Thûtmosis III., 11-15, 57
  Mummy of, 40, 41
Thûtmosis IV., 51
Tihonû, 165, 187
Tii, Queen, 79
Timihû. *See* Libyans
Tuia, 160, 185
Tunipa, 11, 24, 207, 311
Turah, Quarries at, 64, 280
Tûtankhamon, 109, 110
Tyrseni, The, 302, 303

U

Uirimaûnofîrurî, 216
Ushabti ("Respondents"), 72, 104

Z

Zahi, 3, 14, 24, 143
Zakkala (Siculo-Pelasgi), 300, 303, 312, 313

www.ingramcontent.com/pod-product-compliance
Lightning Source LLC
Chambersburg PA
CBHW050924240426
43668CB00020B/2424